JUST THE FACTS ABOUT
WASHINGTON, D.C.

ALBERT E. KENNEDY

A & N BOOKS, LLC

Printed in the U.S.A. by
Signature Book Printing, Inc.
8041 Cessna Avenue
Gaithersburg, MD 20879
301-258-8353

ISBN 1-932433-61-9

PREFACE

As a long time Washington-area resident, I have visited and revisited many of the monuments, memorials, and museums within a short drive from my doorstep. Always on the lookout for interesting information about the places I visit, I assembled facts from many written sources, television, radio, park rangers, tour guides, and even other tourists.

During my research, I noticed two similarities about my sources. First, most of the written sources required that I read several pages of text before finding a single fact of interest, and two, there was no one source that summarized the many facts under one cover.

Just The Facts About Washington, D.C. is intended to be no more than an aid to tourists and amateur history buffs like myself. It provides easy to read summaries about the lives of the people who are celebrated through the monuments and memorials, interesting facts about each of the sites, and a source of information that I hope will answer many questions.

The photographs were taken by this very amateur photographer, and are only intended to provide a limited form of reference.

So enjoy your trip through history....I certainly did!

ABOUT THE AUTHOR

As a Vietnam-era veteran, Albert (Abe) Kennedy retired as a chief master sergeant from the United States Air Force after 22 years of service. He earned a Bachelor of Arts degree in business from Kansas-Newman University, and a Master of Arts degree in business from Central Michigan University. He also earned an Associates of Arts degree in paralegal studies from the Community College of the Air Force, and a teaching certification in social studies through the College of Notre Dame of Maryland.

He continuously spends much of his spare time reading about and visiting places of interest to find that elusive fact about the history of the United States.

Dedicated to Nancy♥♥ – My wonderful and loving wife, terrific travel companion, editor, and invaluable contributor to this book.

And a special dedication to all of the men and women in the United States military who have served, protected, and sacrificed for our country. Thank you.

TABLE OF CONTENTS

FACTS ABOUT THE CITY OF WASHINGTON, D.C.

During the past two centuries, several generations of Americans have witnessed dramatic changes to a city that is located on a site previously occupied by the Manahoac, Monacan, and Piscataway Indian tribes. Its new citizens described the early city as a *"howling and malarious wilderness in the woods."* Not only has Washington, D.C. grown to become one of the most powerful seats of government, it has also become a center for culture; offering visitors from around the world a wide range of attractions and an almost unlimited source of entertainment. Visitors are welcomed to museums ranging from natural science to aviation. They can spend days in the galleries of the U.S. Senate or the galleries of art. And the national shrines and memorials provide unique insights into the lives and accomplishments of national heroes. But before you start your amazing journey through the many attractions offered by the *"City on the Potomac,"* take a few minutes to learn about how this little patch of wilderness evolved into a city that many citizens and visitors believe symbolizes a nation dedicated to democracy....**THE NATION'S CAPITAL**.

SELECTING THE SITE FOR THE CAPITAL OF THE UNITED STATES AND THE CITY'S EVOLUTION

1. The Residence Act of July 16, 1790, directed the federal government to establish a permanent city for the federal government before the year 1800.

2. The Residence Act authorized the President of the United States, who was then George Washington (1789-1797), the power to select the permanent seat of government.

3. President Washington was actively involved in choosing the site for the new city. He was authorized to choose a site from the east bank of the Potomac River between the mouth of the Eastern Branch, to a site nearly 70 miles northwest on the east bank of the Connogocheague Creek (now Conococheague) near Hagerstown, Maryland.

1

4. Other areas seriously considered for the permanent site of the nation's capital were near Germantown, Pennsylvania, and the cities of Baltimore, Maryland, Philadelphia, Pennsylvania, and New York City, New York.

5. The selection of the permanent site of the federal government resulted from a compromise between the southern and northern states. Representatives from the northern states wanted the seat of government to be located at a site further north, the southern states wanted the site further south. As a compromise, one that garnered the support of the northern states for a seat of government further south was the federal government's offer to accept the $21,500,000 in war debts accumulated by both the northern and southern states during the Revolutionary War.

View of Washington, D.C.

6. In 1790, Maryland donated approximately 69 square miles of land, and Virginia added approximately 31 square miles to the federal government for the site of the U.S. Capital. (The original landmass of Washington, D.C. totaled approximately ten-miles-square or 100 square miles.)

7. Because the land offered by Virginia was retroceded (returned) to Virginia in 1846, the land on which the capital now stands rests on soil that was formerly a part of Maryland.

8. President Washington appointed city commissioners to administer the city. The city continued to be administered solely by the city commissioners until the election of a mayor in November 1967.

9. On March 30, 1791, nineteen landowners transferred land to the federal government for the site of the permanent government. It was agreed that the proprietors would receive half the city lots platted on their former holdings, as well as $66.67 an acre for as much land as was needed by the government for public buildings and public improvements. The federal government would retain half the lots and all the land designed for streets. (The government intended to use the sale of the lots to fund the construction of the city.)

10. The site of the new national city was initially referred to as *"Federal City."* A term often credited to George Washington.

11. On September 9, 1791, the new city was officially renamed *"Washington,"* in honor of the first President of the United States, George Washington (1789-1797).

12. Its designation as the District of Columbia (D.C.) honors the memory of Christopher Columbus.

13. Newly elected President Washington selected Pierre Charles L'Enfant to survey and plan the city. However, because of L'Enfant's disagreements with the city's commissioners, he was dismissed in 1792 without fully accomplishing his appointed task.

14. President Washington then chose Andrew Ellicott of Maryland, and his assistant Benjamin Banneker, to survey the land destined to become Washington, D.C. (L'Enfant had his plans engraved in 1792, and had briefed President Washington on their contents.)

15. Benjamin Banneker was a self-educated freed Negro, who was a prominent astronomer and mathematician.

16. On April 15, 1791, surveyor Andrew Ellicott installed the first of several stones that marked the boundaries of the new city. The sandstone markers, rising approximately two feet off the ground, were placed at one-mile intervals around the city during 1791 and 1792. They formed the diamond–shaped territory of the nation's capital.

17. Each marker was inscribed with the magnetic compass reading and the words "*Jurisdiction of the United States*" on the side facing the District of Columbia.

18. Eventually 40 boundary stones marked the perimeter of Washington, D.C. Since 1916, the Daughters of the American Revolution have preserved and maintained the surviving 37 stones.

19. The four corner stones that were installed to mark the boundaries of the city of Washington, D.C. still exist. The north cornerstone is located just off East-West Highway near Silver Spring, Maryland, with the east cornerstone located just off the intersection of Eastern and Southern Avenues near Seat Pleasant, Maryland. The west cornerstone is off Arizona Avenue, near Falls Church, Virginia, and the southern cornerstone (the first cornerstone to be laid) is located at the southern tip of Jones Point, Virginia, near what is now the Wilson Bridge.

20. On December 1, 1800, the federal capital was transferred from Philadelphia, Pennsylvania, to Washington, D.C.

21. At the time of the 1800 census, the population of Washington, D.C. included 10,066 whites, 793 free Negroes, and 3,244 slaves.

THE KEY POINTS ABOUT THE EARLY YEARS OF WASHINGTION, D.C.

1. The first two public schools in Washington, D.C. were opened in 1806.

2. In 1850, Washington, D.C. became the first large city to abolish slave trading. (Slavery was outlawed in Washington, D.C. in April 1862.)

3. In the early 1870's, the Board of Public Works, headed by Alexander R. Shepherd, oversaw the creation of 120 miles of sewers, 150 miles of road improvements, 280 miles of sidewalks, 30 miles of water mains, 39 miles of gas lines, 3.5 million cubic yards of excavation, and the planting of more than 60,000 trees.

4. In 1895, the first underground trolley system was constructed in Washington, D.C. This limited trolley evolved into the current extensive Metro system that speeds workers and visitors to all points within Washington, D.C.

THE KEY POINTS ABOUT THE PRESENT DAY WASHINGTON, D.C.

1. Temperatures in Washington, D.C. average 37 degrees Fahrenheit during January and 78 degrees in July.

2. Washington, D.C. receives an average of 50 inches of precipitation over the course of the year.

View of Washington, D.C. from Arlington Cemetery

3. Since 1938, the flag of Washington, D.C. has consisted of three red stars above two horizontal red stripes on a white field. This pattern is based on the coat of arms used by the family of George Washington.

4. Washington, D.C. is divided into four parts - Southeast, Southwest, Northeast, and Northwest. These four parts meet at the Capitol Building.

5. The District flower is the American Beauty Rose.

6. The District bird is the Wood Thrush.

7. The District tree is the Scarlet Oak.

8. In 1950, the population of Washington, D.C. peaked at just over 800,000 people. (During the past few years the population of the city has averaged between 550,000 and 600,000 citizens.)

FACTS ABOUT THE CAPITOL BUILDING

President George Washington (1789-1797) accepted the challenge of overseeing the construction of the U.S. Capitol Building. To accomplish his goal, a site had to be selected, money appropriated, designers hired, diagrams approved, conflicts resolved, and work completed. However, even with all the problems encountered, the efforts of the president, the members of Congress, and the countless ordinary Americans, saw their ideas evolve into a symbol of democracy that is immediately recognized by visitors to Washington, D.C.

THE CONGRESS OF THE UNITED STATES

1. There are three branches of the United States government. The legislative branch makes the laws (Congress), the executive branch carries out the laws (headed by the president), and the judicial branch (Supreme Court) interprets the laws to determine if they are lawful according to the U.S. Constitution.

2. The Congress of the United States was created by Article I of the United States Constitution.

3. Two houses of government form Congress. These houses are the Senate and the House of Representatives.

4. The Senate consists of 100 senators – two from each of the 50 states.

5. To qualify as a senator, a candidate must be at least 30 years of age and a U.S. citizen for at least nine years.

6. Senators are elected for a period of six years.

7. One-third of the senators are elected/re-elected every two years.

8. There are 435 members of the House of Representatives.

9. Each state of the United States has at least one representative in the House of Representatives.

10. State representation in the House of Representatives is proportional to its population. More representatives are elected to represent the more densely populated states, and fewer representatives are elected to represent the states with smaller populations. (Members of Congress represent districts within their states.)

11. To qualify as a member of the House of Representatives, a candidate must be at least 25 years of age, and a U.S. citizen for at least seven years.

12. The first Congress (1800) to convene in the new Capitol Building consisted of 32 members of the Senate and 106 members of the House of Representatives.

THE LOCATIONS AND EVOLUTION OF THE CAPITOL BUILDING

1. Before 1791, the federal government had no permanent site. The early Congresses met in eight different cities: Philadelphia, Pennsylvania; Baltimore, Maryland; Lancaster, Pennsylvania; York, Pennsylvania; Princeton, New Jersey; Annapolis, Maryland; Trenton, New Jersey; and New York City, New York.

2. Between 1789 and 1790, Congress convened in Federal Hall in New York City, New York.

3. Between 1790 and 1800, Congress convened in Congress Hall in Philadelphia, Pennsylvania.

4. On November 22, 1800, Congress first convened in the current Capitol Building.

5. The Capitol Building is located on Capitol Hill at the east end of the National Mall.

6. The Capitol Building is located on what was formerly known as *"Jenkins' Hill."*

7. The plateau on which the Capitol Building is located is 88 feet above the level of the Potomac River.

8. The boundaries of the Capitol grounds are Independence Avenue on the south, and Constitution Avenue on the north. First Street on the northeast/southeast forms the eastern boundary, and First Street on the northwest/southwest forms the western boundary.

9. The same three commissioners appointed by George Washington to oversee the building of Washington, D.C. also oversaw the building of the Capitol Building.

10. Pierre Charles L'Enfant was initially tasked with designing the Capitol Building, but he was fired when he chose not to accept the authority of the D.C. Building Commission, and to provide the D.C. Building Commission with any designs or drawings. He claimed the plans *"were in his head,"* and the commission should trust him.

The U.S. Capitol Building

11. After L'Enfant was fired, Secretary of State Thomas Jefferson suggested that a $500 prize and a city lot be awarded for the best plans for the Capitol Building.

12. On April 5, 1793, the D.C. Building Commission accepted the plan proposed by Dr. William Thorton from the eighteen submitted plans. Thorton was from the British West Indies.

13. Benjamin Henry Latrobe was appointed the first architect responsible for supervising the construction of the Capitol Building.

14. On September 18, 1793, President George Washington (1789-1797) dedicated the first cornerstone for the Capitol Building in the building's southeast corner.

15. No surviving records have revealed where the first cornerstone was placed, and the cornerstone has never been rediscovered. (The most recent unsuccessful search for the cornerstone was in 1998.)

16. Most of the original Capitol Building was constructed primarily out of sandstone from the quarries at Aquia, Virginia. As the Capitol Building expanded, the sandstone was replaced with marble and granite.

17. On November 22, 1800, Congress (Senate and House of Representatives) convened its first session in the Capitol Building (North Wing).

18. In 1801, the United States Supreme Court and the courts of the District of Columbia occupied the Capitol Building.

19. In 1814, a covered one-story walkway connected the chambers of the House of Representatives and Senate.

20. On August 24, 1814, the British Army burned the Capitol Building.

21. If it had not been for the rain during a very bad thunderstorm soon after the torch was set to the Capitol Building, the building would have sustained considerably more damage.

22. After the burning of the Capitol Building by the British Army, Congress met in a brick building on the site of the present day U.S. Supreme Court. The structure was referred to as the "*Old Brick Capitol.*"

23. On December 6, 1819, five years after the British attack, Congress reoccupied the Capitol Building for a second time.

24. The Capitol Building is the centerpiece of the Capitol Complex, which includes six principal Congressional office buildings and three Library of Congress buildings constructed on Capitol Hill during the 19th and 20th centuries.

25. The cornerstones of the new wings to the Capitol Building, which currently house the Senate and the House of Representatives, were dedicated during ceremonies on July 4, 1851. The House of Representatives occupied its chamber in 1857, and the Senate in 1859.

26. In 1959, President Dwight Eisenhower (1953-1961) dedicated the fourth and final cornerstone of the Capitol Building.

THE DESIGN AND SIZE OF THE CAPITOL BUILDING

1. Through a series of eight major construction projects, the Capitol Building has been expanded from a single small building housing both the Senate and House of Representatives to its current size. Viewing the Capitol Building from the National Mall, the below shaded blocks show the construction of the original building (1st Wing), and five of the seven additions to the exterior as they occurred.

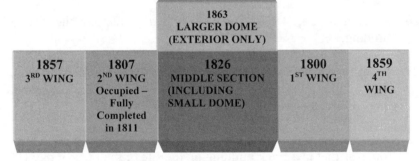

Stages of Construction – U.S. Capitol Building

2. Between 1884 and 1891, the sixth addition, which consisted of adding marble terraces to the north, west, and south sides of the Capitol, was completed.

3. Between 1959 and 1963, the seventh addition saw the construction of the largest modification to the Capitol Building since the exterior of the Capitol dome was finished in 1863. During the four-year project, the old east front of the Capitol Building was torn down, and duplicated in marble. The construction also extended the front of the Capitol Building by 32 feet.

4. In addition to the major projects described above, there have been several other projects to strengthen, renovate, and preserve the Capitol Building.

5. The exterior of the larger dome was completed in December 1863. The interior of the dome was completed in January 1866.

6. The Capitol Building contains 540 rooms, 658 windows, and 850 doorways.

7. Currently, and subject to change because of new construction, the Capitol Building is divided into five levels:

    - Committee rooms occupy the first level of the Capitol Building. In addition, there is space for congressional offices, the Hall of Columns, Brumidi Corridors, the Old Supreme Court Chamber, and the Crypt.

    - The second level of the Capitol Building holds the chambers of the House of Representatives and the Senate, offices of congressional leadership, the Rotunda, and a gallery of paintings and sculptures.

    - The third level of the Capitol Building allows access to the galleries from which visitors to the Capitol Building may watch the proceedings of the House of Representatives and the Senate. It also contains offices, committee rooms, and press galleries.

    - Offices, machinery rooms, workshops, and other support areas occupy the fourth level of the Capitol Building.

    - The fifth level of the Capitol Building consists of the terrace level. This level contains additional offices.

8. The design of the Capitol Building is 19th century neoclassical architecture derived from ancient Greek and Roman designs.

9. The Capitol Building covers 175,170 square feet of the grounds, or approximately four acres.

10. The floors within the Capitol Building cover approximately 16 1/2 acres.

11. The length of the Capitol Building from north to south is 751 feet.

12. The greatest width of the Capitol Building, including approaches, is 350 feet.

13. The height of the Capitol Building from the baseline to the top of the statue of "*Freedom*" is 288 feet.

14. Twenty-four columns grace the west face ("National Mall" side) of the Capitol Building. Each column was constructed from Potomac freestone, which is 240 feet long by 3 feet in diameter.

15. There are pediments over the entrance to the central section of the Capitol Building and the entrances to the House of Representatives and Senate (East Front). (A pediment is a form of classical architecture in a triangular space forming the gable of a pitched room with carved figures in the interior.) (These allegorical figures, representing a symbolic portrayal of an idea or principle, were raised by crane onto their positions.)

16. The primary entrances to the Capitol Building are through three porticos. A portico is a colonnaded (columned) porch found on Classical and Neoclassical buildings, usually with a pediment above. The pediments over the entrances to the Capitol Building are titled, and symbolize the following:

    - Central Portico - The original pediment was completed in 1828. Titled "*The Genius of America*," it is 12 feet high by 60 feet wide. The central figure represents "*America*", with the figure on her right representing "*Hope*" and on her left representing "*Justice.*" The implication is that America may hope for success so long as she cultivates justice. (This is the entrance that was used by most visitors to the Capitol Building prior to the construction of the new visitor center.)

    - In 1959-1960, the Central Portico was replaced with the marble reproduction that is seen today.

- Senate Portico - Completed in 1863, the 12-foot-high by 60-foot-wide pediment is titled *"The Progress of Civilization."* The central figure represents America. The figures on her right represent the confrontation between American pioneers and the American Indians. The figures on her left represent the advantages of liberty and civilization.

- House of Representatives Portico - Completed in 1916, the 12-foot-high by 60-foot-wide pediment is titled *"The Apotheosis of Democracy."* The central figure represents *"Armed Peace,"* and its protection of *"Industry"* on the left, and *"Agriculture"* on the right. The waves on each side of the portico represent the Atlantic Ocean and Pacific Ocean.

17. Beneath the porticos are doors that lead to the Rotunda, House of Representatives, and the Senate. The doors symbolize the following:

- Rotunda - Columbus Doors. Completed in 1858, the doors reflect on the life and accomplishments of Christopher Columbus.

- House of Representatives - American Revolutionary War Doors. Completed in 1905, the 8-foot-wide by 15-foot-high doors reflect on the events of the American Revolutionary War.

- Senate - George Washington and the Revolutionary War Doors. Completed in 1868, the 7-foot-wide by 14-foot-high doors reflect on the life of Washington as a farmer, soldier, and President of the United States. The marble figures over the door symbolize "*Justice*" and "*History.*"

THE CAPITOL GROUNDS

1. The Capitol grounds total 274 acres.

2. The grounds immediately surrounding the Capitol Building are bordered by a stonewall, and cover an area of a little over 58 acres.

3. Law Olmsted designed the grounds around the Capitol Building after his commission in 1874. He is also credited with designing Central Park in New York City.

4. Six massive red granite lamp piers, topped with light fixtures in wrought-iron cages, and sixteen smaller bronze light fixtures, line the Capitol Plaza at the East Capitol Street entrance.

5. The roofed bench at the East Capitol Street entrance was originally a shelter for streetcar passengers.

6. Watchmen started patrolling the Capitol grounds in 1878.

THE SENATE GARAGE FOUNTAIN

1. The Senate Garage Fountain is located between the Capitol Building and Union Station.

2. On July 16, 1932, the fountain operated for the first time.

The Senate Garage Fountain

3. The fountain is a hexagonal monolith constructed from Minnesota Pink granite, Minnesota Green granite, and Mount Airy granite.

4. The hexagon is 25 feet across, and the basin measures 85 feet by 100 feet.

5. The reflecting pool of the fountain measures 180 feet by 80 feet.

6. The fountain's lighting display is comprised of 114 underwater light fixtures with red, green, blue, and clear lens. The computer program, which was started on July 4, 1980, runs every twenty minutes.

7. The fountain pumps up to 3,000 gallons of water per minute.

14

MISCELLANEOUS FACTS ABOUT THE CAPITOL BUILDING

1. The Library of Congress was located in the west wing of the Capitol Building at the time it was gutted by fire in 1851.

2. Running water was installed in the Capitol Building in 1832, gas lighting in the 1840's, electricity in 1885, and steam heat in 1902. The first elevator was operational in 1874, and electric air conditioning was installed in 1929. (Prior to electric air conditioning being installed, a system of using ice and fans under the floors was the primary source for cooling the building.)

3. The Old Supreme Court Chamber, the Old Senate Chamber, and the National Statuary Hall were restored to their mid-19th century appearance for the nation's 1976 Bicentennial celebration.

4. Over thirty layers of white paint have been removed from the Capitol Building.

5. The first Capitol office building was constructed in 1908. Prior to this date, members of Congress rented their own office space in downtown Washington, D.C.

6. In 1897, electric lighting replaced gas lighting on the Capitol grounds.

7. In response to complaints from members of Congress about the poor air quality in their windowless chambers, two air-intake towers were installed to allow fresh air to the chambers of the Senate and the House of Representatives. The tower for the House of Representatives was completed in 1879, and the tower for the Senate was completed in 1889.

8. Over 3,000 soldiers were barracked in the Capitol Building during the early stages of the Civil War. Later it was converted to a hospital with over 1,500 cots for patients. The soldiers referred to the building as the "*Big Tent.*"

9. In 1876, the original Guide Service for the Capitol Building was established as an outgrowth of the Philadelphia Centennial. Until 1971, the guides derived their incomes from a 25-cent fee for the tour. This charge was discontinued when Public Law 91-510 established an organization under Congress to be designated the *"Capitol Guide Service."*

10. In 1844, it was in the Capitol Building that Samuel F.B. Morse first demonstrated the telegraph. Morse tapped out the message *"What hath God wrought?"* from Washington, D.C. to Baltimore, Maryland.

11. The tradition of flying the United States flags over the east and west fronts of the Capitol Building 24-hours a day began during World War I. (It is not known when the tradition of flying the flags over the Capitol Building for any part of the day was begun.)

12. The flags that fly over the east and west fronts to the Capitol Building are 8 feet by 12 feet.

13. There is really no front or back to the Capitol Building. What visitors refer to as the front side (facing the National Mall) is the garden side, and the other side is the carriage side.

14. The Capitol Building was constructed using sandstone, limestone, marble, and concrete.

15. The exterior walls of the Capitol Building's center structure have been treated with special consolidants, and then painted to match the marble wings.

16. Because President James Monroe (1817-1825) did not want to offend the members of the House of Representatives or Senate by taking the presidential oath of office in a particular chamber, he started a tradition in 1817 by taking the oath of office in front of the temporary Capitol Building on the site where the U.S. Supreme Court Building is now located. (This tradition continues as modern-day presidents take the oath of office in front of the current Capitol Building.)

FACTS ABOUT THE ROTUNDA AND CRYPT WITHIN THE UNITED STATES CAPITOL BUILDING

As visitors enter the interior of the Capitol Building, they are immediately presented a colorful lesson in history through paintings, statues, brassware, and woodworks. Abraham Lincoln, Thomas Jefferson, George Washington, Martin Luther King, Pocahontas, and other great contributors to history greet visitors as they enter the Rotunda. Every direction offers visitors an opportunity to learn about the sacrifices and contributions immortalized through the hands of artists who used their considerable talents to craft several beautiful gifts to a grateful nation.

THE ROTUNDA

1. A rotunda is a high ceiling room having a circular space, covered by a dome.

2. In 1818, work on the initial Capitol Rotunda was started, and was completed in 1824. The dimensions of the first rotunda were 96 feet high from floor to ceiling by 96 feet in diameter.

3. In 1824, the original Rotunda was first used for a reception to honor Marquis de Lafayette. (Lafayette, a Frenchman, served under George Washington during the Revolutionary War.)

4. In 1866, the current Rotunda was completed. The Rotunda is 180 feet high from floor to ceiling by 96 feet in diameter.

5. The bronze doors used to enter the Rotunda are known as the *"Columbus Doors."* The doors were sculptured by Randolph Rogers in the 1850's, and are 17 feet high by 10 feet wide. They depict the life of Christopher Columbus.

6. The *"Columbus Doors,"* which weigh ten tons (20,000 pounds), were cast in Germany, and were initially used as the doors to the old House of Representatives Chamber.

7. In 1871, the "*Columbus Doors*" were moved to the Rotunda.

8. The initial height of the Rotunda's sandstone walls was 48 feet. Everything above this height was added between 1855 and 1866.

9. The Rotunda has a sandstone floor.

10. At the top of the Rotunda is the painting *The Apotheosis of George Washington* by Constantine Brumidi (1805-1880). [Apotheosis means glorification.] Brumidi painted the 4,664 square feet of surface in eleven months, completing it in 1866. Most of his painting was completed while he laid on his back beneath the 62 feet, 2-inch diameter of the painting. (Brumidi worked in fresco, a process of applying pigments to fresh plaster. Michelangelo used the same process in the Sistine Chapel in Rome, Italy.)

11. In *The Apotheosis of George Washington,* Washington is sitting between women who represent *Liberty* and *Freedom*.

12. The maidens surrounding Washington in *The Apotheosis of George Washington* represent the thirteen original states.

The Apotheosis of George Washington

13. To ensure the figures in *The Apotheosis of George Washington* could be seen from the floor of the Rotunda, 180 feet below, they were painted oversized, some as tall as 15 feet.

14. There are six scenes surrounding the exterior of *The Apotheosis of George Washington*. The depictions, consisting of Greek and Roman gods with distinguished Americans, represent:

    *   Mercury offering a bag of gold to Robert Morris, considered the Financier of the Revolution.

    *   Vulcan rests his foot on a cannon.

- Ceres rides a reaper as young America.

- Bearded Neptune holds the Atlantic cable.

- Wise Minerva speaks to Benjamin Franklin (statesman), S.F.B. Morse (inventor of the telegraph), and Robert Fulton (inventor of the steamboat).

- Armed Freedom triumphs over Tyranny and Kingly power. (Brumidi's young wife modeled for the figure of Armed Freedom.)

- *The Apotheosis of George Washington* was last cleaned and went through maintenance in the year 2000 by a skilled crew of artists and technicians.

15. For all of his work on *The Apotheosis of George Washington,* Brumidi received a commission of $40,000.

16. There are four relief sculptures above the doors of the Rotunda that show the early relationships between Native Americans and the settlers. They reflect the *Preservation of John Smith by Pocahontas – 1606* (West), *Landing of the Pilgrims – 1620* (East), *William Penn's Treaty with the Indians – 1682* (North), and *Conflict of Daniel Boone and the Indians – 1773* (South).

17. There are eight framed niches holding historical paintings on the walls of the Rotunda. Each painting measures 12 feet by 18 feet, and consist of the following:

- Four scenes from the period of the American Revolutionary War, which were recommended for the Rotunda by James Madison, were painted by John Trumbull between 1819 and 1824. They consist of the *Declaration of Independence in Congress, Surrender of General Burgoyne at Saratoga, Surrender of Lord Cornwallis at Yorktown*, and *General George Washington Resigning his Commission to Congress as Commander in Chief of the Army*. (Trumbull served as an aid to George Washington during the Revolutionary War. He received $8,000 for each of the four paintings.)

19

- Four scenes of early exploration were added to the Rotunda between 1840 and 1855: *Landing of Christopher Columbus* by John Vanderlyn, *Discovery of the Mississippi by De Soto* by William Powell, *Baptism of Pocahontas* by John Capman, and *Embarkation of the Pilgrims* by Robert Weir.

18. In the painting *Baptism of Pocahontas*, one of the Indians has six toes on one foot.

19. If Miles Standish's feet (kneeling figure) were true to size in the Rotunda painting *The Embarkation of the Pilgrims*, they would require size 19 or 20 shoes.

20. Initially, the men seated in the front row of the Rotunda painting *Declaration of Independence* all had their legs crossed in the same manner. A table was inserted to eliminate this prominent feature.

Paintings on the Rotunda Wall

21. Constantine Brumidi was commissioned to complete the frescoed frieze in the belt just below the 36 windows in the Rotunda. The 300-foot panorama, through a series of 14 panels, traces America's history from its discovery by Columbus to the discovery of gold in California.

22. In 1880, at age 74, Brumidi completed all but the last eight depictions in the frieze prior to his death. He died while painting *William Penn's Treaty with the Indians*.

23. In 1889, Filippo Costaggini, Brumidi's understudy, completed the remaining eight panels in the frieze.

24. In 1953, Allyn Cox completed the final 31-foot gap in the frescoed frieze. The additions represent scenes from the Civil War, the Spanish-American War, and the Birth of Aviation.

25. The total length of the frescoed frieze extends 400 feet.

26. In 1835, near the bronze figure of General Andrew Jackson in the Rotunda, an assassin attempted to take the life of President Jackson (1829-1837). Both of the assailant's guns misfired. (This was the first attempt at assassinating a United States President.)

27. Vinnie Ream completed the marble statue of Abraham Lincoln. Ream was the first woman artist to receive a government commission. (Lincoln permitted Ream, just age 17 at the time, to sketch his daily activities when he was informed she was poor. Ream died at age 67, and is buried at Arlington National Cemetery near her husband.)

28. The large statue of three female figures provides the images of suffragists Susan B. Anthony, Elizabeth Cady Stanton, and Lucretia Mott. (The statue was originally in the Rotunda until the 1920s, when it was removed and placed in the Crypt. It was returned to the Rotunda in 1997.)

29. Until the end of the 19th century, visitors could walk the walkway above the Rotunda. However, because several people collapsed from exhaustion on the nearly 300-step walkway, the walkway was closed, and remains closed, to the general public.

30. On July 1, 1852, Henry Clay became the first person to lie in state in the Rotunda.

31. A small circle in the center of the Rotunda marks the spot where the honored dead lie as mourners pay their respects to the deceased for his/her accomplishments and sacrifices.

32. Thirty American heroes and notable citizens have been granted the honor of a public viewing in the Capitol Building. The most recent of these notable Americans was former President Gerald Ford in December 2006.

33. The first woman to be honored with a viewing in the Capitol Building was civil rights activist Rosa Parks in October 2004.

34. As of 2006, the remains of five presidents have lain in state in the Rotunda - Lincoln (1861-1865), Garfield (1881), McKinley (1897-1901), Harding (1921-1923), and Kennedy (1961-1963). There have also been six former presidents who were granted this honor - Taft (1909-1913), Hoover (1929-1933), Eisenhower (1953-1961), Johnson (1963-1969), Reagan (1981-1989) and Ford (1974-1977). (Even though President Franklin Roosevelt (1933-1945) died while he was in office, he had previously requested that his body not lie in state. His request was honored.)

35. A few facts about the military honor guard who pays homage to the deceased as they lie in state:

- The members of the honor guard represent each of the branches of the military - Army, Navy, Air Force, Coast Guard, and Marines.

- Eight body bearers, four body bearers on each side of the casket, carry it into and out of the Capitol Building. If the ceremony is for a former president, an honor guard carries the flag of the United States in front of the casket. Following the casket is the officer in charge, followed by an honor guard carrying the presidential flag.

- Once the casket is placed on the catafalque in the center of the Rotunda, the duties of this team of honor guards are transferred to six other members of the honor guard. (A catafalque is a portable framework on which a casket rests.)

- The members of the honor guard stand at the following positions around the casket:

  - One guard at the head of the casket.
  - One guard at each corner of the casket.
  - One guard near the foot of the casket. This guard is known as the *Supernumerary* or *Super*, and he would take the place of any guard who falls from his position.

- The shifts of honor guards rotate on a thirty minute basis.

- The honor guards at the head and foot of the casket are unarmed.

- The guards at the corners of the casket carry rifles. (The rifles are unloaded and have had the firing pins removed.)

- The flag of the United States is prominently displayed. (Other flags, such as the presidential flag and state flags are also displayed.)

Even though the average casket weighs approximately 400 pounds, many of the caskets containing notable citizens weigh hundreds of pounds more. For example, President Reagan's casket weighed over 700 pounds, and President Kennedy's nearly 1,200 pounds.

Guidance under Title 4 of the United States Code states that when a president or former president dies, the flag of the United States should be lowered to half-staff for 30 days, 10 days for a current vice president, current and former Supreme Court chief justices and speakers of the house. For former vice presidents, associate Supreme Court justices, cabinet secretaries, and governors, the flag is flown at half-staff from their death to their interment.

THE CRYPT

1. The Crypt, which is the center section of the building, was completed in 1827.

2. Despite its name, the Crypt has never been used for a funeral or burial.

3. The 40 Doric columns in the Crypt support the Rotunda above. (This style of columns is the oldest and simplest of the three ancient Greek orders of architecture, usually fluted columns with plain rounded capitols (heads)).

The Crypt – Lower Level of Capitol Building

4. The Doric columns were constructed from brown stone surmounted by groined sandstone arches.

5. The star in the center of the floor denotes the point from which the streets in Washington are laid out and numbered.

6. The Crypt was initially intended to hold the remains of George and Martha Washington.

7. The remains of President and Mrs. Washington were to be enclosed in a memorial that could be viewed through an opening in the Rotunda floor. (The opening has since been enclosed.)

8. The Crypt was also considered for the final resting place of President Abraham Lincoln after his assassination. However, it was later decided to entomb his remains at Oak Ridge Cemetery in Springfield, Illinois.

9. The Crypt contains a velvet-covered catafalque on which Lincoln's coffin rested while in the Rotunda.

10. Benjamin French designed Lincoln's catafalque, which consisted simply of pine boards nailed together and covered with black broadcloth. Over the years the base and platform have been modified to accommodate the remains of the honored dead who lay in state in the Rotunda and nearby locations. The fabric has been replaced, but its draping follows the 1865 style.

11. The same catafalque has been used for other notable Americans who have lain in state.

FACTS ABOUT THE CAPITOL DOME AND STATUE OF FREEDOM OVER THE UNITED STATES CAPITOL BUILDING

The attention of visitors viewing the exterior of the Capitol Building is quickly drawn to the Capitol Dome. Atop one of the most prominent structures in Washington, D.C. is a statue that appears to be welcoming visitors to a house that shelters the governing bodies of the United States. As they view the Dome, and its apparent caretaker, visitors might let their curiosity run wild about how the Dome was constructed, who was responsible for constructing it, and what the statue at the top of the Dome really looks like and represents. The following provides answers to at least a few of these questions.

THE CAPITOL DOME

1. In 1824, the original Capitol Dome, designed after a Roman Temple, was completed. It was constructed from wood covered with copper.

2. In 1855, the old wooden Capitol Dome was removed.

3. In 1856, work on the new Capitol Dome was begun.

4. The architect of the new Capitol Dome was Thomas Walter.

5. Through the fall of 1858, Montgomery C. Meigs, then a captain in the Army Corps of Engineers, was the principal superintendent of construction for the new Capitol Dome. (Meigs was later a key figure in having Robert E. Lee's home at Arlington declared a national cemetery during the Civil War.)

The Capitol Dome

6. William B. Franklin replaced Captain Meigs as the principal superintendent of construction for the new Capitol Dome.

7. The man who had final approval authority over the construction of the Capitol Dome was then Secretary of War Jefferson Davis. (He later became President of the Confederate States of America (1861-1865)).

8. The iron supports that support the Capitol Dome weigh nearly 8.9 million pounds.

9. The iron supports were lifted to the top of the Capitol Dome by steam-powered derricks. (Wood from the original dome was used to power the derricks.)

10. The height of the Capitol Dome, not including the statue of "*Freedom*," is 287 feet.

11. In 1863, the exterior of the current Capitol Dome was completed. In 1866, the interior was completed.

12. The cost of the completed Capitol Dome totaled $1,047,291.

13. There are 108 windowpanes in the Capitol Dome.

14. The top of the Capitol Dome has an inner-shell and an outer-shell, with a flight of stairs in between.

15. The assembly of the Capitol Dome rests on 36 supporting trusses attached to the Capitol's foundation.

16. On very hot days, the Capitol Dome can expand as much as four inches.

17. Electrically charged wires on the Capitol Dome generate mild shocks to discourage birds from roosting on the dome.

18. Thirty-two coats of paint were removed from the Capitol Dome in 1958. It takes 1,750 gallons of paint to repaint the Capitol Dome. A red undercoat of paint protects the iron from the elements.

19. The Capitol Dome is the third largest dome of its kind in the world. The largest domes crown the tops of St. Peter at the Vatican and St. Paul in London, England.

THE STATUE OF "FREEDOM"

1. The statue on top of the Capitol Dome is known as *"Freedom."* (It was initially referred to as *"Armed Freedom."*)

2. Thomas Crawford sculptured the statue of *"Freedom."*

3. *"Freedom"* is often mistaken for the Indian princess Pocahontas. In reality, it is a woman wearing a helmet on which there is a head of an eagle with long feathers and large stars. (To protect the statue from lightning, ten bronze points tipped with platinum are attached to the headdress, shoulders, and shield.)

4. *"Freedom"* wears a brooch (belt) that secures her fringed robe. The letters "U.S." are inscribed on the brooch.

5. *"Freedom's"* right hand rests on a sheathed sword, while her left hand holds a laurel wreath of victory and a shield with thirteen strips representing the original thirteen states of the United States.

The Statue of "Freedom" at the top of the Capitol Building

6. *"Freedom"* stands on a globe that is 7 feet in diameter. Around the sphere is the national motto, *"E Pluribus Unum"* – *"One Out of Many."*

7. The bronze statue of *"Freedom"* is 19 feet, 6 inches tall, and weighs 14,985 pounds.

8. The statue of *"Freedom"* faces east, away from the Mall. This is due to the Capitol Building's east front being planned, and still serves, as the principal entrance to the building, and thus faces those who arrive from this direction.

9. Initially, the headwear worn by *"Freedom"* was that of a figure wearing a softly folded cloth liberty cap. The proposed cap was similar to the cap worn by freed slaves in ancient Rome. However, Jefferson Davis would not accept any figure that suggested freedom for slaves, and he forced Thomas Crawford to modify the design to look like a crested Roman helmet.

10. In 1859, the plaster model of *"Freedom"* was delivered to the United States from Rome, Italy. The statue was then cast in Bladensburg, Maryland. (Bladensburg is located just over the Washington, D.C. border, near the Capital Beltway.)

11. *"Freedom"* was cast in five pieces, bolted together after being lifted to the top of the Capitol Dome.

12. The cost of the statue, excluding installation, was $23,796.

13. In December 1863, a 35-gun salute signaled the dedication of the statue of *"Freedom."* Each cannon shot represented one of the 35 states in the Union at the time of the dedication. (The states consisted of the 34 states in the Union at the start of the Civil War, and West Virginia, which entered the Union in June 1863.)

14. Philip Reid supervised the assembly of *"Freedom"* at the top of the Capitol Dome. (Reid was a former slave who acquired his freedom through the Emancipation Proclamation, which went into effect on January 1, 1863.)

15. In 1993, the statue of *"Freedom"* was removed from the Capitol Dome by helicopter for cleaning. It was replaced in the same manner. Bronze plugs were inserted in several hundred places where pitting was severe. New caulking was added in the gaps of the structure, and wax was layered over the complete statue.

16. Every seven to ten years the statue receives some well-deserved maintenance (while the statue remains on the Dome). This maintenance consists of cleaning the corrosion from the lady, caulking the gaps in the structure, and applying a thick layer of wax over the entire statue.

FACTS ABOUT THE OLD SENATE CHAMBER WITHIN THE UNITED STATES CAPITOL BUILDING

The Old Senate Chamber, modeled after the amphitheaters of antiquity (early years of history), is a two-story semicircular chamber measuring 75 feet long by 50 feet wide. This quick overview of the Old Senate Chamber could be used to describe many rooms within the Capitol Building or similar rooms in many other government buildings constructed during the nineteenth and early twentieth centuries. But it is the architecture of this particular chamber that stirs visitors' imaginations. Visitors might wonder where a particular senator sat, or what laws were passed within the chamber walls, or what treaties those makers of laws approved during a period known for some of the greatest debates. Visitors may never know the answers to these and other questions, but the chamber does provide ample incentives for the mind to wonder.

THE OLD SENATE CHAMBER

1. The chamber, as it exists today, was completed in December 1819. It was the third chamber constructed for the U.S. Senate. The first chamber deteriorated so rapidly that it had to be reconstructed just six years after its completion. The British Army destroyed the second chamber in 1814 during the burning of the Capitol Building.

2. The two-story chamber is semicircular in shape, and is 75 feet long by 50 feet wide.

3. The ceiling of the chamber is a half dome.

4. The domed, white-painted ceiling of the chamber is elaborately coffered and enriched by decorative moldings.

5. Five smaller circular skylights border a central, semicircular skylight. The skylights originally provided the chamber with natural light. It is now artificially lighted.

6. The prestigious Philadelphia firm of Cornelius and Company furnished the large brass chandelier that hangs above the vice president's desk.

7. Two visitor galleries overlook the chamber.

8. Eight Ionic columns of variegated marble support the gallery on the east wall. The columns of the Erechtheion in Athens, Greece, inspired the columns in the chamber. They were constructed from marble quarried along the Potomac River.

9. A second and much larger *"Ladies' Gallery"* follows the curved western wall. The gallery is carried on twelve steel columns encased in cast-iron forms, topped with Corinthian capitals. The columns were designed to simulate the cast-iron originals.

10. A wrought-iron balcony railing follows the contour of the gallery. The crimson fabric backing was intended to accentuate the decorative metal work.

11. Directly above the east gallery hangs an original 1823 *"porthole"* portrait of George Washington. The artist, Rembrandt Peale, had painted Washington from life. The portrait was purchased in 1832, the centennial of Washington's birth, for display in the chamber. (The words under the figure of Washington read "Father of Our Country".)

12. A curved table with richly turned and carved legs and a crimson modesty screen sits on a raised platform in the center of the room.
This is the desk of the Vice President of the United States, who serves as President of the Senate. To symbolize the importance of the desk, an elaborate canopy with a mahogany valance from which crimson fabric hangs covers the desk. A carved gilt (gold surface) eagle and shield stand above the valance. (The desk is the original.)

The Vice President's Desk

13. Directly in front of the vice president's desk, but one tier down, is a larger desk of similar design. The Secretary of the Senate and the chief clerk occupied this desk when it was an active Senate Chamber.

14. A glass screen separates the vice president's dais (series of tiers) from a small lobby. This is where the senators could go to relax, yet still listen to floor proceedings.

15. Two fireplace mantels are located on the east wall behind the screen. Both mantels are originals to the chamber.

16. The two additional mantels on the north and south ends of the lobby are reproductions. The original mantels were replaced with stoves when the Supreme Court started using the chamber.

17. The 64 senators' desks and chairs in the chamber are reproductions.

18. Reproduced from 1819 designs by New York cabinetmaker Thomas Constantine, the original desks and chairs were custom made from mahogany.

19. The original desks each cost $34.00, each chair cost $48.00.

20. Today all of Constantine's desks remain in use in the current Senate Chamber. His chairs have been replaced.

21. A desk's shape reflects its position in the room: aisle desks are narrow and angled, while center desks are wider and more square.

22. The desk of Daniel Webster, which was moved to the current Senate Chamber, is the only desk that is not a lift top desk. It is also the largest desk in the Senate Chamber.

23. As new states entered the Union, desks of similar design were ordered from other cabinetmakers; although, the four newest desks in the current chamber—those constructed for Alaska (1959) and Hawaii (1959)—were built in the Senate Cabinet Shop.

24. Immediately behind the last row of desks is a low paneled wall. The wall separates the senators' space from a third visitor area. Furnished with red-upholstered sofas, this area was reserved for privileged visitors who gained admittance through special invitations from the senators. The niches, one on either side of the main doorway, house reproductions of the stoves that were capable of burning wood or coal.

25. The chamber floor is covered with a carpet woven from long-staple 100% virgin wool. It features a gold star pattern on a red background.

26. Every senator had a spittoon next to his desk.

27. Tradition calls for the Republican senators to be seated on the left side of the chamber, and the Democrats senators on the right.

28. Tradition also calls for the senators to sit by seniority. The most senior senators sit in the front of the chamber, and the junior senators sit in the rear of the chamber.

29. In 1859, the U.S. Senate moved to its current chamber.

30. In 1860, the U.S. Supreme Court was relocated into the vacated Senate Chamber, where it remained until 1935.

31. From 1935 to 1976, the chamber was used as a law library, committee room, meeting room, and storage room. In 1976, it was opened to visitors as part of the nation's bicentennial celebration.

32. The "*Ladies' Gallery*" on the western wall was restored in 1976.

33. Today the restored chamber is used primarily as a museum space open to the public. It is also used periodically for joint House-Senate committee conferences, important meetings, and ceremonial events. (In January 1999, the chamber was used as a meeting chamber for the full body of the U.S. Senate to discuss the possible impeachment trial of President William Clinton (1993-2001).)

FACTS ABOUT THE NATIONAL STATUARY HALL
WITHIN THE UNITED STATES CAPITOL BUILDING

The area in the Capitol Building that currently houses the National Statuary Hall previously housed the House of Representatives. After the House of Representatives moved to its current location, it was decided that the open area would be an ideal location for displaying the likenesses of notable Americans who contributed to the nation's history. Doctors, war heroes, inventors and statesmen adorn the halls. These sculptures, formed from raw pieces of marble and uniformed pieces of bronze, are oversized likenesses of such notable citizens as patriot Ethan Allen of Vermont, New Jersey's Civil War hero Philip Kearny, Pennsylvania's Robert Fulton, the inventor of the steamboat, and Utah's religious leader Brigham Young.

THE NATIONAL STATUARY HALL

1. From 1807 to 1857, the U.S. House of Representatives occupied the chamber that is now known as the *National Statuary Hall.*

2. The Hall was constructed in the shape of an ancient amphitheater, and is one of the earliest examples of Greek revival architecture in America.

3. While most of the Hall surface is painted plaster, the lower gallery walls and pilasters (columns) are sandstone.

4. Around the perimeter of the Hall stand colossal columns of variegated Breccia. The marble for the columns was quarried from along the Potomac River. The Corinthian capitals of white marble were carved in Carrara, Italy.

The National Statuary Hall

5. A lantern in the fireproof cast-steel ceiling admits natural light into the Hall.

6. The floor of the Hall is covered with black and white marble tiles. The black marble was purchased specifically for the Hall, while the white marble was scrap material from the 1857 extension to the Capitol Building.

7. The four fireplaces on the south side of the room, in conjunction with an ingenious central heating system, warmed the room during cold months.

8. Only two of the many sculptures presently in the room were commissioned for display in the House of Representatives Chamber.

   - The first, Enrico Causici's neoclassical plaster *Liberty and the Eagle*, looks out over the Hall from a niche above the colonnade behind what was once the Speaker's rostrum. Giuseppe Valaperta carved the sandstone relief eagle in the frieze of the entablature.

   - The second, which is located above the door leading into the Rotunda, is the *Car of History* by Carlo Franzoni. This neoclassical marble sculpture depicts Clio, the Muse of History, riding in the Chariot of Time while recording events occurring in the chamber below. The wheel of the chariot contains the chamber clock, with works by Simon Willard.

9. The heavy curtains on the walls of the Hall were installed to help suppress the noise. The results were minimal.

10. A small bronze marker marks the spot in the Hall where former President John Quincy Adams (1825-1829) was fatally stricken by a heart attack in 1848. Other markers identify the spots where the desks of important members of Congress were seated. These members included such men as future Presidents Fillmore (1850-1853), Pierce (1853-1857), and Lincoln (1861-1865). (Lincoln's desk was #191.)

11. The statue over the south door of the Hall is of *Lady Liberty*.

12. In 1864, Congress authorized the Statuary Hall in the Capitol Building. Each state was authorized to display no more than two figures of prominent men or women from their respective states.

13. The figures of 93 men and 7 women are displayed in the Hall and throughout the Capitol Building. Each statue must be a gift from a state, not from an individual or group of citizens.

14. The likeness of Nathaniel Green (soldier & politician) was the first statue placed in the Hall. In 1870, it was presented as a gift from the state of Rhode Island.

15. In 2000, Congress enacted a law that permits the states to replace the statues of notable citizens with new statues. As a result, the date and name of the last of the 100 statues in the Capitol Building are subject to change. It should also be noted that the location of the statues within the Hall or other parts of the Capitol Building are subject to change.

16. The largest statue in the Statuary Hall collection is that of King Kamehameha I. The bronze statue is 9 feet, 10 inches tall, stands on a 3 feet, 6 inch granite base, and weighs approximately 15,000 pounds. It was presented as a gift from the state of Hawaii in 1969.

17. In 1933, because the collection of figures in the Hall had grown to 66, and the weight had caused the floor of the Hall to sag, Congress restricted the number of statues to be displayed in the Hall. Currently, there are 38 statues in the Hall.

18. When the Hall was used for the House of Representatives, it so happened that Daniel Webster's desk was in a strategic location. While sitting at his desk, he often heard the whispered conversations of his peers as they planned their strategies in other parts of the room.

19. In 1824, it was in the Hall (then the Chamber for the House of Representatives) that Marquis de Lafayette became the first foreign citizen to address Congress.

20. Of special note is what happened to the statue honoring the notable American politician John Calhoun (located in another part of the Capitol Building). On July 24, 1998, security guards confronted a man trying to force his way into the Capitol Building. When confronted the man shot to death Capitol Police Officer Jacob Chestnut and Detective John Gibson and put a bullet hole in the statue of John Calhoun. <u>The hole is in the right leg of the trousers</u>.

FACTS ABOUT THE OLD SUPREME COURT CHAMBER WITHIN THE UNITED STATES CAPITOL BUILDING

For decades following its formation, the United States Supreme Court was like an orphan without a home as it was moved from one temporary location to another. One of these temporary shelters was in the bowels of the Capitol Building. In a small, poorly lit chamber the Supreme Court convened from 1820 through 1859. As visitors enter the chamber, they view a room that may still echo with the voices of prominent judicial figures as they rendered some of the nation's most notable legal opinions.

THE OLD SUPREME COURT CHAMBER

1. The old Supreme Court Chamber was the first room constructed specifically for use by the nation's highest judiciary body.

2. From 1801 to 1819, the Supreme Court was convened in what became committee rooms S-146 and S-146A of the Capitol Building.

3. Benjamin Henry Latrobe constructed most of the Supreme Court Chamber. In 1815, Latrobe started to construct the chamber for the third time. After Latrobe resigned in 1817, Charles Bulfinch completed the chamber in 1819. (The first chamber had to be replaced because of poor construction, and the second because of the burning of the Capitol Building by the British Army in 1814.)

The Supreme Court Chamber

4. Latrobe's assistant, John Lenthall, was killed when the ceiling of the vaulted chamber collapsed during construction. (The accident occurred when Lenthall removed the supports to the vaulted chamber before the structure had fully dried.)

5. Entrance to the chamber is gained through the robing room at its southern end. The displayed robes are the actual robes of former Justices.

6. In the robing room is a bust of Roger B. Taney, the nation's fifth Chief Justice, who held the post from 1836 to 1864.

7. The coat hooks on the wall opposite the bust carry the names of the Justices on the Supreme Court from 1858 to 1860. The label "*Chief*" indicates the hook was used by Chief Justice Taney.

8. The chamber is in the shape of a semicircle, which measures 74 feet wide by 50 feet deep.

9. The vaulted ceiling of the chamber is divided into lobes by 10 ribs.

10. Originally, the windows on the east wall of the chamber provided a view onto the Capitol Plaza. However, because the 1959-1963 expansion of the Capitol's east front blocked the windows, the windows are now artificially lighted.

11. The four busts displayed in the rear of the chamber are of the first four Chief Justices of the U. S. Supreme Court. From north to south they are John Marshall, John Ruthledge, John Jay, and Oliver Ellsworth.

12. Over the west fireplace stands a clock. It was ordered for the chamber by Chief Justice Taney in 1837.

13. The location of the chamber is near where construction of the Capitol Building was started. A wall at the entrance to the chamber is exposed to show an example of the bricks that were used to construct the building.

14. Above the clock is a plaster relief sculptured by Carlo Franzoni in 1817. The central figure in the relief is *"Justice"*, who is seated holding a pair of scales in her left hand, and her right hand resting upon the hilt of an unsheathed sword. Unlike many depictions of *"Justice,"* she wears no blindfold. The winged youth seated beside her is *"Fame,"* who holds up the Constitution of the United States under the rays of the rising sun. At the right side of the sculpture, an eagle protectively rests one foot upon books containing the written laws.

15. In front of the eastern arcade are mahogany desks for the nine Supreme Court Justices, which are set off from the rest of the room by a mahogany railing. Seven of these desks are 19th-century originals that are believed to have been purchased for the court in the late 1830s. The chairs behind the desks represent various styles used around the year 1860. Each Justice selected the style of his own chair.

16. Court officials used the desks at either end of the Justices' desks. The U.S. Attorney General, the clerk, and the deputy clerk sat to the right of the Justices. The court reporters, the marshal, and the deputy marshal sat to the left of the Justices.

17. The floor in the central area of the chamber is approximately one-foot lower than the level where the Supreme Court Justices sat. In this area stand four baize-covered mahogany tables that were used by lawyers presenting their cases before the Justices. Facing these tables, and lining the area's western end, are the wooden panel-back settees provided for the audience.

18. After the chamber was vacated, it was subsequently used as a reference library until the 1940s, as an office for the Joint Committee on Atomic Energy from 1955 to 1960, and as a storeroom until restoration work began in 1972.

19. In May 1975, the chamber was opened to the public after a $478,000 renovation.

FACTS ABOUT THE LIBRARY OF CONGRESS

Soon after winning their freedom from the British Empire, the members of Congress determined that if they were to be successful in governing the United States, reference materials covering many topics would have to be readily available. In 1783, Congress appointed a Continental Congress committee, chaired by James Madison, to assemble a reference library for members of Congress. Additionally, a bill was passed for establishing a congressional library. As time passed, this small, poorly organized set of reference material grew into the largest library in the world.

THE LIBRARY OF CONGRESS

1. On April 24, 1800, the Library of Congress was founded.

2. A sum of $5,000 was appropriated to purchase a case of maps and 740 books from dealers in London, England.

3. The first Library of Congress was located in New York City, New York.

4. In 1800, the Library of Congress was moved to Washington, D.C. when Congress moved to the new city.

5. On August 25, 1814, the British Army destroyed the first library when the Capitol Building was burned.

6. To replace the destroyed books, Congress purchased over 6,000 replacements from Thomas Jefferson. The 1815 purchase cost $23,950.

7. On Christmas Eve, 1851, 35,000 of the 55,000 assembled library books were destroyed in another fire to the Capitol Building. In 1853, the restored Library was opened.

8. Until 1897, the Library remained in the Capitol Building.

9. Three primary buildings in Washington, D.C. house the Library of Congress.

10. The three buildings (Jefferson, Adams, and Madison) are connected by a series of underground pedestrian tunnels that protect the materials as they are moved from building to building.

11. Initially, access to the Library of Congress was limited to government related research. In 1897, the library was first opened to the general public.

12. In 1870, the Library of Congress was declared the National Copyright Library.

13. The Library of Congress is the world's largest library. It contains over 120 million items (books, maps, etc.) on over 600 miles of shelving.

14. The Library of Congress is the nation's oldest federal cultural institution.

15. In addition to its primary mission of serving the research needs of the U.S. Congress, the Library of Congress serves all Americans through its popular website and twenty-two reading rooms on Capitol Hill.

THE THOMAS JEFFERSON BUILDING

1. The Thomas Jefferson Building was named in honor of President Jefferson (1801-1809), and was the first building constructed specifically as the home for the Library of Congress.

2. Between 1886 and 1887, the Thomas Jefferson Building was constructed. (Keep in mind that Jefferson's sale of his personal library to Congress formed the nucleus of the second Library of Congress after the British Army burned the first library in 1814.)

3. The architects of the Thomas Jefferson Building were John L. Smithmeyer and Paul J. Pelz. (They also designed Georgetown University's Healty Building in 1879.)

4. The design of the building is Italian Renaissance.

5. New Hampshire granite was used for the exterior of the building.

6. Fifteen kinds of marble were used in the interior of the building.

7. Fifty American artists and twenty sculptors provided the works of art within the building.

8. The themes of the artwork within the building are *"Knowledge and Learning."*

The Thomas Jefferson Building

9. Greeting visitors at the entrance to the building is the fountain *"The Court of Neptune."* Constructed in 1897-1898, the fountain represents the events in Neptune's reign as the ruler of the seas.

10. The main entrance to the building consists of three sets of 14 feet by 7 1/2 feet bronze doors. The doors are known as the *"Tradition Doors."* The left door is symbolic of *"Tradition,"* the center door represents *"Printing,"* and the right door *"Writing."*

11. The six female figures over the *Tradition Doors* (main entrance) to the building represent *"Literature," "Composition,"* and *"Reflection."*

12. Above the second-story windows of the building are thirty-six keystones. Each keystone contains a head that represents one of the major races of the world. Completed in 1891, they are known as the *"Ethnological Heads."*

13. Above the main windows on the third-story of the central pavilion of the building is a series of nine circular windows. These windows serve as a background for three-foot high granite portrait busts of men eminent in the history of western literature. The bust of Benjamin Franklin is the central figure. Other figures are Demosthenes, Emerson, Irving, Goethe, Maculay, Hawthorne, Scott, and Dante.

14. On the dome of the building is the *"Torch of Learning."* The torch, which marks the center and apex of the Thomas Jefferson Building, is 15 feet high by 6 1/2 feet in diameter at its base. Originally, the torch was covered with a 23-carat gold leaf. It is now covered with copper.

15. The Main Reading Room in the building is 160 feet high. This room is one of twenty-two reading rooms.

16. The eight statues placed around the reading room symbolize *"civilized life and thought."*

17. In 1997, an $81.5 million, twelve-year renovation was completed on the building.

18. There are hundreds of items on display in the building at any given time. However, because of their age and delicate condition, many of the exhibits are rotated for display. As a result, what is listed below may have been replaced with other exhibits. However, the list does provide an idea of what may be displayed.

- A letter written by Christopher Columbus in 1494.

- Thomas Jefferson's rough draft of the *Declaration of Independence*.

- Thomas Jefferson's design for a macaroni machine.

- The 1640 Whole Book of Psalms.

- Pierre Charles L'Enfant's 1791 plan for the U.S. Capital.

- First edition of Frank Baum's "*The Wizard of Oz.*"

- Maya Lin's 1981 first design for the Vietnam Veterans Memorial.

- Items relating to American Indian and African-American cultures.

THE JOHN ADAMS BUILDING

1. The John Adams Building is the second of three buildings constructed near the Capitol Building to store the contents of the Library of Congress.

2. In 1939, the John Adams Building, named in honor of President John Adams (1797-1801), was completed.

The John Adams Building

3. The exterior facade of the building was constructed from white Georgia marble.

4. In 1938, the Library of Congress Annex Bronze Doors were constructed. These seven sets of doors are twelve feet high and represent the following:

- The center doors (west entrance) depict six figures that represent major contributors to written communication. They are Hermes, the Greek god who served as a messenger; Odin, originator of the Viking alphabet and mythical god of war; Ogma, who performed the same alphabetical task for the Iris; Itzama, chief god of the Mayans; Quetzalcoatone, god of the Aztecs; and Sequoyah, an American Indian.

- There are two figures near the single door to the south entrance. The male is symbolic of "*physical labor,*" and the female is symbolic of "*intellectual labor.*"

- On the east side of the John Adams Building are doors with six more figures of educators who have contributed to the history of the written word. They are Thoth, Egyptian god and conveyor of speech; Ts'ang Chieh, Chinese patron saint of pictographic letters; Nabu Sumero, Akkadian god; Brahma, supreme god of the east Indian trinity; Cadmus of Greece, who planted the dragon teeth from which sprang armedme; and Tamurath, a cultural hero of Persian antiquity.

THE JAMES MADISON MEMORIAL BUILDING

1. The James Madison Memorial Building is the third of three buildings constructed to store the property of the Library of Congress.

2. On April 24, 1980, the building was opened.

The James Madison Memorial Building

3. The building is considered an official memorial to James Madison (1809-1817), the fourth President of the United States.

4. A large marble statue of James Madison greets visitors to the James Madison Memorial Hall.

5. Relatively plain in design, the primary goal of the building is to provide an efficient means of storing materials for easy retrieval.

6. The building contains 2,100,000 square feet of space, and houses administrative offices, the Congressional Research Services, the Law Library, the Office of the Librarian, and the Copyright Office.

THE CENTRAL REPOSITORY FOR THE AUDIOVISUAL WORKS OF CONGRESS

1. In 1997, Congress approved the use of a new repository to store the audiovisual works of the Library of Congress.

2. The structure that stores the Central Repository Audiovisual Works was constructed in the 1960s.

3. The original purpose of the structure was to harbor as many as 125 government officials and civilians from Washington, D.C. and the Federal Reserve Bank in Richmond, Virginia, after a possible nuclear holocaust.

4. The primary purpose of assembling officials at Mount Pony was to provide a *"think tank,"* whose purpose was to help rebuild the economy and banking system of the United States after a nuclear attack.

5. The structure is located approximately 70 miles southwest of Washington, D.C., near Culpeper, Virginia.

6. The 140,000-square-foot, three-level former bunker is carved into the mountainside of Mount Pony.

7. The nearly $10 million needed to purchase equipment and maintain the 41-acre installation was donated by the David and Lucile Packard Foundation.

8. The structure is radiation-proof, and is temperature and humidity-controlled.

9. The former bunker houses the Motion Picture, Broadcasting and Recorded Sound Division of the Library of Congress. Formerly, the recordings were stored in the Jefferson and Madison buildings on Capitol Hill, and within storage vaults in Suitland, Maryland, and Wright-Patterson Air Force Base in Dayton, Ohio.

10. The repository stores and maintains over 150,000 film titles of the Library of Congress.

FACTS ABOUT THE BOTANIC GARDEN
(IN FRONT OF THE CAPITOL BUILDING)

Even though countless visitors drive or walk by the Botanic Garden on their way to the Smithsonian museums on the "*Mall*," very few take notice to one of the most unique and beautiful retreats from the fast pace of Washington, D.C. This building on the west end of the Capitol grounds is one of those little noticed, but unique stops, visitors should take time to enjoy.

THE BOTANIC GARDEN

1. The United States Botanic Garden traces its beginning to 1816, when the constitution of the Columbia Institute for the Promotion of Arts and Sciences in Washington, D.C. proposed the creation of a botanic garden to collect, grow, and distribute plants of the United States and other countries that might contribute to the welfare of the American people.

2. The United States Botanic Garden was founded in 1820, under the auspices of the Columbia Institute for the Promotion of Arts and Sciences.

3. The Columbia Institute ceased to exist in 1837, and the Botanic Garden was abandoned until 1842.

4. In 1842, the United States government provided accommodations for the botanical collections brought to Washington, D.C. from the South Seas by the U.S. Exploring Expedition of 1838-1842.

5. The South Seas exhibit was maintained behind the U.S. Patent Office until 1849, at which time the exhibit was moved to the current site of the Botanic Garden.

6. Work on the initial Conservatory began in 1931, and the building was first occupied on January 13, 1933. Between 1997 and 2002, a $33,500,000 restoration of the Conservatory was completed.

7. The size of the Botanic Garden totals 50,946 square feet. Almost 10,000 square feet of this total were added during the 1997-2002 restoration.

8. The structural design of the Conservatory is of conventional form, with an arched and domed roof frame carrying the great expanse of glass sheathing.

9. The main feature of the building is the one-story loggia or entrance hall that forms the Maryland Avenue front. (A loggia is an arcaded or roofed gallery constructed into or projecting from the side of a building, particularly one overlooking an open court.)

10. Constructed from limestone, the loggia is 40 feet high at its maximum height, with a series of lofty arched doorways.

11. The area of glass sheathing is known as the *"Palm House."* This area of the building is an example of the first use of aluminum for the structural members supporting the building. The addition of steel columns during the 1997-2002 restoration replaced the aluminum columns supporting the new 13,800-pound aluminum *"monitor,"* or peak of the Palm House.

12. The main Conservatory is approximately 262 feet in length by 183 feet in width.

The Palm House of the Botanic Garden

13. The Conservatory also consists of other sites. One is the outdoor garden in the square across Independence Avenue, and another is the Popular Point Nursery adjacent to Anacostia Park.

14. Within the walls of the main building of the Botanic Garden are a wide variety of plants from around the world. These plants are located throughout the building in a maze that offers visitors plenty of opportunity to rest and enjoy the surroundings. Exhibits totaling more than 3,000 plants include the following:

- West Gallery – Features exhibits on the plants' ability to adapt to their environment.

- Garden Court – Features *"economic plants"* – those used in commercial products (fibers, food, beverages, cosmetics, fragrances, wood, spices or herbs).

- Jungle/Palm House – Depicts a jungle growing around an abandoned plantation in a tropical rainforest. This exhibit is under the Palm House, which stands 93 feet high.

- Plant Adaptation – Features a series of changing plant exhibits that show how the plants adapt and evolve in response to environmental factors.

- Garden Primeval – Features primitive fern and plant species that have existed for 150 million years.

- Children's Garden – Offers children an area for play and an opportunity to learn informally about plants.

- Oasis – Features a fertile place filled with dates, palms, figs and other fruit plants. (One exhibit is a palm tree from Arizona named after George Washington.)

- World Desert – Features cacti, succulents, grasses, shrubs and other flowering plants that exist in the deserts of the world. (Exhibit requires a nightly temperature drop of 40 degrees to keep the plants healthy.)

- Medicinal Plants – Features the origin of herbal medicine with a collection of plants from all over the world.

- Orchid House – Features an exhibit of nearly 12,000 orchids of 200 types.

- Plant Exploration House – Features plant related discoveries being made in the wild and in the laboratory.

- Rare and Endangered Species – Features plants that are threatened by habitat destruction.

- Meditation Garden (through the Transition House) – Features an eastern Asian meditative garden using a palette of plants native to North America.

15. Adjacent to the Botanic Garden is a 3-acre National Garden.

16. The National Garden functions as an outdoor annex to the U.S. Botanic Garden's Conservatory, and is meant to be an outdoor classroom for children and adults to learn about nature.

17. The most recent version of the National Garden was open to the public in the fall of 2006. Some of the key attractions within the garden are:

- The Regional Garden – Features flora of the Mid-Atlantic.

- The First Ladies Water Garden – A fountain terrace that features granite mosaics recalling Colonial American quilts.

- Butterfly Garden – Features beds filled with nectar plants to draw butterflies. (This exhibit is dedicated to the Garden Club of America.)

- Rose Garden – Features a selection of roses. (The rose was declared the national flower of the United States in 1986.)

- Amphitheater – Available for outdoor events.

THE BARTHOLDI FOUNTAIN

1. The Bartholdi Fountain is located in the square across from the Botanic Garden in Bartholdi Park, which was named after Frederic Auguste Bartholdi in 1985.

2. The architect of the fountain was Frederic Auguste Bartholdi. (Bartholdi, a French sculptor, also designed the Statue of Liberty in New York City, New York.)

3. In 1876, the fountain was first exhibited at the International Exhibition in Philadelphia, Pennsylvania.

4. In 1877, Congress purchased the fountain for $6,000, and moved it to Washington, D.C.

The Bartholdi Fountain

5. In 1932, the Bartholdi Fountain was placed in its current location.

6. The fountain was constructed from bronzed iron, cast in Paris, France. The fountain is painted black to keep it from rusting.

7. Resting on a 90-foot wide marble base, the fountain is 30 feet high and weighs approximately 80,000 pounds.

8. The fountain has three sections: A base with amphibious creatures and stylized shells, a central section with three curvaceous sea nymphs, and a large basin at the top with twelve lights and three tritons supporting a kind of crown. In 1886, the lights surrounding the basin were added.

9. The central section of the fountain depicts three identical sea nymphs with fish and sea life between their feet, a headdress made of leaves on their heads, and arched backs, which follow a tradition of sculptures founded in classical Greece. These eleven feet high women seem to support the upper basin, which are actually supported by a central column. The nymphs have form-revealing drapery, cinched at the waist by scallop shells.

FACTS ABOUT THE ULYSSES S. GRANT MEMORIAL
(IN FRONT OF THE CAPITOL BUILDING)

Second only to President Abraham Lincoln, General Ulysses S. Grant is credited with saving the Union from destruction during the American Civil War. A man of action, Grant's personality and drive fit perfectly into the mold needed to successfully lead men into battle at Shiloh, Vicksburg, the Wilderness, Cold Harbor, and Appomattox. The final of many generals appointed by Lincoln to lead the Union armies against those of the Confederacy, Grant saw victory in the defeat of the enemy's armies, not the capture of their capital city of Richmond. Confronting the Army of Northern Virginia almost constantly from March 1864 to April 1865, Grant was quick to take advantage of the opportunities offered by Lee, using his superior strength in manpower and overwhelming source of supplies to defeat an army that many believed unbeatable.

Grant was a man of war, not of peace. In the everyday life of peace-time-soldier, farmer, clerk, businessman and president, many historians consider Grant a failure. But it was not the skills of a peacemaker that were needed during 1861 through 1865, but those of a warrior. It is that warrior a grateful nation pays homage to through this memorial.

THE LIFE OF ULYSSES S. GRANT

1. On April 27, 1822, Hiram Ulysses Grant, referred to in history as Ulysses S. Grant, was born in Point Pleasant, Ohio.

2. Grant's parents were Jessie Grant and Hanna Simpson.

3. Grant was not named until six weeks after his birth, when his first and middle names were drawn from a hat by his parents.

4. The names picked from the hat were Hiram (first name), and Ulysses (middle name), not Ulysses Simpson, as he is known.

5. In 1839, at age 17, Grant entered the Military Academy at West Point, New York. (He was only 5 feet, 1 inch tall, and weighed approximately 120 pounds. He eventually grew to 5 feet, 8 inches tall.)

6. Because of confusion on the part of the congressman who appointed him and the administration officer at West Point, Grant was listed in the academy's records as Ulysses S. Grant. The "*S*" representing the maiden name of Grant's mother "*Simpson*."

7. Grant was listed on the rolls of new cadets as U.S. Grant. An upper classman by the name of William T. Sherman (a future Union general) jokingly stated that the letters "*U*" and "*S*" represented Uncle Sam. Thereafter, Grant's friends and relatives often used the name "*Sam*."

8. In 1843, Grant graduated from West Point with a class standing of 21st out of 39 graduates. He also received 290 demerits during his four years at the academy. (Comparing Grant with Lee - Lee graduated 2nd in a class of 46, with no demerits.)

9. Grant fought in the Mexican War of 1846-1848. It was while they served in Mexico that Lee met Grant for the first and only time prior to Lee's surrender at Appomattox, Virginia. On that occasion, Colonel Lee reprimanded Grant for a sloppy uniform. (Lee did not remember the encounter when reminded by Grant at Appomattox.)

10. In 1854, at age 32, and after four years at the Military Academy at West Point and eleven years as a commissioned officer in the quarter master corps, Captain Grant resigned from the U.S. Army.

11. Even though Grant the general was victorious in many battles during the Civil War, his attempts at other trades usually resulted in failure. These professional failures included:

    • Because he could not stand the sight of blood or to kill animals, Grant hated working at this father's tannery.

- While stationed in Oregon, Grant tried his hand at shipping ice to San Francisco. Businessmen from Alaska edged him out.

- Grant couldn't sell the cattle, hogs, and sheep he raised.

- The chickens Grant raised died on their way to market.

- Grant's attempt as a merchant resulted in his partner stealing his money and leaving town.

- A billiard room he started went bankrupt.

- Grant was fired from a job as a realtor and rent collector when he failed to collect the rent.

- As a clerk in a leather goods store, Grant often charged the wrong amounts to customers. (Usually in favor of the customer.)

- Grant lost his job in a customs house.

- As a farmer, Grant only raised 75 bushels of grain when his neighbors were raising as much as 500 bushels on similar acreage.

- Selling cut wood drew very few customers for Grant.

- Grant lost most of his money in an investment scheme after he left the presidency.

12. At the beginning of the Civil War in 1861, Grant worked as a clerk for the Union Army for $2.00 a day.

13. When the Civil War began Grant made several unsuccessful attempts at getting a commission in the Union Army. These attempts included commissions in the Illinois Volunteers, Illinois Regulars, Missouri Volunteers, and the Ohio Volunteers.

14. In 1861, Grant finally received a commission in the 21st Illinois as a colonel. (When he accepted the commission, Grant was believed to be wearing the same suit of clothes he had worn almost continuously for nearly a year.)

15. In 1864, Grant was promoted to the rank of lieutenant general (three stars). It was the first time the rank had been held by an officer in the United States Army since George Washington.

16. On March 12, 1864, soon after his appointment as General-in-Chief of the Armies of the United States, Grant started a campaign against the Confederacy that resulted in the surrender of General Lee at Appomattox, Virginia, on April 9, 1865.

17. In 1866, Grant was promoted to the rank of full general (four stars). This promotion was the first time the rank of full general had been awarded to any officer in the United States Army.

18. In March 1869, Grant was sworn in as the 18th President of the United States. His second term ended in 1877.

19. Largely due to Grant's lackadaisical attitude, his presidency is considered one of the most corrupt in U.S. history. (Grant appointed twenty-four family members to government positions after his election. Grant's normal workday was from 10 a.m. to 3 p.m. Many of his appointees were forced to resign from office.)

20. On July 23, 1885, at age 63, Grant died of throat cancer. (Lee had died at the same age in 1870.) Grant and his wife, Julia, are buried in a tomb in New York City.

THE ULYSSES S. GRANT MEMORIAL

1. In 1901, Congress authorized the memorial. Funding totaled $250,000.

2. In 1903, sculptor Henry Shrady and architect Edward Casey were commissioned to design and execute the memorial. (Shrady designed and executed the sculptured elements, while Casey designed the marble plaza and pedestal elements.)

3. In 1906, the site for the Grant Memorial in front of the Capitol Building at the east end of the *"National Mall"* was approved.

4. Shrady and Casey's design was selected over 26 other design submissions.

5. The statue of Grant and the accompanying works total 252 feet in length by 71 feet in depth.

6. Four lions, which guard the flag of the United States and the flags of the Union Army, are located around the base of the memorial.

7. Grant is riding his favorite horse *"Cincinnati"*. (The horse was presented to him in 1864 when he was a lieutenant general, and was one of seven horses he rode during the Civil War.)

The Grant Memorial in front of the Capitol Building

8. To better understand the movements of the men and horses in battle, Shrady observed staged cavalry drills at the West Point Military Academy in New York.

9. To better understand the physiological structure of horses, Shrady dissected several horses.

10. Shrady modeled the lead horse in the memorial nine times before he was satisfied.

11. In order to better reveal the rippling of their muscles, the horses used as models were sprayed with water.

12. Shrady's fingerprints, some observers say thumb prints, can be seen in the body of the lead horse.

13. The truck carrying the plaster molds to the foundry caught fire, but the molds were not damaged. The finished bronze figures also survived a fire at the foundry.

14. In 1912, the 30,000-pound Artillery Group was placed on the site, the Cavalry Group in 1916, and in late 1920, the 10,000-pound equestrian statue of Grant was erected on the pedestal.

15. The large bronze panels on Grant's pedestal portray the U.S. Infantry. The panels, installed in 1924, were started by Shrady, but were completed by sculptor Sherry Fry after Shrady's death.

The Artillery Group

16. West Point cadets Fairfax Ayres, James Chaney, and Henry Weeks, class of 1908, modeled for the soldiers depicted in the relief portraying the artillery.

17. The name *"Grant"* on the pedestal is the only inscription found on the memorial that identifies the person the memorial honors. (Other inscriptions are carved in the marble or in bronze, including identifying Shrady and Casey, and dedicating a section of the memorial to Shrady's friends Alice Morris and Dave Morris.)

18. The main figure showing Grant on his horse is 17 feet high. (Forty feet above the marble platform.)

19. On April 27, 1922, the memorial was dedicated. The date marked the 100th anniversary of Grant's birth.

20. It took Shrady and Casey nearly twenty years to complete the memorial.

21. Shrady died just two weeks prior to the dedication of the memorial.

22. The statue of Grant is the largest equestrian statue in the United States, and the second largest in the world after the monument to King Victor Emanuel in Rome, Italy. (The Grant Memorial features thirteen horses.)

23. In 1970-1971, the Capitol Reflecting Pool in front of the statue of General Grant was added. Looking down on the pool it would appear to be in the shape of a fan.

FACTS ABOUT THE UNITED STATES SUPREME COURT
(LOCATED BEHIND THE CAPITOL BUILDING)

Commonly referred to as the *"highest court in the land,"* the United States Supreme Court symbolizes a legal body that has been entrusted with protecting the rights of all citizens. Located behind the U.S. Capitol Building, nine of the best legal minds in the United States make decisions regarding matters ranging from such in-depth issues as race, capital punishment, and abortions, to religious freedom, taxes, and the limitations of the government. This large marble building projects an image befitting a legal body that influences the lives of every citizen of the United States.

THE HISTORY OF THE U.S. SUPREME COURT

1. The United States (U.S.) Supreme Court is the only court that is required by the United States Constitution. (Congress creates all other federal courts.)

2. In 1789, the Supreme Court was formed, and the first six Justices were appointed.

3. On February 1, 1790, the Supreme Court convened its first session under the U.S. Constitution in the Merchants Exchange Building, New York City, New York.

4. In 1790, the Supreme Court moved with the federal government to Philadelphia, Pennsylvania.

5. In 1800, the Supreme Court moved with the federal government to Washington, D.C.

6. John Jay was appointed the first Chief Justice of the U.S. Supreme Court.

7. Between 1815 and 1819, after the Capitol Building was burned by the British Army, Congress was convened on the current site of the Supreme Court Building in what was referred to as the "old brick building."

8. During the Civil War the "old brick building" was used to confine Confederate captives and suspected collaborators. After the Civil War the building was converted into residences until it was removed in October 1932 for the construction of the new Supreme Court Building. (Captain Henry Wirz, the commandant of the Confederate prisoner of war camp at Andersonville, Georgia, was hanged on this site on November 10,1865, for *"murder in violation of the laws and customs of war."*)

THE PRESENT DAY SUPREME COURT BUILDING

1. In 1935, the United States (U.S.) Supreme Court was relocated to its current location at 1st and East Capitol Streets, NW, Washington, D.C.

2. President William Taft (1909-1913), later a Justice, then Chief Justice of the U.S. Supreme Court (1921-1930), was one of the key figures in obtaining funding for the new Supreme Court Building.

3. Cass Gilbert was the primary architect of the Supreme Court Building. (Neither Taft nor Gilbert lived to see the building completed. Taft died in 1930, and Gilbert died in 1934.)

4. Robert Aitkin, Herman MacNeil, John Donnelly, and James Fraser were the primary sculptors of the Supreme Court Building.

5. On October 13, 1932, the cornerstone of the current Supreme Court Building was dedicated. Among the items placed in the cornerstone were a photograph of former Chief Justice Taft and a copy of the 1932 World Almanac.

The United States Supreme Court Building

6. In 1935, the Supreme Court Building was completed at a cost of $9,700,000. (This was the 146th year of the Supreme Court's existence.)

7. On October 7, 1935, the first term of the U.S. Supreme Court in its new building was convened.

8. The Supreme Court was moved from what is now the Old Senate Chamber in the U.S. Capitol Building.

9. The Supreme Court Building is five stories high. (Terrace/ground floor, and four stories above.)

10. The Supreme Court Building consists of a central building in the Corinthian architectural style, with two wings.

11. The Supreme Court Building measures 304 feet from north to south by 385 feet from east to west (front to back).

12. The plan of the first floor is based on a Greek temple.

13. The exterior of the Supreme Court Building was constructed from Vermont, Alabama, and Georgia marble. The interior of the building was constructed from Spanish, Italian, Honduran, and African marble.

14. Sculptured from Vermont marble, the double rows of sixteen Corinthian marble columns are a prominent part of the Supreme Court Building's exterior.

15. The architrave above the sixteen columns is inscribed with the phrase "*Equal Justice Under Law*."

16. In 1935, the two light fixtures at the west entrance to the Supreme Court Building were installed. (The turtles at the base of the lights symbolize the slow, but sure, movement of justice.)

17. The base of the two flagpoles in front of the Supreme Court Building consists of nine levels. These levels are swags of drapery, shields, thorns, shells, dolphins, cherubs (which symbolize justice) acantus leaves and pinecones, egg and dart molding, and an anthemion (design of palmettes). An eagle sits on the top of each pole.

18. White oak is the primary wood used in the interior of the Supreme Court Building.

19. Two 45-ton cheek blocks on each side of the main west entrance steps act as pedestals for two large figures. The male figure represents "*The Authority of Law*," the female figure represents "*The Contemplation of Justices*." The male figure holds a tablet backed by a sheathed sword - symbolic of "*law and its execution*." The miniature figure the female figure holds in her hand represents "*Justice*."

20. There are two pediments over the porticos of the east and west entrances to the Supreme Court Building.

- The pediment over the east entrance is titled "*Justice, The Guardian of Liberty*." Moses, with the tables of Hebraic law, is the central figure of the 18 feet by 60 feet symbol of law. On Moses' left is Confucius, representing the laws of China. On Moses' right is Solon, representing Greek law. The figure of a man holding a child represents the enforcement of the law, and the figure of a woman holding a baby represents tempering justice with mercy. The left soldier represents the settlement of disputes between states, and the other represents the protection of maritime and other laws. The tortoise and hare symbolize the slow, but sure, course of justice.

- The pediment over the west (main) entrance is titled "*Equal Justice Under Law*." Liberty, who is looking into the future and has the scale of justice on her lap, is the central figure of the 18 feet by 60 feet symbol of law. The Roman soldiers represent "*Order and Authority*." The remaining figures are symbolic of "*Council*."

21. The 17 feet high by 9 1/2 feet wide bronze doors on the west side of the Supreme Court Building are titled "*The Evolution of Justice.*" The pair of doors, which face the U.S. Capitol Building, weigh about 13 tons (each door weighs 13,000 pounds).

22. On the other side of the above bronze doors is the main corridor. It is known as the "*Great Hall*," and features a carved and painted ceiling of loral plagues. Busts of former Chief Justices also line the corridor.

23. At the end of the Great Hall, on the other side of the large oak doors, is the Court Chamber where the Justices hear arguments. The sides of the chamber are 82 feet by 91 feet, which rise 44 feet to the ceiling.

24. The 24 columns that stand around the chamber were constructed from Old Convent Quarry Siena marble from Italy. The walls and friezes are Ivory Vein marble from Spain, and the floor boards are Italian and African marble.

25. The high windows along the north and south sides of the chamber were designed to ensure sunlight would not shine directly into the eyes of the Justices on the bench, nor the counsel facing them.

26. The chamber is decorated with drapes and a mould plaster ceiling picked out in gold leaf.

27. A frieze runs around the top of all four sides of the chamber. It depicts various ancient and modern legal themes.

28. The bench behind which the Justices sit, and the other furniture in the courtroom, were constructed from mahogany. In 1972, the bench was altered to its current half-hexagon shape to provide the Justices with better sight and sound advantages.

29. The chairs for the Justices are constructed in the court's own carpentry shop, and are retained by the Justices upon their retirement.

30. The Justices are assembled behind the bench in the following order. The Chief Justice sits in the center of the bench, with the most senior Justice on his/her right, and the next in precedence on his/her left. The rest sit in similar alternating fashion so the most junior Justice sits on the far right (left as visitors face the bench).

31. The two central figures above the bench depict the Majesty of the Law, and the Power of the Government.

32. Representatives of the press are seated on the red benches along the left side of the chamber. The benches on the right are reserved for the guests of the Justices.

33. The chamber has 230 seats for the public, more if you consider the chairs in the far back of the room where visitors can sit for just 3-5 minutes during a busy session, and then must surrender their seats to other temporary visitors.

34. There are two elliptical staircases in the Supreme Court Building. These self-supporting, hand-carved staircases were constructed from Alabama marble and bronze. The spiral staircases, which are embedded into the wall 17 inches, spiral through all five levels of the Supreme Court Building.

35. On the ground floor of the Supreme Court Building is another *"Great Hall."* This Hall is overseen by a large statue of Chief Justice John Marshall. (The statue of Justice Marshall was completed in 1883, and stood on the west lawn of the Capitol Building until 1981.)

THE SUPREME COURT JUSTICES AND PROCEEDINGS

1. The United States Constitution requires a United States Supreme Court. Congress has the responsibility for determining the number of Justices on the court.

2. The maximum number of Justices appointed to the United States Supreme Court may not exceed nine (one Chief Justice and eight Associate Justices). Initially, the Supreme Court consisted of six Justices. Then, it was increased to seven, then nine, then ten, then back to seven, and finally to nine in 1869.

3. President Franklin Roosevelt (1933-1945) made an unsuccessful attempt at increasing the number of Justices to fifteen. (Even though Roosevelt failed in his attempt at increasing the number of Justices, he eventually appointed eight of the nine Justices who comprised the court. More than any other president.)

4. Supreme Court Justices are appointed by the President of the United States, and confirmed by the U.S. Senate.

5. Supreme Court Justices are appointed to their positions for life. However, the Justices may elect to retire or step down from their positions due to ill health or other personal reasons.

6. Supreme Court Justices do not have to be lawyers, but almost all have been members of the bar.

7. The court's term begins on the first Monday in October (required by statute), and generally alternates between two weeks of sitting and two weeks of recesses through the end of April. The Justices release their orders and opinions during the months of May and June. The court ends the term in June, but the Justices continue to work on new petitions, motions, applications, and cases scheduled for the fall.

8. The Justices hear an average of four oral arguments each day on Monday, Tuesday, and Wednesday, two weeks out of a month. The arguments are presented at 10 and 11 a.m., and 1 and 2 p.m.

9. Each argument session is limited to one hour. (Thirty minutes for each side to present their argument and to answer questions from the Justices.)

10. The attorneys to speak first during the morning and afternoon sessions are seated at the table on the left (10 a.m. & 1 p.m.), and the attorneys to speak second are seated at the table on the right (11 a.m. & 2 p.m.).

11. White and red lights are located before the attorney pleading his case. The lights are controlled by the Marshall of the Court, and are used to signal the speaker when his time for oral argument has expired. The white light indicates that the speaker has five minutes to complete his argument. When the red light is switched on, the speaker must stop talking immediately. (The speaker can save his last five minutes for rebuttal.)

12. With few exceptions, Justices vote on a case the same week the oral argument is presented.

13. Between 7,000 and 8,000 petitions are presented to the Supreme Court for review each term. Of this total, the Justices hear fewer than 100 petitions.

14. At least four Justices must vote to hear an argument.

15. There must be at least five Justices present for an argument to be presented.

UNIQUE FACTS ABOUT THE SUPREME COURT

1. A new group portrait of the Justices is taken whenever a new Justice is appointed. (Updated versions are taken on an "as needed" basis.)

2. In 1981, the first female Justice, Sandra Day O'Connor, was appointed by President Reagan (1981-1989). (She retired in 2006.)

3. The library of the Supreme Court has a collection of more than 450,000 volumes of law and reference books. Microfilm collections and electronic retrieval systems supplement this vast collection.

4. The tradition of the Justices wearing black robes dates back to 1800.

5. Another tradition is the placing of white quills on the tables for the counsels each day the court hears arguments.

6. In the 1800s, Chief Justice Melville Fuller started the tradition of the Justices shaking hands prior to convening court sessions and private conferences to discuss decisions. It is believed that this tradition helps keep harmony among the Justices. (The thought is "It's more difficult to hold a grudge against another Justice if contact is made with each other.")

7. As a tradition, there is a green porcelain spittoon by each of the Justices' chairs. (They are used as wastepaper baskets.)

8. The Supreme Court has a traditional seal, which is similar to the Great Seal of the United States, but which has a single star beneath the Eagle's claws, symbolizing the Constitution's creation of "one Supreme Court."

FACTS ABOUT THE WHITE HOUSE

The most popular residence in the United States is also a seat of power where decisions not only influence the policies of the United States, but the lives of countless men, women, and children worldwide. This large white structure on Pennsylvania Avenue has come to symbolize for generations of Americans the closeness between one of the most powerful leaders on earth and the average citizen who elected him to office. To many Americans, it matters not how many men or women serve as President of the United States, nor does it matter how many of them fulfill their quest for greatness. It does matter that this feeling of closeness remains, nurtured by a short, but impressive visit to the *"White House."*

THE EARLY YEARS OF THE PRESIDENTIAL MANSION (WHITE HOUSE)

1. The Presidential Mansion was constructed at 1600 Pennsylvania Avenue.

2. President George Washington (1789-1797) played an instrumental part in deciding where the Presidential Mansion would be located. He approved the site on June 28, 1791.

The Garden Side of the White House

3. In 1791, it was agreed that the Presidential Mansion would be constructed one mile east of the Capitol Building. It was actually constructed nearly 1.5 miles from the Capitol Building.

4. The Presidential Mansion was the first large public building constructed in Washington, D.C.

5. A contest was used to encourage the submission of designs for the Presidential Mansion. The winner was to receive $500 or a medal of equal value.

6. President George Washington (1789-1797) selected James Hoban's design for the Presidential Mansion. A native of Ireland, Hoban resided in Charleston, South Carolina. (Hoban also designed the state Capitol Building in Columbia, South Carolina.)

7. It is believed Hoban patterned his design of the Presidential Mansion after the Leinster House in his native country of Ireland.

8. After his death on December 8, 1831, at age 69, James Hoban was buried at Mount Olivet Cemetery in Washington, D.C.

9. The initial design of the Presidential Mansion called for 36 rooms. Of the 36 rooms, three were to be oval in shape. George Washington wanted the oval shape so the president and his visitors could better face each other. (Upon completion, the structure was only one-fifth the size of its original design.)

10. There are actually four oval rooms in the Presidential Mansion - the Blue, Green, and Yellow rooms, and the oval office for the president.

11. Congress appropriated $50,000 for construction of the Presidential Mansion. The final cost of the Presidential Mansion was $250,000.

12. On October 13, 1792, construction on the Presidential Mansion was started.

13. The Presidential Mansion was constructed primarily by Irish and Scottish immigrants, and by slave labor. The white workers were paid wages for their labor. The owners of the slaves were paid for the labor of their slaves.

14. The exterior of the Presidential Mansion was constructed from Arkose sandstone from the Aquia Creek quarry in Virginia.

15. Because sandstone is weak, a combination of materials, consisting primarily of salt and glue, was used to cover the exterior of the Presidential Mansion.

16. Prior to the War of 1812, two large stone eagles guarded the north entrance to the Presidential Mansion.

17. The roof of the Presidential Mansion was originally slate. Then it was changed to iron sheets, and finally to steel in 1927.

18. The initial exterior color of the Presidential Mansion was light yellow, which was applied in 1797. After the British burned the mansion in 1814, it was reconstructed and painted white in 1818. (The British Army burned Washington, D.C. in retaliation for the American Army burning the city of York in Canada the same year.)

19. From 1818 to 1979, there were at least 32 coats of whitewash and white paint applied to the exterior of the Presidential Mansion/White House. In 1979/1980, these coats were removed at a cost of nearly $3,000,000.

20. There are a few places on the walls of the White House where the burn marks from the 1814 fire remain. One is near the kitchen, the other is near the Truman Balcony. (The Truman Balcony, added to the White House in 1948, was constructed because Truman missed sitting on his porch in Independence, Missouri.)

21. On November 1, 1800, President John Adams (1797-1801) became the first president to occupy the Presidential Mansion. He and his family resided in the Presidential Mansion for approximately four months at a time when there were only six usable rooms. All other presidents following Adams have occupied the Presidential Mansion/White House. (Washington has been the only president who has not lived in the Presidential Mansion/White House. Washington left office in March 1797.)

22. In 1815, after the British Army had burned the Presidential Mansion in 1814, James Hoban was again hired to reconstruct the mansion he had originally designed and constructed. It cost $300,000 to reconstruct the Presidential Mansion.

23. The Presidential Mansion was vacant from 1814 to 1817 while it was being reconstructed. President James Monroe (1817-1825) was the first president to reside in the Presidential Mansion after its destruction by the British Army.

24. In 1824, Hoban constructed the south portico to the Presidential Mansion during the presidency of James Monroe (1817-1825), and the north portico in 1829 during the presidency of Andrew Jackson (1829-1837).

25. Until after the American Civil War, the Presidential Mansion was the largest residence in the United States.

26. The White House currently sits amid eighteen acres of greenery known as the *President's Park*.

THE PRESENT DAY WHITE HOUSE

1. The current White House has 132 rooms, 35 bathrooms, 147 windows, 412 doors, 28 fireplaces, 8 staircases, and 3 elevators.

2. The White House is 170 feet long by 85 feet wide.

The Carriage Side of the White House

3. The White House initially consisted of a ground floor level (formerly the basement), and two upper level floors. In 1927, during the presidency of Calvin Coolidge (1923-1929), a third upper level floor was added to the White House. Eliminating the large attic and raising the roof added eighteen new rooms to the White House. (It was also during this renovation that the solarium or "*sky parlor*" over the south portico was constructed.)

4. Of the four upper floors, the ground and first floors are used for public functions.

5. The third and fourth floors of the White House are the living quarters for the First Family.

6. Beneath the ground floor are two sub-floors that were constructed as bomb shelters. (The floors are now used largely for storage.)

7. There are four entrances to the White House (excluding service doors; i.e. kitchen, etc.)

8. The East Room is the largest room in the White House. It was in the East Room where Mrs. Adams hung her laundry to dry, and it was also where seven presidents have lain after their deaths, including Presidents Lincoln and Kennedy. Because of its size (80 feet long by 40 feet wide, with a 22-foot ceiling), the East Room is usually used for performing arts presentations attended by the president, first lady and their guests. (Through the use of bleachers that reached nearly to the ceiling, the East Room held nearly 600 mourners during the funeral services for President Lincoln in April 1865.)

9. It was in the East Room that Merriweather Lewis (famed explorer) lived while he was the private secretary of President Thomas Jefferson (1801-1809).

10. Because of its use for large gatherings, the only piece of permanent furniture in the East Room is usually a 1938 Steinway piano.

11. The Blue Room is used for receptions. It was in the Blue Room that President Franklin Roosevelt (1933-1945) transmitted his *"fireside chats."*

12. Prior to becoming a reception room, the Blue Room was a boiler and furnace room. In 1837, President Martin Van Buren (1837-1841) began the tradition of referring to the room as the *"Blue Room."*

13. The Yellow Room is located on the third floor and is part of the private residence of the president and his family. The yellow motif was due to the influence of Jackie Kennedy.

14. The colors of the Green Room and Red Room became predominant during the presidency of James Monroe (1817-1825).

15. In 1862, it was in the Green Room that the body of President Abraham Lincoln's son William (Willie) was embalmed after his death.

16. President Thomas Jefferson (1801-1809) used the Green Room as his dining room.

17. In 1902, the east terrace was added to the White House. In 1942, the west terrace was added.

18. Designed by Edith Wilson to display a growing collection of White House china, the China Room was constructed in 1917 during the presidency of Woodrow Wilson (1913-1921).

19. The Map Room:

    • Was used by President Franklin Roosevelt (1933-1945) as a situation room to show the status of military actions during World War II. (The current Situation Room was created in 1962 during the presidency of Kennedy (1961-1963), and is located in the basement of the West Wing of the White House.)

    • Contains the last situation map prepared for President Roosevelt during World War II. The map is dated April 3, 1945.

    • Contains a sandstone mantel constructed from stone removed from the White House during the 1948-1951 renovation.

- Contains a 1755 French version of a map that was charted by Peter Jefferson, the father of Thomas Jefferson.

- The room was decorated in 1970, and again in 1994, as a sitting room in the Chippendale style, which flourished in America during the last half of the 18th century. (The Chippendale style was named after English furniture designer Thomas Chippendale.)

20. The first time the State Dining Room was referred to as the "*State Dining Room*" was during the presidency of Andrew Jackson (1829-1837). A portrait of Abraham Lincoln is a prominent part of the room.

21. The White House Library was started during the presidency of Millard Fillmore (1850-1853).

22. The room containing the current White House Library has a long history. A few facts about the Library are:

- Used as the White House laundry until the presidency of Theodore Roosevelt (1901-1909).

- Dedicated as a Gentleman's Ante-Room (waiting room) in 1902.

- Designated as the White House Library in 1935.

- Completely redecorated in 1961. Nearly 2,800 books are on the shelves of the Library. Several writings relating to American thought and traditions have been added to the Library.

23. The Lincoln Bedroom is the only room in the White House that is named after a president. Abraham Lincoln was President of the United States from March 1861 through April 1865. A few facts about the Lincoln Bedroom are:

- What is now known as the Lincoln Bedroom was used as a Cabinet Room during Lincoln's presidency.

- The Lincoln Bedroom is in a Victorian style, which is known for heavy furniture, formal fabrics, and elaborate trimmings.

- The Lincoln bed, which was constructed from dark rosewood, was purchased by First Lady Mary Lincoln in 1861.

- The headboard of the Lincoln bed is six feet high.

- Over the headboard, and attached to the wall, is a carved canopy in the shape of a crown. The previously removed crown was reinstalled in 2004.

- Hanging from the crown is regal purple satin cloth over white lace.

- Other furniture consists of dark rococo revival furniture that was constructed by cabinetmaker John Belter.

- The carpet is a combination of emerald green, golden yellow, and deep purple.

- The walls are painted in a cream tone.

- Over the two windows are elaborate cornices (an ornamental band for covering a curtain rod). They were installed in 2004.

- The mantel over the fireplace, constructed from Opulent White marble, was installed in 2004.

- In the room is a copy of the Emancipation Proclamation, which was signed in the room by President Lincoln on September 22, 1862. (The Emancipation Proclamation went into effect on January 1, 1863.)

- Winston Churchill, the notable Prime Minister of Great Britain, stayed in the Lincoln Bedroom during his many visits to the White House during World War II. (Churchill swore he saw the image of President Lincoln in this room on more than one occasion.)

24. Prior to the additions to the White House during Theodore Roosevelt's administration (1901-1909), the administrative offices were on the second floor of the White House.

25. During the presidency of Theodore Roosevelt (1901-1909), the West Wing (the first addition) was added to the White House.

26. President William Taft (1909-1913) doubled the size of the West Wing, and acquired the use of two office buildings for the White House staff. The size of the presidential administrative staff during Taft's administration reached 3,000.

27. Under the direction of President Taft, architect Nathan C. Wyeth of Washington, D.C. designed the expansion of the West Wing.

28. The oval office is modeled after the original oval-shaped Blue Room of the White House.

29. The oval office was constructed in 1909 during the administration of President William Taft (1909-1913).

30. The oval office was originally located in the center of the West Wing. In 1934, it was moved to its current location on the southeast corner of the West Wing.

31. The oval office is decorated to suit the tastes of the current president.

32. Features that remain constant in the oval office are the Presidential Seal inlaid in the ceiling, the white mantel, and the United States and Presidential flags behind the president's desk.

33. The East Wing, as it exists today, was added to the White House in 1942, and serves as office space for the first lady and her staff. The East Wing also includes the president's theater, the visitor's entrance, and the east colonnade.

34. In 1902, President Theodore Roosevelt added the third floor living quarters.

35. Extensive renovations to the White House were started in 1948, during the presidency of Harry Truman (1945-1953).

36. The cost of the 1948-1951 renovations totaled $5,700,000.

37. The renovations, completed in 1951, consisted of gutting out the insides of the White House, leaving the outside walls, installing steel beam supports, and rebuilding the insides to the specifications of the earlier White House. The number of rooms of the main structure increased from 48 to 54. Six-hundred-sixty tons of steel support the inner walls and floors, with some of the steel bracing being set on concrete piers as deep as 27 feet below ground level.

38. The renovation of Pennsylvania Avenue in front of the White House was completed in November 2004, at a cost of $23,000,000. This was the most significant improvement since it was paved with asphalt in 1876. It is now paved with gray granite along a 1,600 foot-long stretch of the avenue between 15th and 17th streets. Eighty-eight elm trees were also planted along the sides of the avenue.

UNIQUE FACTS ABOUT THE WHITE HOUSE

1. In 1826, Congress passed a law requiring that as much as possible, the furniture purchased for the White House must be of American origin and manufactured by Americans.

2. The furniture in the White House is polished with lemon oil. No wax is used.

3. In 1801, the first toilets were installed in the White House at the insistence of President Thomas Jefferson (1801-1809). It called for water to be flushed into the bowl from a large bucket over the toilet.

4. President Thomas Jefferson (1801-1809) opened the Presidential Mansion to public tours.

5. The White House is the oldest public building in Washington, D.C.

6. In 1901, President Theodore Roosevelt (1901-1909) established the formal name by having the *de facto* name "White House–Washington" engraved on the stationery.

7. In 1902, Congress formally designated the Presidential Mansion as the White House.

8. Only two known objects that survived the 1814 burning of the Presidential Mansion remain in the White House. These items are:

   - Gilbert Stuart's portrait of George Washington was purchased for the White House in 1800 at a cost of $800. Dolley Madison saved the painting when the British captured and burned Washington, D.C. (Look at the books on the shelf behind Washington - The one titled *"Constitution of the United Sates".*" The word *"States"* is misspelled as *"Sates."*)

   - In the 1930s, a small medicine box was returned to the White House by a descendent of a British soldier who was present at the burning of the Presidential Mansion.

9. President Andrew Jackson (1829-1837) had running water installed in the White House - hand pumps.

10. The Magnolias planted by President Andrew Jackson (1829-1837) are the oldest trees surrounding the White House.

11. In 1913, the White House rose garden was started by Ellen Wilson, the wife of President Woodrow Wilson (1913-1921).

12. Until the presidency of Millard Fillmore (1850-1853), all cooking in the White House was accomplished over an open fireplace. It was during his presidency that the fireplace in the kitchen was replaced with a cast-iron stove.

13. In 1879, President Rutherford Hayes (1877-1881) had a telephone installed in the White House. The one line was 500 yards long and transmitted to the office of the Treasury Secretary.

14. In 1879, the tradition of the annual Easter Egg Roll/Hunt was begun during the presidency of Rutherford Hayes (1877-1881). As many as 15,000 to 20,000 guests participate in this annual event.

15. The first president to display a public Christmas tree in the White House was President Franklin Pierce (1853-1857).

16. In 1923, the tradition of the president lighting the National Christmas Tree was begun. President Calvin Coolidge (1923-1929) lit the first national tree, a 48-foot Balsam Fir.

17. A painting of every former U.S. President hangs in the White House. The painting is completed during the presidency or after the president leaves office. Each president selects the artist who will paint the portrait. If a president dies prior to the painting being completed, the spouse or other close relative selects the artist and approves the painting.

18. As with former presidents, a painting of every former first lady hangs in the White House.

19. The small kitchen in the president's living quarters was installed during the presidency of John Kennedy (1961-1963). (Mrs. Kennedy found it convenient when cooking for the Kennedy children.)

20. It was during the presidency of Benjamin Harrison (1889-1893), that a flagpole flying the flag of the United States was installed on the roof of the White House.

21. On September 4, 1970, Presidential Proclamation 4000 was signed by President Richard Nixon (1969-1974). The proclamation proclaimed that the flag of the United States would be displayed at (over) the White House at all times except during inclement weather.

22. In 1911, the Wright Brothers flew over the White House during the presidency of William Taft (1909-1913).

23. It was also during the presidency of William Taft that the first three automobiles were purchased for the president's use; an electric runabout, a gasoline-powered sedan, and a White steamer.

24. Until 1917, it was considered rude to protest in front of the White House. It was during the Woodrow Wilson presidency (1913-1921) that women suffragettes protested for the right to vote. On January 10, 1917, during a protest by several women, President Wilson offered the ladies tea and a place to get in out of the rain. After the ladies rejected his offer, he had 97 women arrested. The women spent six months in jail before Wilson pardoned them. (Women won the right to vote in 1920.)

25. In 1902, President Theodore Roosevelt (1901-1909) set aside a place for the press. President Dwight Eisenhower (1953-1961) made this area a permanent press area.

26. On March 15, 1913, President Woodrow Wilson (1913-1921) held the first presidential press conference.

27. In 1901, as the guest of President Theodore Roosevelt (1901-1909), Booker T. Washington, a notable scientist, became the first African-American guest at the White House.

28. President Woodrow Wilson (1913-1921) authorized the grazing of sheep on the south lawn during World War I. The wool was sold for $52,823 to benefit the American Red Cross.

29. The current Press Room once held the swimming pool used by Presidents Franklin Roosevelt (1933-1945) through Richard Nixon (1969-1974). It was Nixon who had it covered over. (In 1975, President Gerald Ford (1974-1977) had the current White House swimming pool constructed. It is 22 feet wide by 55 feet long, and is located outside on the White House grounds.)

30. Bullet-proof glass and a bomb shelter were installed in the White House during World War II.

31. A tunnel was dug from the White House to the Treasury Department soon after the start of World War II. One of the Treasury's safest vaults, 30 feet below Pennsylvania Avenue, was converted into a bombproof shelter for the president and his staff. (The shelter was never used, and in a modern war could not withstand a nuclear blast.)

32. Prior to World War II, visitors could just walk into the White House for a visit. Picnics were allowed on the south lawn.

33. A system to detect gas was installed in the White House during the presidency of Harry Truman (1945-1953).

34. Because the White House had deteriorated so much by 1947, President Harry Truman (1945-1953) moved into the Blair House until 1951. (At one point, the piano in the living quarters dropped through a White House floor and the ceilings sagged 18 inches.)

35. Television was installed in the White House during the presidency of Harry Truman (1945-1953).

36. Even though it is often thought that President John Kennedy (1961-1963) was the first to use helicopters for short trips to and from the White House, it was actually President Dwight Eisenhower (1953-1961).

37. In 1995, the section of Pennsylvania Avenue that runs in front of the White House was closed to motor vehicle traffic.

38. The use of *"Hail to the Chief"* was begun during the presidency of James Polk (1845-1849).

39. *"Hail to the Chief"* was discontinued by the direction of President Jimmy Carter (1977-1981), but was resumed three months later when his staff informed the president that many guests failed to notice his entrance into formal gatherings.

40. The White House household staff grew from 16 to the current number of between 85 and 100. Many presidents from the South brought their slaves to the White House. President Zachary Taylor (1849-1850) was the last to use slaves as servants in the White House.

41. Until 1910, the presidents had to pay the salaries of the White House household staff out of their own pockets. The White House household staff consists of cooks, bakers, plumbers, electricians, chefs, doormen, maids, etc.

42. The person in charge of the White House household staff is known as the *"Chief Usher."*

43. In 1842, during the presidency of John Tyler (1841-1845), guards were first assigned to the White House.

44. In 1922, the modern White House guards were established during the presidency of Warren Harding (1921-1923). The guards, originally known as the *"White House Police,"* were renamed the *"Uniformed Division of the U.S. Secret Service"* in 1977.

45. During the presidency of Richard Nixon (1969-1974), the uniforms worn by the security staff were changed. However, they made the staff look like toy soldiers, and the 130 uniforms were quickly turned over to a Washington high school as band uniforms after only one week.

46. The iron railing fence that surrounds the White House is eight feet high.

47. There are ten vehicle entrances to the White House grounds. The gates are made of steel.

48. The large flower planters surrounding the White House were constructed to stop a nine-ton truck traveling 30 mph.

49. In 1898, the first War Room, which is now known as the Situation Room, was installed in the White House during the Spanish-American War.

50. The largest number of children to reside in the White House at one time was six. They were the children of Theodore Roosevelt (1901-1909), and were known as the *"White House Gang."*

51. The White House staff can feed a maximum of 140 guests at a single setting in the State Dining Room.

52. The presidential china consists of 1,500 pieces.

53. The Marine Band often plays at the White House. Established in 1798, the Marine Band is nicknamed *"The President's Own."* It has performed at every presidential inauguration since 1801.

54. In 1961, President John Kennedy (1961-1963) directed the establishment of the formal reception that is now observed when the president and first lady meet foreign dignitaries at the White House.

55. As with the Capitol Building, there is really no front or back to the White House. What visitors refer to as the backside (facing the National Mall) is the garden side or south facade, and the other side is the carriage side or north facade.

56. It takes 570 gallons of paint to paint the exterior of the White House.

57. At one time, old furniture and pieces of presidential china were sold to pay for repairs to the White House, replace furniture, or replace the china. This changed when Edith Roosevelt, the wife of Theodore Roosevelt (1901-1909), saw pieces of the presidential china and furniture for sale in pawnshops. As a result, china that has been broken or is no longer in use is totally smashed. All other items are transferred to the Smithsonian for disposition.

58. In addition to a tennis court and swimming pool, the White House offers a president the use of a two-lane bowling alley and a 65-seat theater. The president also has the use of a putting green and a track for running. (The running track was installed during President William Clinton's (1993-2001) administration.)

59. Seventeen White House weddings have been documented. The first occurred on March 29, 1812, during the presidency of James Madison (1809-1817) between Lucy Washington (the sister of Dolley Madison) and Thomas Todd.

60. President Richard Nixon's (1969-1974) daughter, Patricia, was the most recent daughter of a president to be married on the grounds of the White House. She married Edward Cox in the Rose Garden on June 12, 1971.

61. The latest couple to be formally married in the White House was Tony Rodham, the brother of First Lady Hillary Clinton, and Nicole Boxer. They were married in 1994.

62. President James Monroe's (1817-1825) daughter, Maria, was the first Presidential daughter to be married in the White House.

63. Only three presidents have been sworn into office during ceremonies held in the White House. They were Rutherford Hayes in 1877, Franklin Roosevelt in 1945, and Harry Truman in 1945.

64. By marrying Frances Folsom on June 2, 1886, Grover Cleveland (1885-1889) (1893-1897), at age 49, became the only president to be married in the White House.

65. At age 22, Frances Cleveland has been the youngest first lady.

66. Esther Cleveland, the daughter of President Grover Cleveland (1885-1889) (1893-1897) has been the only child of a president to be born in the White House. She was born in 1894.

67. The first child born in the White House was the grandson of Thomas Jefferson. Jefferson's daughter, Patsy, then Mrs. Thomas Mann Randolph, Jr., gave birth to a son named James Madison Randolph in 1806. (The child was named after future president James Madison.)

68. Of the seven presidents who have lain in state in the White House, only two actually died in the White House - William Harrison (1841) and Zachary Taylor (1849-1850).

69. Two first ladies have actually died in the White House - Caroline Harrison in 1892, and Ellen Wilson in 1914. Their funeral services were held in the East Room.

70. Because of his size (332 pounds), President William Taft (1909-1913) had a bathtub installed in the White House that was 41 inches wide and held 65 gallons of water. (The average bathtub is 21 inches wide.)

71. President James Madison (1809-1814) has been the shortest president, 5 feet tall, and the lightest, weighing 100 pounds.

72. On a daily basis, between 250 and 500 letters were received at the White House daily during President Abraham Lincoln's administration (1861-1865).

73. The salaries of the presidents have been slowly raised at the following increments:

- From President George Washington (1789-1797) through the first four years of Ulysses Grant's presidency (1869-1873), the annual salary was $25,000.

- From Grant's second term (1873-1877) through the presidency of Theodore Roosevelt (1901-1909), the annual salary was $50,000.

- From President William Taft (1909-1913) through the first term of President Harry Truman (1945-1949), the annual salary was $75,000.

- From Truman's second term (1949-1953) through the presidency of Lyndon Johnson (1963-1969), the annual salary was $100,000.

- From President Richard Nixon (1969-1974) through President William Clinton (1993-2001), the annual salary was $200,000.

- Starting with President George W. Bush (2001-Present) the president's annual salary is $400,000.

(Limited by the U.S. Constitution, a president's annual salary may not be raised during a president's current term.)

74. The youngest president to **hold** the office of the presidency was Theodore Roosevelt (1901-1909). He was age 42 when he assumed the office on September 14, 1901, after the assassination of President William McKinley (1897-1901).

75. The youngest president to be **elected** to the office of the presidency was John F. Kennedy (1961-1963). He was age 43 when he took the oath of office on January 20, 1961.

76. The oldest president to be elected to the presidency was Ronald Reagan (1981-1989). He was age 73 in 1985, when he was sworn into office for his second term, and age 77 when he left office.

77. There have been four former presidents who have lived to be at least 90 years of age. John Adams (1797-1801), Herbert Hoover (1929-1933), Ronald Reagan (1981-1989) and Gerald Ford (1974-1977).

78. As of 2006, President Gerald Ford lived longer than any other former or current U.S. President. He died on December 26, 2006, at age 93 years, 165 days. (This was 45 days longer than Ronald Reagan, who died at age 93 years, 120 days; John Adams, who died at age 90 years, 247 days; and Herbert Hover, who died at age 90 years, 71 days.)

79. The oldest former or current first lady has been Bess Truman, the wife of President Harry Truman (1945-1953). She died on October 18, 1982, at age 97.

80. President William Harrison (1841) served the shortest term as president, just 32 days.

81. President Franklin Roosevelt (1933-1945) served the longest term in office, 12 years and 39 days.

82. The 22nd Amendment to the Constitution, which was ratified in 1951, states that no U.S. President may serve longer than ten years. (Two 4-year terms plus a maximum of 2 years having acceded as U.S. President under some other U.S. President's term.)

83. The only bachelor president was James Buchanan (1857-1861).

84. The U.S. Constitution stipulates that a person must be at least 35 years old and be born in the United States to serve as president.

85. Every year on their respective birthdays, the presiding President of the United States sends a commemorative wreath to the graves of each deceased former president. (There has also been a tradition observed by some U.S. Presidents to place a wreath at the Confederate Memorial at Arlington Cemetery on the birthday of former Confederate President Jefferson Davis.)

86. John Quincy Adams (1825-1829) was the first President of the United States to have his photograph taken.

87. Gerald Ford has been the only person to have served as vice president (1973-1974) and president (1974-1977) without having been elected to either office.

88. President Gerald Ford (1974-1977) was named Leslie Lynch King, Jr. at the time of his birth on July 14, 1913. After his mother's divorce and subsequent remarriage, he was referred to as Gerald R. Ford, Jr., after his step-father. Ford changed his name legally in 1935.

89. President William Clinton (1993-2001) was named William J. Blythe IV at the time of his birth on August 19, 1946, a few months after his father was killed in a car accident. He assumed his step-father's name Clinton after his mother's marriage, and legally changed his name to Clinton at age 15.

FACTS ABOUT THE VICE PRESIDENT'S RESIDENCE AND DWIGHT D. EISENHOWER EXECUTIVE OFFICE BUILDING

It is common knowledge that the President of the United States resides and works at 1600 Pennsylvania Avenue, Washington, D.C., or as it is better known – "*The White House.*" However, very few visitors know where the Vice President of the United States resides and works.

As to where the vice president and his family reside, the answer until 1976 was almost anywhere he pleased. The vice president, or the federal government on his behalf, would lease a residence to meet the vice president's needs. The government would pay the majority of the costs, but often the vice president would add to the allotted amount so he and his family could live in the style they had become accustomed to living. However, it was not the cost of actually leasing the residence that prompted the government to find a permanent residence for the vice president, it was the cost and effort of installing security measures at each residence. As a result, the vice president now resides on the grounds of the Naval Observatory.

As to where the vice president conducts his day-to-day business, he has an office in the West Wing of the White House. In addition, the vice president has offices in the Capitol Building, and a ceremonial office in the Dwight D. Eisenhower Executive Office Building (formerly known as the Old Executive Office Building).

THE VICE PRESIDENT'S RESIDENCE

1. The vice president's residence is located at Number One Observatory Circle, Massachusetts Avenue at 34th Street, NW, Washington, D.C.

2. Margaret and Cornelius Barber, wealthy Georgetown landowners, originally owned the land on which the residence is located.

3. In 1893, the house was constructed.

4. The house is in the Victorian style (painted white with green shutters).

5. When constructed, the house consisted of 21 rooms.

6. The house currently consists of 32 rooms on four stories, with a pool house. (Due to security concerns and the possible addition or deletion of unknown rooms, the current number of rooms may not be correct.)

7. The house is owned by the United States Navy and is staffed by Navy personnel. (Security is provided by both the Navy and Secret Service personnel.)

8. The house was originally constructed for the superintendents of the Naval Observatory, who occupied the quarters from 1893 to 1923.

9. From 1923 to 1974, the house was used by the Chiefs of Naval Operations, United States Navy, and was designated the *"Admiral's House."*

10. In 1974, Congress designated the former *"Admiral's House"* as the first official residence of the Vice President of the United States.

The Vice President's Residence

11. The Navy's Chief of Naval Operations now resides on the Washington Navy Yard, near South Capitol Street.

12. Gerald Ford was appointed vice president under President Richard Nixon (1969-1974) on December 6, 1973, after the resignation of Spiro Agnew on October 10, 1973. Ford was the first vice president eligible to reside in the house. However, the resignation of Nixon on August 9, 1974, occurred before renovations on the house were completed, and the then President Ford and his family moved into the White House.

13. The next vice president eligible to reside in the vice president's residence was Nelson Rockefeller, vice president under President Gerald Ford (1974-1977). However, because he was already living in a large residence in the Washington, D.C. area, he elected not to move into the vice president's house, but did use it to entertain guests.

14. The first vice president to actually move into the vice president's residence was Walter Mondale. He was vice president under President Jimmy Carter (1977-1981).

15. The vice presidents usually furnish the residence with their own furniture.

16. In addition to being the site of the vice president's residence, the U.S. Naval Observatory is the preeminent authority in the areas of Precise Time and Astrometry, and distributes Earth Orientation parameters and other Astronomical Data required for accurate navigation and fundamental astronomy.

THE DWIGHT D. EISENHOWER EXECUTIVE OFFICE BUILDING (OLD EXECUTIVE OFFICE BUILDING)

1. The Dwight D. Eisenhower Executive Office Building is located on Pennsylvania Avenue and Seventeenth Street, N.W., next to the West Wing on the White House grounds.

2. Previously known as the Executive Office Building, it was officially designated the "*Dwight D. Eisenhower Executive Office Building*" in May 2002, in honor of President Dwight Eisenhower (1953-1961). (President Eisenhower worked in the building while serving as a military aid to General Douglas MacArthur during the 1930s.)

Dwight D. Eisenhower's Executive Office Building

3. The president's stable once occupied the site on which the building now sits.

4. The building was constructed in the following multiple stages:

    - South Wing (1871-1872)
    - East Wing (1872-1879)
    - North Wing (1879-1882)
    - West & Central Wings (1884-1888)

5. The new wing of the Louvre in Paris, France, inspired the design of the building.

6. The design of the building is referred to as the "*Second Empire Style.*"

7. The building is rectangular in shape, with four wings, and two large interior courts separated by a central wing.

8. The building has more than 500 rooms.

9. There are ten acres of floor-space within the walls of the building.

10. There are 900 freestanding exterior columns to the building.

11. Many of the ceilings are 18 feet high, and the granite walls are 4 feet thick.

12. There are nearly two miles of black-and-white marble halls.

13. Most of the interior detail was constructed using plaster and cast iron. (The thickness of the walls and the use of plaster and cast iron were all intended as fire prevention measures.)

THE HISTORY OF THE DWIGHT D. EISENHOWER EXECUTIVE OFFICE BUILDING

1. The departments of State, War, and Navy were the initial occupants of the Old Executive Office Building.

2. The Navy Department moved out of the Executive Office Building in 1918, the War Department left in 1938, and the State Department moved to other buildings in 1948.

3. In 1939, the White House began using the Executive Office Building for offices for the White House staff.

4. In 1949, the Executive Office Building was turned over to the executive office of the president.

5. During the time the Office of the Secretary of State was in the building, over 1,000 treaties were signed in the Executive Office Building.

6. Six future presidents worked in the Executive Office Building prior to being elected to or assuming the office of the president. Theodore and Franklin Roosevelt worked there as assistant secretaries of the Navy, William Taft performed duties as Secretary of War, Dwight D. Eisenhower worked for General Douglas MacArthur as a military aid, and Vice Presidents Lyndon B. Johnson and George H. W. Bush had offices in this building.

7. In Room 208, Secretary of State Cordell Hull received the Japanese ambassadors on December 7, 1941. It was on this date the Japanese Navy attacked Pearl Harbor, Hawaii.

THE VICE PRESIDENT'S OFFICE IN THE DWIGHT D. EISENHOWER EXECUTIVE OFFICE BUILDING

1. In addition to the Vice President's Office in the West Wing and offices in the Capitol Building, the vice president and his staff maintain a set of offices in the Eisenhower Executive Office Building (EEOB), which is located next to the West Wing on the White House premises.

2. The vice president's office in the Eisenhower Executive Office Building is known as the "*Vice President's Ceremonial Office.*"

3. The office is currently being used for meetings and press interviews.

4. William McPherson, a well known Boston painter and decorator, designed the room.

5. From 1879 until 1921, sixteen secretaries of the Navy occupied the office.

6. From 1921 until 1947, General John Pershing occupied the room as Army Chief of Staff and as Chairman of the Battle Monuments Commission.

7. In 1929, General Pershing's occupancy of the office was interrupted when President Herbert Hoover (1929-1933) was forced to relocate his offices following a Christmas Eve fire in the West Wing of the White House.

8. In 1961, the vice president's office was moved to the building. Lyndon Johnson, vice president under President John Kennedy (1961-1963), was the first to occupy an office in the Executive Office Building as vice president. With the exception of Hubert Humphrey, vice president under President Lyndon Johnson (1963-1969), all the vice presidents since Johnson have occupied the room.

9. In the 1980s, the office underwent an extensive renovation.

10. Some of the notable features of the room are:

    • Part of one wall is decorated with ornamental stenciling and allegorical symbols of the Navy Department. (The designs have been replicated on canvas throughout the rest of the room.)

    • A floor constructed from mahogany and cherry wood, and white marble.

    • Two fireplaces constructed from Belgian black marble.

- Chandeliers that are replicas of circa 1900 gasoliers.

- A bust of Christopher Columbus (original to the building).

- The vice president's desk. Theodore Roosevelt was the first to use the desk. All vice presidents who have occupied this room have used the same desk. (Various users have signed the inside of the top drawer since the 1940s.)

FACTS ABOUT THE BLAIR HOUSE

Just across the street from the White House is what appears to be a small unassuming building known as the *"Blair House."* Within its walls, military leaders, politicians, and heads of states stay during their visits to the Nation's Capital and the President of the United States. It is believed that the Blair House was purchased and renovated by the government at the request of Eleanor Roosevelt to house high-level dignitaries visiting her husband President Franklin Roosevelt (1933-1945). The house has welcomed visitors from around the world since the early days of World War II.

THE HISTORY OF THE BLAIR HOUSE

1. In 1824, the building at #1651 Pennsylvania Avenue was constructed for Doctor Joseph Lovel, the first Surgeon General of the U.S. Army.

2. Francis Preston Blair, a notable journalist and powerful advisor to President Andrew Jackson (1829-1837) and President Martin Van Buren (1837-1841), purchased the house in 1836 for $6,500. And in 1837, Blair, his wife Eliza, and three children moved into the house that later became known as the "Blair House."

The Blair House

3. Montgomery Blair, the son of Francis Blair, and former Post Master General under President Abraham Lincoln (1861-1865), inherited the house in 1876. He expanded the presence of the Blair family on Pennsylvania Avenue by constructing #1653 Pennsylvania Avenue for his daughter Elizabeth Blair Lee and her husband Samuel Lee.

4. In 1942, the federal government purchased the house (#1651-1653 Pennsylvania Avenue) for $175,000. The purchase included much of the furniture in the house at the time.

5. The current Blair House is actually four interconnected townhouses forming a 110-room complex totaling 70,000 square feet. The original Blair House, from which the entire complex takes its name, appears on Pennsylvania Avenue as a yellow masonry structure in the late federal style.

6. It continues to be used by high-level dignitaries visiting the president.

Note: Facing Lafayette Circle and adjacent to the Blair House is Trowbridge House, which is being renovated for use by former U.S. Presidents visiting Washington, D.C.

THE NOTABLE EVENTS THAT HAVE OCCURRED IN THE BLAIR HOUSE

1. Before the American Civil War, such notable men as John Calhoun, Henry Clay, Daniel Webster, and Jefferson Davis used the house as a meeting place.

2. In 1850, future Civil War general William Tecumseh Sherman was married in the house.

3. In 1861, at age 54, Robert E. Lee was offered command of the Union forces in the field. He declined the position, resigned from the Union Army the next day, and then accepted a commission in the Confederate Army.

4. Between 1948 and 1951, President Harry Truman (1945-1953) and his family resided in the Blair House during the renovation of the White House.

5. On November 1, 1950, two Puerto Rican nationalists attempted to enter the Blair House in an attempt to kill President Harry Truman (1945-1953). One federal officer (Leslie Coffelt) and one assailant were killed, and two officers were wounded. (Mr. Coffelt is buried at Arlington Cemetery. The event is described on the back of his headstone.)

Visitors to Washington, D.C. soon become aware of how much a trip to the *"National Mall"* contributes to the enjoyment of their trips to the nation's capital. No matter what their interests, this exciting place offers something for everyone. Whether they are children or adults, are interested in aviation or American history, or are experts in realistic or modern art, there is much to see and learn in the museums and galleries surrounding the *"National Mall."*

THE HISTORY OF THE "NATIONAL MALL"

1. The *"National Mall"* was created from Pierre Charles L'Enfant's 1791 plan.

2. In 1932, the landscaping of the Mall was completed. Frederick Law Olmstead was the consultant for the landscaping.

3. In 1933, the Mall was established as a National Park.

4. Originally, the Mall encompassed the area from between the United States Capitol Building to the Washington Monument. It now also includes the area from the Washington Monument to the Lincoln Memorial.

5. The distance between the steps of the Capitol Building and the Washington Monument is 1.1 miles.

6. The distance between the steps of the Capitol Building and the Lincoln Memorial is 1.9 miles.

7. The total acreage of the Mall is 309.17 acres. (From General Grant's statue in front of the Capitol Building to the Lincoln Memorial.)

. Pierre Charles L'Enfant's Plan of 1791 for developing the Mall was replaced by Andrew Jackson Downing's 1851 Plan.

9. Downing's Plan for developing the Mall was replaced by the 1901-1902 McMillan's Park Commission Plan.

10. The McMillan Plan, named after Michigan Senator James McMillan, called for a monumental and symbolic space. It led to what visitors see as the Mall today - a broad grassy expanse lined with non-residential buildings.

11. The McMillan Plan was designed in such a way that if lines were drawn from one point to another it would form a rectified axis, which looks like "*a child's paper kite*." The Capitol Building rests at the bottom and the Lincoln Memorial at the top. The Jefferson Memorial is angled outward to the extreme left looking from the bottom to the top, and the White House is angled outward to the extreme right looking from bottom to top. At an angle slanting inward from the Jefferson Memorial to the Lincoln Memorial is the FDR Memorial, and at an angle slanting inward from the White House to the Lincoln Memorial is the Vietnam Memorial.

12. Until 1854, a small creek, known as "*Tiber Creek*," flowed from a site near the Washington Monument to the Potomac River. (The creek was named after the Tiber River, which runs through Rome, Italy.)

13. Until 1850, there were slave pens along the Mall.

14. During the Civil War (1861-1865), soldiers camped and trained on the Mall. Cattle also grazed near the Washington Monument.

15. In 1847, the first gaslights (streetlights) were installed on the Capitol grounds and along Pennsylvania Avenue.

16. The Tiber Creek, along the north side of the Mall, was filled in when the railroad was constructed. It is now Constitution Avenue.

17. Between 1854 and 1855, the tracks and terminals of the B&O Railroad were constructed around the Mall. They were removed in 1901.

18. On July 2, 1881, it was at the Baltimore and Potomac (B&P) depot in front of the Capitol Building that President James Garfield (1881) was shot by an assassin.

19. Until 1868, notorious slum communities occupied a large area of what is now known as the "Mall." These communities were known by such names as *"Swamppoodle"* and *"Murder Bay."*

20. Until 1901, a Central Market, which was a very convenient place to sell and buy goods, was among the sites on what is now the Mall.

THE SMITHSONIAN INSTITUTION BUILDING

1. The Smithsonian Institution Building was designed in 1847, and dedicated in 1855.

2. The building is the final resting place of James Louis Macie Smithson, an English chemist and mineralogist. His donation to the U.S. Government led to the founding of the Smithsonian.

3. Smithson was an English citizen who was born in France in 1765, who died and was buried in Italy in 1829, and was reburied in the United States in 1904.

4. Until 1801, Smithson's legal name was James Louis Macie. Smithson was the illegitimate son of Hugh Smithson, the first Duke of Northumberland. When James Macie was nearly 50 years of age, he was granted permission to take his father's name.

The Crypt of James Louis Macie Smithson

5. Smithson's will provided that if his nephew Henry James Hungerford died without an heir, all of Smithson's property would be bequeathed to the United States. (Hungerford died childless in 1835.)

6. In 1838, the Smithson estate was settled.

7. The Smithson estate of 104,000 gold coins totaled $500,000 (some estimates made the total $550,000). In gratitude for his generous gift to the United States for an *"Establishment for the increase and diffusion of knowledge,"* In 1904, Smithson's remains were brought from Genoa, Italy, to Washington, D.C. He lies in the Crypt Room of the Smithsonian Institution Building.

8. By law, the money bequeathed by Smithson is loaned to the United States government. The government pays the Smithsonian Institution interest on the loan.

9. The government decided in 1840 that the gift would be used to start a National Institute, which would house botanical and scientific specimens donated to the national government.

The Smithsonian Institution Building

10. A board of regents, whose chancellor is the Chief Justice of the United States, governs the Smithsonian Institution. The regents include the Vice President of the United States, three U.S. Senators, three members of the House of Representatives, and nine private citizens.

11. Because of its prominent towers, the Smithsonian Institution Building is often referred to as the *"Castle."*

12. During the Civil War, President Abraham Lincoln (1861-1865) occasionally watched from the top of the Castle as Union troops drilled on the Mall.

13. The Smithsonian Institution Building is now largely used for the administration of the Smithsonian Institution and its holdings.

THE ARTS AND INDUSTRIES BUILDING

1. In 1881, the Arts and Industries Building was completed.

2. It took 15 months to build the Arts and Industries Building.

3. The architects of the Arts and Industries Building were Adolph Clues and Paul Schulze.

The Arts and Industries Building

4. Civil War General Montgomery C. Meigs drew up the original concept of the Arts and Industries Building.

5. The style of the Arts and Industries Building has been described as *"Modernized Romanesque."*

6. The interior of the Arts and Industries Building consists of a four-square-plan leading to a central rotunda.

7. The exterior of the Arts and Industries Building was constructed from red brick, sandstone, tile, and slate.

8. The statue on the Jefferson Drive side of the building is of Joseph Henry (1797-1878). He was a noted American scientist and the first Secretary of the Smithsonian Institution.

9. The group of three female figures over the entrance to the building is titled *"Columbia Protecting Science and Industry."* The figures were constructed from zinc coated with plaster.

10. In 1881, the Arts and Industries Building was used for President James Garfield's inaugural ball.

11. Displays within the Arts and Industries Building include:

- Machinery, gizmos, and exotica celebrating the best the world had to offer in 1876 at the Centennial Exhibition held in Philadelphia, Pennsylvania.

- *Jupiter*, a restored locomotive engine constructed for the Santa Cruz Railroad of California in 1876.

- Other exhibits on a rotating basis.

12. The event that led to the building of the Arts and Industries Building was the 1876 Philadelphia Centennial. To spare themselves the cost of shipping their exhibits home, almost all of the exhibitors at the World Fair presented their exhibits to the United States government. Several historians believe this event is how the Smithsonian got to be known as the *"Nation's Attic."* (Some historians credit Mark Twain for first using this term.)

13. Federal laws now restrict these mass presentations.

THE NATIONAL GALLERY OF ART, WEST BUILDING

1. John Russell Pope designed the National Gallery of Art, West Building.

2. In 1941, the West Building was opened to the public.

3. The top of the building's dome stands 109 feet above the ground elevation.

The National Gallery of Art, West Building

4. The West Building consists of a central rotunda on the 6th Street axis, and two windowless wings stretching a total of 780 feet.

5. The exterior walls of the West Building were constructed from five different shades of pink Tennessee marble.

6.	Within the walls of the West Building are 100 rooms of paintings.

7.	The circular hall of the West Building is 100 feet in diameter.

8.	Twenty-four green/black columns capped by white Ionic capitals support the circular hall of the West Building. The Carrara marble used to construct the columns is from Lucca, Italy.

9.	The floor of the circular hall in the West Building was constructed of marble from Vermont.

10.	The bronze statue in the circular hall of the West Building represents Mercury, the messenger of the pagan gods.

11.	The first curator of the West Building was John Walker.

12.	Andrew Mellon was one of the biggest benefactors to the West Building. He presented the building to the nation.

13.	In 1854, a terminal for the Baltimore & Ohio (B&O) railroad was on the site of the West Building. It was removed in 1901.

THE NATIONAL GALLERY OF ART, EAST BUILDING

1.	In 1978, the building containing the National Gallery of Art, East Building, was completed.

2.	Paul Mellon and his family foundation funded the East Building

The National Gallery of Art, East Building

3.	The East Building cost nearly $95,000,000.

4.	The exterior walls of the East Building were constructed from three different shades of Tennessee marble.

5.	The top of the East Building stands 180 feet above the ground elevation, one foot less than the West Building.

THE NATIONAL AIR AND SPACE MUSEUM

1. The Smithsonian's aeronautical collection began in 1876, when it was presented a group of Chinese kites after the Philadelphia Centennial Exhibition.

2. In 1946, Congress chartered the National Air Museum.

3. A national armory, constructed in 1855, was on the site of the museum until 1964.

4. In 1966, Public Law 89-509 changed the museum's name to the National Air and Space Museum.

The National Air and Space Museum

5. On July 1, 1976, the current home of the museum was opened to the public.

6. The ribbon cutting ceremony, which opened the museum, was accomplished by using a 10-foot arm identical to the one on the *Viking Lander*. The *Viking Lander* was on its way to the planet Mars. The arm was activated by a signal from the *Viking Lander*. It took only eighteen minutes for the signal to travel from Mars to the museum.

7. The museum is 685 feet long by 225 feet wide.

8. The exterior walls of the museum were constructed from pink marble from Tennessee.

9. The museum contains 200,000 square feet of exhibit space.

10. The architects of the museum were Hellmuth, Obata, and Kassabaum.

11. The federal government funded for the museum.

12. The structural system of the museum consists of steel framing and tubular trusses.

13. Just twenty-five days after it was opened, the museum greeted its one-millionth visitor.

14. The museum on the Mall contains only a portion of the air and space collection. A second display may be seen at the National Air and Space Museum's Steven F. Udvar-Hazy Center, near the Washington Dulles International Airport. The center was opened to the public on December 15, 2003, and contains more than 200 aircraft and 100 space artifacts.

15. In an effort to protect the displays made of cloth from damaging sunlight, all of the glass windows in the building, including the three-story sheets that face the Mall and Capitol Building, were replaced between 1999 and 2001.

16. Important displays at the National Air and Space Museum include:

- An **unmanned research model plane,** which was launched from a houseboat on the Potomac River in 1896, and flew for a minute and a half.

- The **Wright brothers' 1903 Flyer**, which made the first manned flight in 1903. (The first aviation fatality was Lt. Thomas E. Selfridge, who died in a plane crash piloted by Orville Wright on September 17, 1908. The site of the accident occurred on Fort Myer, adjacent to Arlington Cemetery.)

- **Planes and rockets of World Wars I and II**, including the 1909 Military Flyer, the world's first military airplane, and a Messerschmitt Me 262, the world's first operational jet fighter.

- The **largest plane hanging from the ceiling** is the 17,500-pound Douglas DC-3.

- **Charles Lindbergh's Spirit of St. Louis**, which made the first solo, nonstop transatlantic flight in thirty-three-and-a-half hours in 1927. (On the underside of the engine cover are the signatures of everyone associated with the construction of the plane, including the office secretaries.)

The Spirit of St. Louis

- **Space rockets, modules, guided missiles, and manned spacecraft**, including the sixty-foot-tall Minuteman III.

THE NATIONAL MUSEUM OF AMERICAN HISTORY

1. In 1964, the National Museum of American History was opened to the public.

2. Until 1980, the National Museum of American History was called the National Museum of History and Technology.

The National Museum of American History

3. The exterior of the museum was constructed from Tennessee pink marble.

4. The fountain steps of the museum were constructed from Minnesota pearl granite.

5. Displayed in the museum is a wide variety of items that reflect the history of the United States. Two of the most interesting and widely visited displays are:

- **The American flag, which flew over Fort McHenry during the night of September 13, 1814, as the British Navy bombarded the fort**. The flag....

- Was hand-stitched in Baltimore, Maryland, in 1813 by 34-year-old Mary Pickergill, with the assistance of her 13-year-old daughter Caroline.

- Was purchased for $405.90.

- In 1813, was presented to Major George Armistead, Commander of Fort McHenry during the War of 1812.

- Remained in the family of Major Armistead until 1907, at which time it was loaned to the Smithsonian by Armistead's grandson Eben Appleton.

- Appleton gifted the flag to the United States in 1912.

- Was sewn from 266 yards of English wool with 15 cotton stars and stripes.

- Weighs about 45 pounds without backing. With the old backing it weighed approximately 150 pounds.

- Has a red "V" on one of the white stripes. No one knows its origin, but experts believe that it might be part of an "A" for Armistead, which was sewn on by his widow, or it could be just an attempt at repairing a tear.

- Was originally 30 feet by 42 feet in size.

- Because 8 feet of the flag has been snipped from its length by souvenir hunters. it has been reduced to 30 feet by 34 feet in size.

- Has 15 stripes and 15 stars, one for each state in the Union at the time. (By 1818, Congress had limited the number of stripes on the flag of the United States to 13, one for each of the original 13 states.)

- Has had one of the original stars removed.

- Has had 27 patches added.

- Was designed to fly from a 90-foot flagpole.

- Had a new backing of Irish linen attached in 1914.

- Was installed in the Museum of History and Technology in 1963.

- Had a protective cover installed after a 1982 study.

- Was displayed every hour on the hour for most of the day until it was removed for repairs.

- During 1998-2006, extensive repairs were made, which affected some of the repairs described above. The new repairs included the removal of 1.7 million old stitches and material, while attaching a new, light-weight backing.

- **The First Ladies Hall**....

  - Is intended to provide a broad history of the contributions of the first ladies.

  - Was started in 1912, when Mrs. William Taft presented a dress she had worn at the White House to the Smithsonian.

The First Ladies Hall

  - Was the primary idea of two people - Rose Hoes, who was a descendant of President Monroe, and Julian James.

- Consists of the dresses worn at the inaugural balls, personal items, letters, recorded speeches, and other items that provide insight into the contributions and personal lives of the first ladies. (Many of the dresses are displayed on mannequins from the neck down. However, several other mannequins have different hairstyles, coloring, and sizes, but all of the earlier faces were modeled after an 1863 bust of Cordelia, daughter of Shakespear's King Lear, by Louisiana sculptor Pierce F. Connelly.)

- Only one dress is displayed for each first lady, no matter how many times her husband was re-elected.

THE NATIONAL MUSEUM OF NATURAL HISTORY

1. In 1910, the National Museum of Natural History was opened to the public. In the 1960s, the east and west wings were added.

2. The museum was originally called the *"new"* Natural Museum.

The National Museum of Natural History

3. The Washington firm of Hornblower and Marshal designed the museum in a classical style. The exterior of the building is granite.

4. The total area of the museum is larger than eighteen football fields.

5. The museum contains more than 125 million specimens.

6. A large African elephant greets visitors in the rotunda. The specifics about the elephant are:

   - It weighs eight tons as shown.

   "Harry" The Elephant

109

- It is 13 feet, 2 inches tall.

- J.J. Fenykovi killed it in Angola on November 13, 1955.

- It took sixteen bullets from a .416 Rigby rifle to kill.

- It is the second largest elephant ever killed, and the largest ever mounted. The largest elephant ever killed was six inches taller, and was killed in 1974 in Angola.

- The hide weighed more than two tons (over 4,000 pounds) when it was removed from the carcass.

- The tusks are seven feet long. (The shown tusks are plastic, the real ones are in storage.)

- It is often referred to as "*Harry*."

THE NATIONAL MUSEUM OF THE AMERICAN INDIAN

1. Congress passed a bill for the construction of the National Museum of the American Indian in 1989.

2. In 1995, the architectural team began work on the museum.

3. In 2000, ground was broken for the museum.

4. On September 21, 2004, the museum was dedicated.

5. The cost of the museum totaled nearly $199,000,000.

The National Museum of the American Indian

6. The museum is located on a 4.25-acre site.

7. The museum building totals approximately 450,000 square feet.

8. The museum was constructed from gold-tone Minnesota limestone.

9. The exterior of the museum is intended to look like a canyon wall.

10. The museum is a curving, five-story structure.

11. The shape of the museum is intended to look as if it was formed by wind and water.

12. The museum faces east toward the rising sun.

13. The rotunda at the entrance to the building is 120 feet high.

14. Scattered throughout the forest, wetlands, meadowlands, and crop areas are more than forty "grandfather rocks", which are seen as elders of the landscape, and speak to the longevity of the Native people.

15. The water feature, which runs along the north side of the museum site recalls the tidal waterway of Tiber Creek. (The Tiber Creek once flowed along what is now the National Mall.)

16. Approximately 7,500 objects are displayed in the museum through three major exhibits and other exhibits. These major exhibits are beadwork, baskets, and pottery.

17. Other exhibits address the lives and trials of the Indians of North, Central, and South Americas.

FACTS ABOUT THE NATIONAL ARCHIVES

No building within Washington, D.C. is more important to the history of the United States than the National Archives. This building has within its walls the documents that declared the United States free from England, to set to paper the rights of its citizens, and to record for posterity historical treaties, explorations, discoveries, laws, and special events. Most visitors to the National Archives come to view the Declaration of Independence, Bill of Rights, and the Constitution of the United States. Indeed these pieces of history are important parts of American heritage. However, the building itself is a part of history, and the many documents not on display add even more to the distinct characteristic of the nation's *"safe deposit box."*

THE NATIONAL ARCHIVES

1. For many years prior to the ground breaking, the site of the National Archives was used for a large and busy market (Center Market).

The National Archives

2. Architect John Russell Pope designed the neoclassical structure. It is an example of the *beaux-arts* style.

3. In 1926, Congress authorized construction of the National Archives Building. (A total of $8,500,000 was appropriated for construction.)

4. On September 9, 1931, the ground for the National Archives Building was broken.

5. On February 20, 1933, President Herbert Hoover (1929-1933) dedicated the cornerstone for the National Archives.

6. A total of 8,575 piles were driven twenty-one feet into the ground to support the building, before pouring a huge concrete bowl as a foundation.

7. In November 1935, 120 staff members of the Archives started working in the building.

8. In 1937, the Archives Building was completed.

9. The Archives Building is fireproof and had large pumps installed at the time of construction to deal with possible flooding.

10. The Archives Building is 330 feet long by 213 feet wide, and is 166 feet high.

11. The exterior superstructure of the Archives Building was constructed from limestone, and the base was constructed from granite.

12. There are 72 Corinthian limestone columns surrounding the exterior of the Archives Building. Each column is 53 feet high by 5 feet, 8 inches in diameter, and weighs 95 tons. (The columns were formed in sections, and as each section was finished, it was hoisted into place on top of earlier sections.)

13. On the Constitution Avenue and Pennsylvania Avenue sides of the Archives Building are four statues. The statues were carved from 125-ton blocks of limestone.

14. The figures on the Constitution Avenue side of the Archives Building represent *"Heritage"* (female), and *"Guardianship"* (male). The female holds a child and a sheaf of wheat in her right hand as symbols of growth and hopefulness. In her left hand she protects an urn, symbolic of the ashes of past generations. The male uses martial symbols, such as the helmet, sword, and lion skin to convey the need to protect the historical records for future generations.

15. The figures on the Pennsylvania Avenue side of the Archives Building represent *"Past"* (male), and *"Future"* (female). The inscription, *"Study the Past,"* on the male figure is from a quotation by the Chinese scholar, Confucius: *"Study the past, if you divine the future."*

16. The pediment of the Archives Building facing Constitution Avenue is 18 feet high in the center by 118 feet wide. The figures were carved from individual stone blocks weighing between 13 and 50 tons each. The central figure in the pediment represents the *"Recorder of the Archives."* The frieze above the figures is based on the flower of the papyrus plant, which is the symbol of paper. The rams represent parchment (parchment is made from the skin of sheep). The other figures represent citizens holding documents, such as the U.S. Constitution and the Declaration of Independence. The dogs symbolize *"guardianship,"* and the winged horses symbolize *"inspiration."*

17. The pediment of the Archives Building facing Pennsylvania Avenue is 18 feet high in the center by 118 feet wide. The central figure represents *"Destiny."* This figure is flanked by eagles, which represent *"strength through unity."* The male and female figures on the left of the central group symbolize *"The Art of Peace."* The warriors on the right of the central group symbolize *"The Art of War."* The group of four people on the right represents *"The Romance of History."* The group of four people on the opposite side represents *"The Song of Achievement."*

18. The 12-foot limestone eagles on top of the Archives Building symbolize *"Guardians."*

19. There are thirteen, 8-foot-high medallions on the attic frieze of the Archives Building. One represents the House of Representatives, one the Senate, and the ten cabinet-level executive departments of the federal government that surrendered their records into the keeping of the National Archives. The thirteenth medallion is the Great Seal of the United States.

20. The two, 9-foot figures in Roman armor on the sides of the central doorway of the Archives Building (Pennsylvania Avenue) represent "*The Guardians of the Portal.*"

21. The storage space of the Archives Building is 757,000 square feet. The opening of an additional storage building in College Park, Maryland, added an additional 1.9 million square feet.

22. The entrance doors to the Archives Building from the Constitution Avenue are each nearly 10 feet wide, 11 inches thick, and 38 feet, 7 inches high. Each door weighs 6 1/2 tons (13,000 pounds), and are the largest bronze doors in the world.

23. The bronze design on the floor (entrance) of the Archives Building represents *"Legislation," "Justice," "History,"* and *"War and Defense."*

24. The Rotunda of the Archives Building is 75 feet high from the floor to the ceiling.

25. The mural on the left side of the Rotunda is titled *The Declaration of Independence.*

26. Barry Faulkner completed the mural titled *The Declaration of Independence.* It shows 28 delegates to the 1776 Continental Congress. Thomas Jefferson is presenting the Declaration of Independence to John Hancock.

Mural – Declaration of Independence

27. The mural on the right side of the Rotunda is titled *The Constitution.*

28. The mural titled *The Constitution,* was completed by Barry Faulkner, and depicts George Washington and the 28 delegates to the United States Constitutional Convention. James Madison is presenting the Constitution to George Washington.

29. Each mural weighs 340 pounds.

30. The major holdings of the National Archives date back to 1775.

31. There are billions of pages of textual material and millions of still pictures in the Archives Building.

32. The Archives Building stores only those federal records that are judged to have historical/legal value. This number totals about 1 to 3 percent of the records generated by the federal government during any given year.

33. In November 2004, the National Archives opened its document warehouse to visitors. The $7,000,000 exhibit consists of a dozen alcoves ("Public Vaults") that display over 1,100 items.

THE DOCUMENTS ON PERMANENT DISPLAY IN THE NATIONAL ARCHIVES

1. On permanent display are the Declaration of Independence, the Constitution of the United States, and the Bill of Rights.

2. Between June 11, 1776 and June 28, 1776, the "*Committee of Five*", consisting of two New England men, John Adams of Massachusetts and Roger Sherman of Connecticut; two men from the Middle Colonies, Benjamin Franklin of Pennsylvania and Robert R. Livingston of New York; and one southerner, Thomas Jefferson of Virginia, drafted the Declaration of Independence.

3. On June 28, 1776, the committee's initial draft of the Declaration of Independence was submitted to Congress.

4. Prior to voting for independence, 47 alterations were made to the draft of the Declaration of Independence by Congress.

5. On July 2, 1776, Congress voted for independence.

6. From July 2nd through July 4th 1776, Congress made an additional 39 alterations to the draft, for a total of 86 alterations to the original draft proposed by the committee charged with drafting the Declaration of Independence.

7. On July 4, 1776, twelve of the thirteen colonies (New York did not vote), approved the Declaration of Independence, but it wasn't actually signed by all the delegates until August 2, 1776.

8. Fifty-six members of Congress signed the Declaration of Independence.

9. The Declaration of Independence is written on parchment, which is an animal skin specially treated with lime and stretched to create a strong, long-lasting document.

10. The parchment on which the Declaration of Independence is engrossed, which is a process of preparing an official document in a large, clear hand, measures 29 3/4 inches by 24 1/4 inches.

11. The Declaration of Independence consists of 1,458 words, plus signatures.

12. On the back of the Declaration of Independence are penned the words "Original Declaration of Independence, dated 4th July 1776."

13. The first formal use of the term "*United States of America*" was in the Declaration of Independence.

14. On May 14, 1787, the Constitutional Convention first met in Philadelphia, Pennsylvania, to discuss the formation of the Constitution, but a quorum was not present until May 25, 1787. (Rhode Island chose not to attend the convention.)

The Constitution of the United States

15. On August 6, 1787, the Constitutional Convention accepted the first draft of the Constitution.

16. On September 17, 1787, the Constitutional Convention approved the United States Constitution.

17. Article VII of the United States Constitution required the approval of at least 9 states for the Constitution to be considered established. This occurred on June 21, 1788, when the ninth state, New Hampshire, voted to ratify the Constitution.

18. Listed below is the order in which the states ratified the Constitution:

STATE	DATE RATIFIED	VOTE
Delaware	December 7, 1787	Unanimous
Pennsylvania	December 12, 1787	46-23
New Jersey	December 18, 1787	Unanimous
Georgia	January 2, 1788	Unanimous
Connecticut	January 9, 1788	128-40
Massachusetts	February 6, 1788	187-168
Maryland	April 28. 1788	63-11
South Carolina	May 23, 1788	149-73
New Hampshire	June 21, 1788	57-47
Virginia	June 25, 1788	89-79
New York	July 26, 1788	30-27
North Carolina	November 21, 1789	194-77
Rhode Island	May 29, 1790	34-32

19. Each of the four pages of parchment on which the Constitution is written measures 28 3/4 inches by 23 5/8 inches.

20. The Constitution consists of 4,543 words, plus signatures.

21. On September 25, 1789, the first United States Congress met to discuss twelve amendments to the Constitution. Congress ratified ten of the twelve proposed amendments, which are known as the *Bill of Rights*.

22. On December 15, 1791, the first ten amendments to the Constitution were ratified by three-fourths of the states.

23. Congress has ratified only 27 amendments to the Constitution.

24. The Declaration of Independence, the Constitution, and the Bill of Rights are known collectively as the "*Charters of Freedom*."

25. Through much of the 19th century, the Declaration of Independence and Constitution were displayed in the Old Executive Office Building (renamed the Eisenhower Executive Office Building) near the White House.

26. From 1924 through 1951, and with the exception of the documents being stored in vaults at Fort Knox, Kentucky, during World War II, the Declaration of Independence and Constitution were exhibited at the Library of Congress.

27. From 1952 through 2000, the Declaration of Independence and Constitution were displayed in a special helium-filled glass and bronze case in the Archives Building. (Because of space limitations, only two of the four pages of the Constitution were displayed.)

28. A special yellow filter protects the Declaration of Independence and Constitution from light.

29. As the result of a 2001-2003 renovation to the Archives Building, all pages of the Declaration of Independence, Constitution, and Bill of Rights are displayed in an encasement that consists of an aluminum base and a titanium frame. A 3/8 inch-thick laminated tempered glass covers the documents. The encasements are filled with argon gas with a controlled amount of humidity to keep the parchment flexible.

30. It is believed that each evening, the Declaration of Independence, Constitution, and Bill of Rights are lowered 25 feet into a 5-ton concrete vault. (However, for the sake of security, this may not be the final secured site.)

FACTS ABOUT THE FORD'S THEATER
(SITE WHERE PRESIDENT LINCOLN WAS SHOT)

On April 14, 1865, sensing the end of the Civil War, President Abraham Lincoln turned his attention to the reunification of the Union. After working a full day, the 16th President of the United States and his wife, Mary, took what was to be their last ride together. During the carriage ride and at stops along the way, they discussed what the future might bring to them. Among their plans were their return to Springfield, Illinois, and trips to Europe and the Holy Lands of the Middle East. Lincoln thought about returning to the practice of law, and his wife would be happy just to get away from a city whose people she considered cruel and unsympathetic. However, neither the president nor Mrs. Lincoln could ever envision that in less than six hours after this quiet ride through the Maryland countryside their plans would be destroyed by a single shot at Ford's Theater.

THE FORD'S THEATER

1. Ford's Theater is located at 511 Tenth Street, Washington, D.C.

2. In 1833, the First Baptist Church of Washington was constructed on the future site of Ford's Theater.

3. In 1859, the church was vacated when the First Baptist congregation merged with the Fourth Baptist congregation.

The Ford's Theater

4. In December 1861, John T. Ford purchased the Tenth Street Church building for use as a theater.

5. In February 1862, and after its initial success, Ford invested $10,000 into new renovations and the remodeling of the theater.

6. On March 19, 1862, the theater was reopened as *"Ford's Athenaeum."*

7. On December 30, 1862, the theater was gutted by fire.

8. On February 28, 1863, the cornerstone for the present structure was laid.

9. On August 27, 1863, the theater was reopened under the name *"Ford's New Theater."*

10. On April 14, 1865, John Wilkes Booth assassinated President Abraham Lincoln (1861-1865) during the performance of *"Our American Cousin."* The theater was closed on the same day.

11. The performance of April 14, 1865, was the last of 495 performances of various types between 1863, when the theater was reopened, and the shooting of President Lincoln.

12. Ford's plan to reopen the theater was thwarted by Secretary of War Edwin Stanton, who stationed troops outside the building on July 7, 1865. (The same day that four of the Lincoln conspirators were hanged.)

13. On July 8, 1865, the War Department began leasing the building from Ford.

14. In August 1865, the War Department began converting the theater into a three-story office building at a cost of $28,000.

15. In December 1865, the U.S. Surgeon General started using the building as an Army Medical Museum.

16. On April 7, 1866, Congress appropriated $100,000 for the purchase of the building.

17. In July 1866, the Treasury Department paid Ford the final installment for the purchase of the building.

18. From 1866 through 1887, the building was used as an office building. The War Department Records Office occupied the first floor, the Library of Medicine was located on the second floor, and the Army Medical Museum was located on the third floor.

19. In 1887, the Library of Medicine and Army Medical Museum were moved to a new building on the Mall. All three floors of the building were subsequently used by the War Department.

20. On June 9, 1893, the collapse of the building's floors resulted in 22 government clerks being killed and 68 others injured.

21. During the period of 1893-1931, the building served as a warehouse and a publications depot for the Adjutant General's Office of the War Department.

22. On July 1, 1928, the building was transferred from the War Department to the Offices of Public Buildings and Public Parks.

23. On February 12, 1932, a museum about the life of Lincoln was opened on the first floor of the building.

24. On August 10, 1932, the building was transferred to the National Park Service.

25. In 1946, Senator Milton Young of North Dakota introduced the first legislation for the restoration of Ford's Theater.

26. In 1954, President Dwight Eisenhower (1953-1961) signed a Congressional Act to restore the theater.

27. On July 7, 1964, after the completion of a restoration study, Congress authorized $2,073,000 for the restoration of the theater.

28. Between January 1965 and December 1967, Ford's Theater was restored.

29. On January 21, 1968, the National Park Service held dedication ceremonies for the restored Ford's Theater.

30. February 5, 1968, a select group saw the first performance held at Ford's Theater since 1865. The name of the play was *"John Brown's Body."*

31. On February 13, 1968, the restored Ford's Theater was opened to the general public.

32. In 1930, the Star Saloon, which was adjacent to Ford's Theater and the site where Booth had a number of drinks prior to shooting the president was demolished.

THE LINCOLN ASSASSINATION

1. As early as August 1864, Booth had gathered around him a group of boyhood friends and other accomplices in an effort to capture President Lincoln. (His goal was to exchange President Lincoln for Confederate prisoners of war.)

2. The final unsuccessful attempt at capturing President Lincoln occurred in March 1865.

3. It is believed Booth was in the crowd in front of the White House when President Lincoln made his speech after the surrender of Robert E. Lee's army on Palm Sunday, April 9, 1865. It is also believed that Booth, irritated by Lincoln's remarks, decided on that date to assassinate the president.

4. After deciding to kill President Lincoln, Booth assigned George Atzerodt the task of killing Vice President Andrew Johnson, and Lewis Powell to kill Secretary of State William Seward.

5. On the night of April 14, 1865 (Good Friday), President Lincoln and his wife went to Ford's Theater to watch the play *"Our American Cousin."* Major Henry Rathbone and Clara Harris accompanied them. (These guests of the Lincoln's were related through the marriage of Harris' father to Rathbone's mother – step-brother/step-sister.)

6. President Lincoln entered Ford's Theater at 8:30 p.m., an hour after the play had begun.

7. Prior to going to Ford's Theater, Booth stopped at the Star Saloon near the theater for a few drinks.

8. Just prior to 10 p.m., Booth made the last of several trips to the theater. He walked to the back entrance of the theater and asked Edman Spangler, a handyman at the theater, to hold his horse. After several minutes, and because he wanted to return to work, Spangler turned the horse over to a young man by the name of Joseph *"Peanuts"* Burroughs to hold.

9. After entering the theater, Booth took the back stairs to the level of the President's State Box. Seeing no guards in the immediate vicinity, the assassin walked to the door separating the hallway from the president's box. He then peered through a small hole in the door. (Some historians believe Booth bored the hole through the door. Other historians feel Booth had insufficient time to bore the hole.)

10. Waiting for a scene in the play where he knew there would be a loud response from the crowd, Booth stepped through the door and shot President Lincoln once behind the left ear with a .44 caliber derringer.

The President's State Box

11. Responding to the shot, Major Rathbone struggled with Booth. Having the gun knocked from his hand, Booth pulled a knife and stabbed Rathbone in the forearm.

12. While jumping from the state box to the stage floor, a drop of eleven feet, Booth caught his spur on the Treasury flag hanging over the front of the president's box. This misstep caused Booth to land off-balance, breaking a small bone in the lower part of his left leg near the ankle.

13. Even with his injury, Booth took time as he raced to his horse in the alley to shout *"Sic Semper Tyrannis."* A Latin phrase on Virginia's state flag meaning *"Thus always unto tyrants."*

14. Escaping through Baptist Alley behind Ford's Theater, Booth started his twelve-day escape attempt.

15. While Booth was escaping, shouts from the state box to the crowd of 1,700 called for a doctor. In response, Dr. Charles Leale, a 23-year-old surgeon, rushed to the box, and had the president placed on the floor. President Lincoln had stopped breathing, but his labored breaths started again. (The capacity of Ford's Theater today is limited to 700 people.)

16. Determining that the president's wound was too severe for him to survive a trip to a hospital or to the White House, Dr. Leale decided to take the president some place near Ford's Theater. The Petersen Boarding House across the street was chosen as the most suitable place to administer medical aid.

17. Major Rathbone, even though seriously injured by Booth's knife, escorted Mrs. Lincoln to the Petersen House, where he collapsed from a loss of blood.

THE AFTERMATH OF THE ASSASSINATION

THE MEMBERS OF THE LINCOLN FAMILY

1. After his death on April 15, 1865, President Lincoln, age 56, was buried in a tomb in Springfield, Illinois, with his two sons, Edward (Eddie) who was age 4 when he died in 1850, and William (Willie), who was nearly age 12 when he died in 1862. (President Lincoln was buried in the same suit that he wore to his second inauguration just a few weeks prior to his assassination.)

2. Mary's son, Robert, had Mrs. Lincoln committed to a sanitarium. After gaining her release, Mary lived until 1882, when at age 64 she passed away in Springfield, Illinois. She is buried in a crypt near her husband's sarcophagus.

3. In 1872, Thomas (Tad) Lincoln died at age 18, and is buried near his father and mother.

4. Robert Todd Lincoln, who was present at his father's death, became a lawyer, a successful businessman, Secretary of War, and Minister to England. He was also present at the dedication of the Lincoln Memorial in 1921. Robert died in 1926 at the age of 82, and is buried with his wife, Mary, and son, Abraham, at Arlington Cemetery at a site overlooking the memorial to his father.

(Why was Robert buried at Arlington versus next to his parents and siblings in Illinois? The answer was revealed in his wife's words, when in a letter she stated that Robert *"was a personage, made his own history, independently of his great father, and should have his own place in the sun!"*)

THE CONSPIRATORS

1. John Wilkes Booth was shot and killed by Union troops on April 26, 1865, a few days from his 27th birthday. It was not until 1869 that his remains were returned to his family for burial at Greenmount Cemetery, in Baltimore, Maryland.

2. Mary Surratt (age 42), Lewis Powell (age 21), David Herold (age 23), and George Atzerodt (age 30) were hanged on July 7, 1865, at a site on Fort McNair in Washington, D.C., that is now a tennis court for post personnel. (The remains of Surratt are buried in the Mount Olivet Cemetery, Washington, D.C., and Herold's last resting place is in the Congressional Cemetery, Washington, D.C. Atzerodt is buried in Maryland. No one claimed the remains of Powell after his execution, and in 1992, Powell's skull was discovered in a desk drawer in the Anthropology Department of the Smithsonian Institution. In 1994, the skull was released to his relatives, who buried it in a cemetery in Geneva, Florida.)

3. Dr. Samuel Mudd (who treated Booth's broken leg), Michael O'Laughlen, and Samuel Arnold were sentenced to life in prison at Fort Jefferson, Florida. O'Laughlen, at age 27, died of yellow fever in 1867 at the prison. Mudd and Arnold were released in 1869. Mudd died in 1883, at age 49, Arnold in 1906, at age 68.

4. Edman Spangler, who held Booth's horse at Ford's Theater, was sentenced to six years in prison. He was released from Fort Jefferson in 1869, and lived the remainder of his days with the Mudd family in Maryland. He died in 1875, at age 49.

5. John Surratt, the son of Mary Surratt and an admitted co-conspirator in the kidnapping attempt of President Lincoln, escaped to Canada, then to England, then Rome, Italy. He was arrested in Alexandria, Egypt in 1866, and tried in 1867 for the murder of Lincoln. The civil trial ended in a deadlock (four votes guilty and eight votes not guilty). He was never tried again, and died in 1916, at age 72.

HENRY RATHBONE AND CLARA HARRIS

1. Henry Rathbone and Clara Harris were married in 1867. However, while serving as the United States Consul to Germany, Rathbone stabbed his wife to death in 1883. She was age 38. For his crime, Rathbone was placed in a mental asylum for the criminally insane, where he died in 1911, at age 74. (Rathbone blamed himself for not preventing the murder of Lincoln.)

JOHN F. PARKER – THE GUARD AT FORD'S THEATER

1. John F. Parker, the Washington, D.C. police officer who was assigned to protect President Lincoln at Ford's Theater, was tried for neglect of duty, but the complaint was dismissed. He was fired from the police force in 1868 for sleeping on duty. He died in 1890, at age 60.

THE DISPOSITION OF THE ARTIFACTS RELATING TO THE LINCOLN ASSASSINATION

1. The portrait of George Washington and the small sofa are the only two remaining items in the state box that were actually located there on the night of April 14, 1865. Major Rathbone sat on the sofa near the president. The other items are reproductions.

2. The .44-caliber derringer used to kill President Lincoln is on display in the Ford's Theater Museum.

3. The knife used to stab Major Rathbone is on display in the Ford's Theater Museum.

4. The boot removed from Booth's leg, when Dr. Mudd set it, is on display in the Ford's Theater Museum.

5. The federal government confiscated the rocker on which President Lincoln was sitting at the time he was shot. Secretary of War Edwin Stanton kept the rocker in his office until 1866. In 1866, the rocker was given to the Smithsonian, where it was placed in storage. In 1921, Blanche Chapman Ford, Harry Ford's widow, petitioned the federal government for the return of the rocker. It was returned in 1929. An agent of Henry Ford's (Ford Motors Company) bought the rocker for $2,400 at an auction. The rocker is currently on display in the Henry Ford's Museum in Dearborn, Michigan.

6. The suit of clothing worn by President Lincoln at the time he was assassinated is on display in the Ford's Theater Museum.

7. The Treasury flag on which Booth caught his spur when he jumped from the balcony is on display in the Ford's Theater Museum.

8. The bullet that killed President Lincoln, a small section of his skull, and a few strands of his hair, are on display at the National Museum of Health and Medicine on the grounds of Walter Reed Medical Hospital.

9. Booth's diary is on display in the Ford's Theater Museum.

10. A portion of Booth's vertebrae was at one time on display at the National Museum of Health and Medicine, but has since been put in storage at the museum.

11. The couch on which Booth sat, while Dr. Mudd set his leg, is on display at the Dr. Samuel Mudd Museum near Waldorf, Maryland.

FACTS ABOUT THE PETERSEN HOUSE
(BUILDING WHERE PRESIDENT LINCOLN DIED)

After President Abraham Lincoln (1861-1865) was shot by John Wilkes Booth on the night of April 14, 1865, the doctors who examined the president determined that the wound to the back of his head was too serious for him to survive a trip over cobblestoned streets to either the White House or to a hospital. As a result, President Lincoln was carried to the street in front of Ford's Theater, as witnesses to this tragedy searched for a suitable place to treat the president's wound. Their search ended at the Petersen Boarding House, a small establishment almost directly across the street from Ford's Theater. It was in a back bedroom of this unassuming boarding house that at 7:22 a.m. on April 15, 1865, President Lincoln labored with his final breath. President Lincoln was age 56 at the time of his death.

THE PETERSEN BOARDING HOUSE

1. In 1849, William Petersen had the Petersen Boarding House constructed.

2. The house is a three-story brick building across the street from Ford's Theater.

3. The Petersen Boarding House, at the time of President Lincoln's assassination, was a well-kept establishment used by both men and women for single or multiple-nights of lodging.

The Petersen Boarding House

4. The room in which President Lincoln died is relatively small, approximately 9 feet wide by 17 feet long.

5. A Union soldier, Private William Clark, was the guest who occupied the room the night President Lincoln was shot.

6. The spool bed on which President Lincoln died was very small for a man 6 feet, 4 inches tall. President Lincoln was placed diagonally across a bed that was only six feet long. (An unsuccessful attempt was made to remove the headboard.)

7. In 1871, the bed was sold for $80 to William H. Boyd. Boyd also purchased a bureau, gas jet, rocking chair, and engraving. In 1889, the collection, including the bed, was sold to Charles F. Gunther for $5.000. In 1920, the bed and related furnishings were sold to its current owner, the Chicago Historical Society, Chicago, Illinois, for $250,000. (A replica of the bed is displayed in the Petersen House.)

8. The blood-spotted pillow on which President Lincoln's head rested was displayed on the bed in the Petersen House for several years. It is now on display in the Ford's Theater Museum.

9. The wallpaper in the room where Lincoln died is a reproduction of the original wallpaper.

10. Just a few weeks prior to the assassination of the president, John Wilkes Booth had actually slept on the same bed that President Lincoln died on during the morning of April 15, 1865.

11. The parlor, a common area used by all the boarding house guests, looks today very much like it did the morning of April 15, 1865. The reproductions of Victorian style furnishings consist of a couch, chairs, small tables, writing desk, and fireplace. The wallpaper in the room is a pattern from the time period. (Mrs. Lincoln spent much of the night in this parlor, often crying hysterically in between trips to see her husband. Her bereavement reached such a hysterical pitch that Secretary of War Stanton limited her access to the bedroom.)

12. The house remained in the Petersen family until 1878, when it was sold to Louis Schade for $4,500.

13. The Schade children used the bedroom where Lincoln died as a playroom.

14. The basement of the house was used by Schade to publish the *"Washington Sentinel"* newspaper.

15. In 1893, Osborn H. Oldroyd rented the house to display his Lincoln artifacts.

16. In 1896, the federal government purchased the house for $30,000.

17. In 1927, for $50,000, the federal government purchased from Osborn Oldroyd a large collection of artifacts about the life of Abraham Lincoln. This collection included dozens of items associated with the Lincoln assassination. The eighty-eight year old Oldroyd spent a life time collecting the artifacts, which formed the nucleus of the Lincoln exhibit in Ford's Theater.

FACTS ABOUT THE WASHINGTON MONUMENT

Farmer, statesman, soldier, and first President of the United States - George Washington is revered as the *"Father of Our Country."* This man of many talents served his country during the Revolutionary War by leading an army that was little more than a skeleton of the British Army he defeated. Not only did he not accept the $500 monthly salary as Commander of the Continental Army, he also spent over $160,000 of his own money toward the cause of independence. After the Revolutionary War, Washington was called upon to serve as a member of the U.S. Congress and as the first President of the United States from 1789 to 1797.

Among the many duties Washington performed as the first President of the United States was to use his position to influence the decisions as to where the permanent site of the nation's capital was to be located, and where within the city many of the primary government buildings were to be constructed. Because of his influence on Washington, D.C., it is only appropriate that a tribute to this honored citizen be constructed on a site of prominence in the city that bears his name.

THE LIFE OF GEORGE WASHINGTON

1. In 1656, the Washington family immigrated from England to America after the English Civil War.

2. On February 11, 1732, Mary (Ball) Washington gave birth to George Washington on the Pope's Creek Plantation in Virginia. His birth date was changed to February 22, when England adopted the Gregorian calendar in 1752. (The site of Washington's birth is near the site of General Robert E. Lee's birth.)

3. George Washington had no middle name or initial.

4. As an adult, Washington was 6 feet, 2 inches tall, weighed approximately 175 pounds, and had reddish brown hair and blue eyes.

5. In 1743, Washington's father, Augustine Washington, died when George was only age 11. His mother, Mary, died in 1789.

6. In 1745, Washington moved in with his brother, Lawrence, at Mount Vernon, Virginia.

7. Between 1754 and 1759, Washington served as commander of the Virginia militia. He played an active part in the French and Indian War during this period.

8. In January 1759, Washington married Martha Dandridge Custis, a wealthy widow with two children, John Parke Custis and Martha Parke Custis.

9. From 1775 through 1783, Washington served as Commander-in-Chief of the Continental Army.

10. In 1787, Washington presided over the Constitutional Convention that drafted the United States Constitution.

11. On April 30, 1789, Washington was inaugurated as the first President of the United States. Washington's second term started on March 4, 1793, and ended on March 4, 1797.

    (March 4th remained the inauguration date for elected U.S. Presidents until the 20th Amendment to the U.S. Constitution was ratified in 1933. This amendment changed the beginning of the president's and vice president's terms to noon on January 20th following the date of their elections.)

12. On December 14, 1799, Washington died at age 67 from complications of a throat infection. He and his wife Martha are buried at Mount Vernon, Virginia. (Historians believe Washington would have probably lived longer, but the practice of bleeding was still being used to treat sickness. Bleeding is when a patient is intentionally cut to allow the sickness to flow from the body.)

13. Washington did not attend college or a university.

PLANNING THE WASHINGTON MONUMENT

1. In 1783, a monument honoring George Washington was first considered by Congress.

2. Because George Washington was still alive at the time the first efforts to build a tribute to him were started, the structure is considered a *"monument"* rather than a *"memorial."*

3. After George Washington died on December 14, 1799, Congressman John Marshall, later Chief Justice of the Supreme Court, lead an effort to construct a monument to contain the body of Washington.

4. In 1833, Congress authorized the construction of the Washington Monument.

5. In 1836, Robert Mills designed the monument. He also oversaw the initial stages of its construction. Mills died in 1855, and did not see the completion of the monument.

6. The initial design for the monument provided for a decorated obelisk 600 feet high and 70 feet square at the base. It was to rise from a circular colonnaded building 100 feet high and 250 feet in diameter, surrounded by 30 Doric columns, each 12 feet in diameter and 45 feet high.

Sketch of the initial design of the Washington Monument by Robert Mills – Courtesy of the National Archives

7. It was later decided that the best shape for the tower of the monument would be that of an Egyptian *"obelisk."* (An obelisk is an upright four-sided pillar, gradually tapered as it rises, with the top terminating in a pyramid.)

8. Planners proposed that the money to construct the monument would be donated by U.S. citizens, and were optimistic about each citizen offering a $1.00 donation. The results were less than successful. By 1847, only $87,000 had been collected for the construction of the monument.

THE CONSTRUCTION OF THE WASHINGTON MONUMENT

1. On July 4, 1848, using the same trowel that was used by George Washington to dedicate the cornerstone of the U.S. Capitol Building in 1793, Grand Master Benjamin B. French dedicated the first of two cornerstones installed in the monument.

2. The first cornerstone weighs 24,500 pounds, and is located 36 feet under the northeast corner of the monument.

3. As a member of the House of Representatives, Whig representative Abraham Lincoln was a guest at the dedication of the first cornerstone to the monument. Other guests included Dolley Madison, Mrs. John Quincy Adams, President James Polk, and former President Martin Van Buren.

4. In 1849, the state of Alabama offered a large stone to be used in the construction of the monument. This act prompted several other states and societies (including American Indian tribes) to offer similar stones. Presently there are **193 inscribed memorial stones** and **2 description stones** installed around the interior steps of the monument, for a **total of 195 stones**.

5. The construction of the monument progressed at the following pace during the given years:

- 1848-1854 - 0 to152 feet
- 1855-1858 - 153 to 176 feet
- 1880 – 150 to 176 feet (removed)*
- 1880 - 150 to 172 feet
- 1881 - 173 to 250 feet
- 1882 - 251 to 340 feet
- 1883 - 341 to 410 feet
- 1884 – 411 to 555.5 feet and 1/8 inch

The Washington Monument

*In 1880, an inspection of the 26 feet of secondary stones that had been set in 1858 atop the original 150 feet level revealed the shaft had disintegrated, and the facing stones had been displaced and were chipped and crumbled. As a result, between July 15, 1880, and August 7, 1880, three courses of stone were removed from the monument.

This alteration was to leave a permanent dividing line on the monument at the 150-foot level, which is particularly noticeable in damp weather.

6. The monument consists of the following materials at various levels:

   • From the ground level to a height of 150 feet – there are two walls. The inner-wall was constructed from gneiss and the outer-wall from Ashlar marble. The area between the inner-wall and exterior-wall is filled in.

   • From 150 to 450 feet – there are two walls. The inner-wall was constructed from granite and the outer-wall was constructed from Ashlar marble. The area between the inner-wall and exterior-wall is not filled in, and the walls butt-up against each other.

   • Above 450 feet – there is a single wall constructed from Ashlar marble.

7. Due to the lack of money and the event of the Civil War, construction on the monument was halted between 1858 and 1880.

8. In 1876, a Congressional act was passed to complete the monument. The act transferred responsibility for completing the monument from the Washington National Monument Society to the U.S. Army Corps of Engineers.

9. Colonel Thomas Casey, Army Corps of Engineers, was instrumental in reinforcing the base of the monument, and completing the structure above the 150-foot level. (The 150-foot level is marked by a change in the color of the marble.)

10. The engineers inspected the foundation, and determined that it was too weak to support the proposed structure. The problem was corrected by using a new building material known as concrete to reinforce the foundation. The concrete pad is over 13 feet thick and extends out 23 feet from the previous edge of the foundation.

11. On December 6, 1884, construction on the outside of the monument was completed when a marble capstone was placed on the top of the monument.

12. On February 21, 1885, the Washington Monument was dedicated - a day before the anniversary of Washington's 153rd birthday. (The Saturday ceremony was because Sunday was considered a day of rest and religion.)

13. The final cost of the monument totaled $1,187,000.

14. The monument was finally opened to the public on October 9, 1888. It remained the tallest man-made structure in the world until the Eiffel Tower in Paris, France, was completed one year later.

THE CHARACTERISTICS OF THE WASHINGTON MONUMENT

1. The shape of the monument is of an Egyptian "*obelisk*." (An obelisk is an upright four-sided pillar, gradually tapered as it rises, with the top terminating in a pyramid.)

2. Because obelisks are of Egyptian origin, construction of the Washington Monument in this style showed the Masons' mystic connection with the Egyptian stone builders. Washington became a mason at age 20, and was a master mason at the time of his death.

3. The Egyptian "obelisk" is also referred to as "*Cleopatra's Needle*," in reference to the notable Queen Cleopatra.

4. The monument was constructed on a 41-acre site.

5. The original foundation of the monument was constructed of massive blocks of gneiss (blue stone). Some of the stones weigh six to eight tons.

6. The square or footing of the original foundation for the obelisk was 80 feet each way, and rising by offsets or steps 25 feet high.

7. The height of an obelisk is usually ten times its width. Thus the height of the monument is its width at 55 feet times 10 = 555 feet, 5 1/8 inches.

8. The height of the monument equals the height of a 55-story building. (From the base of the monument to the tip of the monument.)

9. Most of the monument's exterior marble came from a quarry near Baltimore County, Maryland. Other marble came from a quarry near Sheffield, Massachusetts.

10. The interior granite came from a quarry in Maine.

11. The width of the monument at the observation level is 34 feet, 5 1/2 inches.

12. The walls at the base of the monument are 15 feet thick.

13. The walls at the observation level are 18 inches thick.

14. The walls at the top of the monument are as thin as 6 inches thick.

15. The depth of the monument's foundation is 36 feet, 10 inches.

16. The monument's foundation covers an area of 16,002 square feet.

17. Each side of the capstone is 3 feet wide.

18. There are 897 steps leading to the top of the monument.

19. The shade of the monument changes at the 150-foot level.

20. There is a total of 93,600 square feet of monument surface.

21. There are 36,491 stone blocks in the monument. Of this number, 11,098 blocks are on the face of the monument.

22. The pyramidion, the area at the top of the monument that slants inward to a peak, consists of white marble stones 7 inches thick, supported by 12 "*ribs*" that rise from the walls of the shaft.

23. The combined weight of the structure totals 128,066 tons. (The monument weighs 90,854 tons, the pyramidion weighs 300 tons, the foundation weighs 36,912 tons, and the capstone weighs 3.300 pounds.)

24. At the very top of the monument is a 100-ounce pyramid tip constructed from solid aluminum. The height of the aluminum is 8.9 inches. The width of the aluminum is 5.6 inches. Engraved on the four sides of the capstone are the official records of the monument's construction. The west face reads "*Cornerstone laid on bed of foundation, July 4, 1848. First stone at height of 152 feet laid August 7, 1880. Capstone set December 6. 1884*". The east face reads the Latin words "*Laus Deo*" meaning "*Praise be to God.*" On the north face are the names of the monument's commission members, and on the south face are the names of Thomas Casey, Chief Engineer and Architect, and his assistants: George Davis, Bernard Green, and P.H. McLaughin. (Aluminum was used as the top of the monument because it would not deteriorate and stain the monument.)

UNIQUE FACTS ABOUT THE WASHINGTON MONUMENT

1. The Washington Monument stands 555 feet high, the Capitol Building stands 288 feet high, which makes the Washington Monument 267 feet higher that the Capitol Building. Because the base of the Washington Monument is 30 feet above sea level, and the base of the Capitol building is 88 feet above sea level, the top of the Washington Monument is 209 feet higher than the top of the Capitol Building.

2. In 1854, a group of citizens who were against immigration, especially against Catholic immigrants, stole the stone donated by Pope Pius IV. It is believed the stone was broken into pieces and thrown into the Potomac River. In 1982, a replacement stone was installed in the monument.

3. During the Civil War, the grounds surrounding the unfinished monument were used as a site to slaughter army beef and drill Union troops.

4. Construction on the monument had been delayed so long that it became known as the "*Deep Hole*" monument.

5. On August 7, 1880, a second cornerstone was dedicated at the 150-foot level of the Washington Monument. At the ceremony, President Rutherford Hayes (1877-1881) scratched his initials and the date on a coin, and placed it in the mortar.

6. Visitors enter the monument through the east side.

7. The monument is the highest freestanding masonry structure in the world.

8. Major repairs were made to the monument during the years 1934-1935, 1964, and 1998 through 2000.

9. Lightning has hit the monument several times, causing severe damage. In 1934-1935 a 1,200-pound block of marble had to be replaced because of lightning strikes.

10. In 1931, aircraft signal lights were installed on the monument cap.

11. The observation area is located at the 500-foot level. Visitors may enjoy the view from this level through eight observation windows – two on each side of the monument.

12. An exhibit room is located at the 490-foot level.

13. Five suicides have taken place at the Washington Monument. Two men jumped out the windows at the top of the monument in 1926, and three jumped down the elevator shaft in 1915, 1923, and 1949. A woman accidentally fell down the shaft in 1923.

14. In 1926, as a result of men jumping to their deaths from the monument's observation level, bars were installed over the windows of the monument.

15. In 1958, safety glass was installed over the windows on all sides of the observation level to keep people from throwing objects out the windows.

16. In 1975, bullet proof glass was installed over the windows.

17. In 1937, the circle of 48 U.S. flags, one for each of the states in the Union at the time, was added to the site. The circle now contains 50 flags, one for each of the 50 states.

18. In 1901, the first electric elevator was installed in the monument. In 1959, a replacement elevator was installed, and 1998 saw the completion of the current elevator.

19. The 25-passenger elevator cab, installed in 2002, has glass panels in the doors. These panels allow the passengers to view 45 of the 193 commemorative stones on the 290 and 160-foot levels as the elevator descends. The trip up the monument takes 70 seconds, and the trip down takes 2 minutes and 18 seconds.

20. In 1971, visitors were no longer allowed to walk up the stairway. In 1976, the same restriction was placed on walking down the stairway. However, the Park Service still provides limited escorted tours.

21. One of the 193 memorial stones is the "*Alaska Memorial Stone*." This solid green jade stone, measuring 3 feet by 5 feet by 61 feet is estimated to be worth several million dollars. It is located on the west wall of the monument, near the 450-foot level.

22. Sealed in the first cornerstone of the Washington Monument is a zinc box. The box contains money – bills and coins, a bible, newspapers, reports of the government agencies, and the first Program of the Smithsonian.

23. In August 1998, due to the possibility of the terrorist acts against the United States, a series of concrete barriers were erected around the monument. The initial barriers were replaced with the barriers that fold into the landscape as is seen today.

FACTS ABOUT THE WORLD WAR II MEMORIAL

No other event in history has been more catastrophic than World War II. Lead by the dictators of Germany, Italy, and Japan, Germany's invasion of Poland on September 1, 1939, signaled a period of destruction that engulfed the world. This violent armed conflict left an estimated 60 million men, women, and children dead, and countless others displaced and homeless.

Just prior to World War II, ten other countries had larger military forces than the United States, including Greece and Belgium. From this small beginning of ill-equipped soldiers, sailors, and airmen grew one of the largest and best-equipped military the world has ever known. Drawn from the ranks of farmers, factory workers, coal miners, secretaries, and businessmen, these men and women set aside their way of life to become what author Stephen Ambrose described as *"Citizen Soldiers."*

The World War II Memorial honors all of these *"Citizen Soldiers,"* as well as the citizens on the home front, the nation at large, and the highly moral purpose and idealism that motivated the nation's call to arms.

THE PARTICIPATION OF THE UNITED STATES IN WORLD WAR II

1. Hostilities for the United States during World War II officially started on December 7, 1941, when the Empire of Japan attacked the Pacific Fleet at Pearl Harbor, Hawaii. The attack left the United States with 2,433 dead and 1,178 wounded. It also resulted in the sinking of 18 warships and 188 planes destroyed.

2. On December 8, 1941, the United States declared war on Japan.

3. On December 11, 1941, Germany and Italy declared war on the United States.

4. Some of the major battles the United States fought in during World War II included the naval battles of the Coral Sea and Midway (1942), invasions of North Africa (1943), Sicily (1943), and Normandy (1944), and the battles for the Philippines (1944) and Iwo Jima (1945).

5. On September 3, 1943, Italy agreed to surrender to the Allies. (The formal surrender occurred on September 8, 1943.)

6. On May 7, 1945, German forces surrendered to the Allies. (Victory in Europe (VE-Day) occurred on May 8, 1945.)

7. On August 15, 1945, Japan agreed to surrender to the Allies. (The formal surrender occurred on September 2, 1945.)

8. On December 31, 1946, President Harry Truman's Presidential Proclamation officially terminated hostilities by the United States.

9. World War II lasted 2,193 days, and claimed an average of 27,600 lives each day.

10. The U.S. Presidents during World War II were President Franklin D. Roosevelt (1933-1945) from December 7, 1941 through April 12, 1945, and President Harry S. Truman (1945-1953) from April 12, 1945, through the end of the war.

11. The population of the United States at the end of World War II (1945) totaled 140,000,000.

12. The strength of the United States military in 1940, the year prior to the United States entering World War II, totaled approximately 457,000 officers and enlisted personnel.

13. A total of 16,353,659 Americans, 11.7% of the population of the United States, served in the military during World War II (1941-1945).

14. Approximately 1,100,000 African-Americans served in the military during World War II.

15. Approximately 250,000 Hispanic Americans served in the United States military during World War II.

16. Approximately 44,000 Native Americans served in the United States military during World War II.

17. Approximately 25,000 Asian Americans (Chinese, Japanese, and Hawaiians) served in the United States military during World War II.

18. Over 200,000 American women served in uniform during World War II. The women who served included:

    • Over 150,000 - Women's Army Corps (WAC) (Of this total 60,000 served in the Army Air Force.)
    • 18,000 - Navy's Women Accepted for Voluntary Emergency Service (WAVES)
    • 1,074 - Women Air Service Pilots (WASPS) flyers, plus support personnel
    • 50 – Women Auxiliary Ferrying Squadron (WAFS) flyers, plus support personnel
    • 10,000 - Coast Guard (SPARS)
    • 22,000 - Marine Corps Reserves

19. The average enlisted soldier during World War II was 26 years of age. After completing basic training he averaged 5 feet, 8 inches in height, weighed 151 pounds, had a 35-inch chest, and a 31-inch waist.

20. Nearly half of the soldiers were high school graduates, and one in ten had at least some college education.

21. Military personnel during World War II spent an average of thirty-three months on active duty.

22. Approximately 73% of the military personnel served overseas.

23. Military personnel deployed overseas spent an average of 16 months overseas.

24. The following table provides statistics about the men and women who served in the United States military and merchant marines during World War II.

Military Branch/ Mariners	Number Who Served	Battle Deaths	Other Deaths *	Wounded – Not Mortal	Total Casualties
Army (Including the Army Air Force)	11,260,000 (Including 3.4 million in the Army Air Force	234,874	83,400	565,861	884,135
Navy	4,183,466	36,950	25,664	37,778	100,392
Marines	669,100	19,733	4,778	68,207	92,718
Coast Guard	241,093	574	1,343	-	1,917
Sub-Total	16,353,659	292,131	115,185	671,846	1,079,162
U.S. Mariners	215,000	9,300	Unknown	11,000	20,300
Total	16,568,659	301,431	115,185	682,846	1,099,462

  *Accidents, sickness, etc.

25. The following table provides statistics about the percentages of combat deaths and wounded versus the number of men and women who served in the United States military and merchant marines.

Military Branch/ Mariners	Number Who Served	Battle Deaths	% of Combat Deaths vs. Served	Wounded Not Mortal	% of Wounded vs. Served
Army (Including Army Air Force)	11,260,000	234,874	2.09%	565,861	5.03%
Navy	4,183,466	36,950	0.88%	37,778	0.90%
Marines	669,100	19,733	2.95%	68,207	10.19%
Coast Guard	241,093	574	0.24%	-	0%
Sub-Total	16,353,659	292,131	1.79%	671,846	4.11%
U.S. Mariners	215,000	9,300	4.32%	11,000	5.11%
Total	16,568,659	301,431	1.81%	682,846	4.12%

26. Of the men and women who served in the United States military and merchant marines during World War II, 416,616 lost their lives. Of this total 72% were battle deaths.

27. Of the 416,616 men and women who lost their lives, 78,976 were declared missing in action.

28. A total of 130,201 U.S. military personnel became prisoners of war (POW) during World War II. Of this total 14,072 died while they were POWs, nearly 11% of the total number of POWs.

29. Nearly 40% of the U.S. military personnel held as POWs by Japan died while in captivity. A little over 1% of the POWs held by Germany died in captivity.

30. There were 19,000 American civilian internees during World War II.

31. Approximately 11% of the American civilian internees held by Japan died while in captivity. Nearly 3.5% of the American civilian internees held by Germany died in captivity.

32. Of the servicemen and servicewomen who died overseas during World War II, 233,181 were returned to the United States for reburial.

33. Specially designed metal transportation caskets were used to transport the remains home. Many of these same caskets were first used to transport home the remains of the soldiers killed during World War I.

34. Over 400 servicewomen, including 38 WASPS, died while serving their country during World War II.

35. The Medal of Honor was awarded to 464 men for acts of valor during World War II. Of this total, 286 served in the Army, 82 served in the Marine Corps, 57 served in the Navy, 38 served in the Army Air Corps, and 1 served in the Coast Guard.

36. Of the 464 Medals of Honor awarded, 22 were to Asian-Americans, 12 to Hispanic-Americans, 7 to African-Americans, and 3 to Native-Americans.

37. Fifty of the Medal of Honor recipients were still living at the time the memorial was dedicated.

38. The first eight Presidents of the United States who were elected to the presidency after President Truman (1945-1953) all served in the military during World War II. These men were Eisenhower, Kennedy, Johnson, Nixon, Ford, Carter, Reagan, and George H. W. Bush. (Carter was in the Naval Academy during the war.)

THE WORLD WAR II MEMORIAL

1. The World War II Memorial is located on the National Mall at the site of the Rainbow Pool and east end of the Reflecting Pool.

2. In 1987, the idea of a World War II Memorial was conceived.

3. On Veterans Day, November 11, 1995, President William Clinton (1993–2001) dedicated the memorial site.

4. On August 27, 2001, preparation work for the memorial was started.

5. In September 2001, construction of the memorial was started.

6. On May 29, 2004, the memorial was dedicated.

7. President George W. Bush (2001-Present) accepted the memorial on behalf of the citizens of the United States.

The Entrance to the World War II Memorial

8. Former Presidents George H. W. Bush (1989-1993) and William Clinton (1993-2001) attended the ceremony.

9. It was noted during the ceremony that May 29th would have been the 101st birthday anniversary of the great American comedian Bob Hope, who often entertained the troops during World War II, the Korean War, and the Vietnam War. It also marked the 87th birthday anniversary of former President John F. Kennedy (1961-1963), who served in the Navy during the war.

148

10. Approximately four million veterans of World War II were living at the time of the memorial's dedication. The average age of the remaining veterans was 82 years.

11. In October 1996, architect Friedrich St. Florian, the former Dean of Rhode Island School of Design, was chosen to design the memorial. His design was selected over nearly 400 other designs.

12. Raymond Kaskey, whose deceased father was a veteran of World War II, sculptured every bronze piece of the memorial, including the 4,000 gold stars on the Freedom Wall.

13. The memorial is on a 7.4-acre site.

14. Two-thirds of the acreage consists of grass, planting, and pools.

15. The memorial includes 17,000 pieces of granite.

16. The largest stone weighs 17 tons.

17. The memorial consists of two primary granite stones. The "Kershaw" from South Carolina is used for the vertical elements, and the "Green County" from Georgia for the main plaza paving stone.

The World War II Memorial

18. Two green stones, "Rio Verde" and "Moss Green," have been used to accent paving on the plaza. Both were quarried in Brazil.

19. The bronze figures were cast in a foundry in Chester, Pennsylvania.

20. The main entrance (Ceremonial Entrance) to the memorial is on 17th Street.

21. The Ceremonial Entrance is 48 feet, 3 inches wide by 147 feet, 8 inches long (curb to plaza).

22. The following words greet visitors to the World War II Memorial at the Ceremonial Entrance:

"HERE IN THE PRESENCE OF WASHINGTON AND LINCOLN, ONE THE EIGHTEENTH CENTURY FATHER AND THE OTHER THE NINETEENTH CENTURY PRESERVER OF OUR NATION, WE HONOR THOSE TWENTIETH CENTURY AMERICANS WHO TOOK UP THE STRUGGLE DURING THE SECOND WORLD WAR AND MADE THE SACRIFICES TO PERPETUATE THE GIFT OUR FOREFATHERS ENTRUSTED TO US: A NATION CONCEIVED IN LIBERTY AND JUSTICE".

23. At the Ceremonial Entrance to the memorial are three wide steps that descend into the heart of the memorial.

24. Three large lawn panels break up the three steps. This space can be used to seat as many as 3,000 attendees during ceremonial events.

25. Two United States flags fly over the Ceremonial Entrance. Located at the base of each flagpole are the crests for each branch of the military and the merchant marines.

26. Along the steps are 24 bas-relief panels (12 for the Atlantic theater of the war and 12 for the Pacific theater). The panels depict America's vast agricultural, industrial, military, and human resources at the time of the war.

27. Each bas-relief contains a minimum of eight figures, which took approximately 250 hours to sculpt.

28. Raymond Kaskey sculptured the bas-relief panels. The depicted human elements of the war are based on archival photographs taken during the war.

29. There are 276 faces in the bas-relief panels. Kaskey used living
persons as models for the faces
of the people in the panels,
including six World War II re-
enactors, his assistant, himself,
and even the UPS deliveryman.

Bas-Relief Panel of D-Day Invasion at Normandy

30. The dimensions of the memorial are:

- Length from the back of the Pacific Arch to the back of the
Atlantic Arch: 384 feet.

- Width from the back of the basin behind the Freedom Wall to
the bottom of the Ceremonial Entrance: 279 feet.

31. The two, 49-foot memorial arches
(pavilions) to the north and south
represent the Atlantic and Pacific
theaters of the war.

32. Each arch is 43 feet above grade and
23 feet square.

Arch – Representing the Pacific Theater

33. Each arch has four bronze pillars, four bronze eagles, and one
bronze laurel.

34. The four pillars within the arch represent each major military
branch - Army, Army Air Force,
Navy, and Marines. An eagle rests
on each of the pillars.

35. Each eagle weighs about 2,600
pounds, and has a wingspan of
about ten feet. The eagles hold a
ribbon that supports a laurel wreath,
commemorating victory.

Eagles holding the Victory Wreath

36. An X-ray machine was used to ensure the welds holding the eagles and wreaths to their supports were welded correctly.

37. The inlaid on the floor beneath the wreath and eagles is the World War II victory medal with the inscription *"Victory on Land,"* *"Victory at Sea,"* and *"Victory in the Air."*

38. In front of each arch is a semicircular fountain that lists the names of major battles for that theater of the war.

39. The 56 stone pillars in the memorial are 17 feet above grade, 4 feet, 4 inches wide, and 3 feet deep.

The Stone Pillars

40. The pillars represent the states, territories, and the District of Columbia at the time of the war. (There were 48 states at the time of the war. Alaska and Hawaii became states in 1959.)

41. The names on the pillars start with the original 13 states from the right side of the Freedom Wall (facing 17th Street), and alternate from right to left in the order the states ratified the U.S. Constitution – Delaware, Pennsylvania, etc.

42. The opening in each pillar behind the wreaths symbolizes the loss of military members from each state, territory, and the District of Columbia.

43. Each pillar is adorned with two sculptured bronze wreaths, one on each side, for a total of 112 wreaths. The oak leaves in the wreaths represents the industrial strength of the United States, and the wheat represents the agricultural strength.

44. There are 56 bronze ropes between the pillars. This arrangement signifies the unprecedented unity of the nation during the war.

The Bronze Ropes

45. The curved Freedom Wall, centered at the back of the memorial, pays tribute to the Americans who lost their lives during the war.

46. The Freedom Wall is 84 feet, 8 inches wide, 9 feet high from the plaza floor, with a radius of 41 feet, 9 inches.

47. There are 4,000 sculptured gold stars on the Freedom Wall. Each star represents the death of about 100 Americans in the war. The stars are set against a textured bronze background.

The Freedom Wall – With the inscription "Here We Mark the Price of Freedom"

48. The use of a star is symbolic of service to the nation. If a family member was serving in the military, a blue star was displayed in the window of the family's house for each family member serving. A gold star was displayed for each family member who had died serving his/her country.

49. The Circle of Remembrance is located in the northwest corner of the memorial.

50. The Circle of Remembrance is a circular garden of about 38 feet in diameter that is enclosed by a two-foot high stone wall. (Wooden benches are available for rest and taking time to remember the events of the war and the people who participated in the war.)

51. The Plaza was designed to fit around the Rainbow Pool.

52. The Plaza is 337 feet, 10 inches long, 240 feet, 2 inches wide, and 6 feet below grade.

53. In the center of the Plaza is the Rainbow Pool.

The Rainbow Pool

54. The Rainbow Pool was initially completed in the early 1920's. (It was reduced in size by 15% for the memorial.)

55. The Rainbow Pool and fountains symbolize the significance of the oceans and seas during World War II.

56. The Rainbow Pool is 246 feet, 9 inches long by 147 feet, 8 inches wide. The two fountains in the Rainbow Pool shoot water 30 feet into the air.

57. To help ensure visitors aren't showered by the flow of water from the fountains on windy days, an automatic system controls the height of the spray. On the top of the Atlantic Arch is a wind gauge. It signals an underground system to lower or raise the height of the water as the wind increases or decreases.

58. The 900 bronze-green drain grates surrounding the plaza allow for drainage. They are in the shape of a star within a star, surrounded by a circle. The symbol of a white star within a white circle was the identification marking placed on American vehicles (tanks, jeeps, etc.) during the war. A star within a dark background with bars on both sides of the star was the identification marking placed on American planes during the war.

59. The bronze-green color of the bronze wreaths, figures, grates, etc. is the result of rubbing chemicals on the bronze.

60. On the walls are portions of speeches made by notable participants of the war (i.e. Presidents Roosevelt and Truman, and Generals Eisenhower and MacArthur).

D-DAY JUNE 6, 1944
YOU ARE ABOUT TO EMBARK UPON THE GREAT CRUSADE TOWARD WHICH WE HAVE STRIVEN THESE MANY MONTHS. THE EYES OF THE WORLD ARE UPON YOU... I HAVE FULL CONFIDENCE IN YOUR COURAGE, DEVOTION TO DUTY AND SKILL IN BATTLE.

Eisenhower's D-Day Speech

61. See if you can locate an engraving of "Kilroy" on the memorial (on the outside wall near the pillar for the state of Delaware). This engraving consists of a bald little man peeking over a wall with the comment "Kilroy was here" over his head. This form of graffiti was drawn on structures by servicemen as they battled through countries during World War II.

154

FACTS ABOUT THE THOMAS JEFFERSON MEMORIAL

During his long life, Thomas Jefferson accomplished more than almost any other ten people combined. As a statesman, he drafted the Declaration of Independence, served in Congress, performed duties as secretary of state and vice president, and was twice elected to the presidency. As an inventor, he is credited with inventing many effort saving devices, and as a horticulturist, he experimented with many fruits, vegetables, and herbs. Jefferson was also paradoxical. He wrote that "*all men are created equal,*" but owned slaves. Prior to becoming president, he believed periodic revolts by citizens were good for a country, but had citizens imprisoned for protesting his presidential policies. He believed personal property should be protected by the government, but forced the American Indian from their lands in the East. He was appalled by the decadency he found in Paris, but participated in and enjoyed many of the large parties.

Even with his faults, many Americans, including some of the nation's greatest presidents, considered Jefferson second only to Washington as the nation's best president. The Jefferson Memorial is a tribute to the man and his accomplishments.

THE LIFE OF THOMAS JEFFERSON

1. On April 13, 1743, Thomas Jefferson was born at Shadwell, Albemarle County, Virginia.

2. Jefferson's father was Peter Jefferson, a land surveyor and landowner. His mother was Jane Randolph, the daughter of a prominent Virginia family.

3. Jefferson was a good reader and writer at the young age of 6. His studies included Greek and Latin.

4. Jefferson taught himself how to play the violin, and eventually became very good at playing the works of Mozart.

155

5. On August 17, 1757, Jefferson's father, Peter, died at age 49. Thomas was only 14 years of age at the time of his father's death. On March 31, 1776, his mother, Jane, died at age 56.

6. In 1759, at age 16, Jefferson entered William and Mary College in Williamsburg, Virginia.

7. In 1767, at age 24, Jefferson was admitted to the Virginia bar as a lawyer.

8. In 1769, at age 26, Jefferson was elected to the Virginia House of Burgesses.

9. In 1772, Jefferson married Martha Wayles Skelton. He was age 28 and she, 25.

10. Jefferson fathered six children - five girls and one boy. With the exception of his first born, Martha (Patsy), and another daughter, Mary (Polly), all of his children died during infancy or childhood.

11. On September 6, 1782, at age 34, Martha died from weakness incurred from giving birth to a child. Jefferson never remarried.

12. In 1775, Jefferson was selected to represent Virginia in the Congress of the United States. He helped draft 160 bills while a member of this governing body.

13. In 1776, at age 33, Jefferson was credited with being the primary author of the Declaration of Independence. (With alterations, the Declaration of Independence was approved by Congress in 1776.)

14. From 1779 through 1781, Jefferson served as governor of Virginia. While governor of Virginia, Jefferson pushed for and was very successful in ensuring religious freedom. (Being an atheist was a capital offense in Virginia, and no Jew, Catholic or Quaker could hold government positions in Massachusetts.)

15. In 1783, Jefferson was elected to the Congress of the Confederation of States.

16. In 1784, Jefferson was appointed the U.S. Minister to France.

17. In 1789, President George Washington (1789-1797) appointed Jefferson the first Secretary of State for the United States.

18. In 1797, Jefferson became Vice President of the United States under John Adams (1797-1801), after losing to Adams by only three electoral votes in the presidential election. (Election rules at that time directed that the presidential candidate who received the most votes from the U.S. Electoral College was elected president, and the presidential candidate who received the next highest number of votes was elected vice president. This selection system was changed in 1804, when the 12th Amendment to the Constitution required separate ballots for the president and vice president.)

19. In 1801, Jefferson became the 3rd President of the United States by defeating Raymond Burr for the presidency. He was later elected to a second term, which ended in 1809.

20. It was very likely Jefferson would have been elected for a third term to the presidency, but like Washington, he believed two terms would limit a president's ambitions.

21. Among his accomplishments while President of the United States, Jefferson started the military academy at West Point, purchased the Louisiana Territory from France for $15,000,000 (1803), and directed the Lewis and Clark expedition to explore the purchased land (May 1804-September 1806).

22. At the end of his presidency (1801-1809), Jefferson left Washington, D.C., never to return to the city during the remaining seventeen years of his life.

23. In 1819, Jefferson founded the University of Virginia.

24. On July 4, 1826, Jefferson died at age 83. He and John Adams (2nd U.S. President), age 90, both died on the 50th anniversary of the signing of the Declaration of Independence. (Jefferson died a few hours prior to Adams, and he had lost most of his wealth.)

UNIQUE FACTS ABOUT THOMAS JEFFERSON

1. Jefferson was freckled and sandy-haired, and was considered rather tall and awkward.

2. Jefferson considered himself a scientist, first; a farmer, second; and a statesman, third.

3. All through his adult life, Jefferson rose from bed before daylight, and seldom stayed up after 10 p.m.

4. Jefferson was considered a very poor public speaker, which probably contributed to his skills as a writer. He was known as the "silent member" of the Continental Congress.

5. Jefferson was mostly a vegetarian, using meat as a condiment.

6. As a result of Jefferson bringing certain foods from Paris when his term as U.S. Minister to France ended, he is credited with introducing ice cream, macaroni, and waffles into the United States.

7. Jefferson was the first president to take the oath of office in Washington, D.C. He was also the first to introduce the custom of men shaking hands versus bowing stiffly.

THE JEFFERSON MEMORIAL

1. In 1913, when Franklin Roosevelt made his first trip to Washington, D.C. as Assistant Secretary of the Navy, one of his first actions was to view the tribute to Thomas Jefferson. To his surprise and dismay, he discovered no such tribute.

2. In 1933, when Franklin Roosevelt returned to Washington, D.C. as the 32nd President of the United States, he and other admirers of Jefferson took steps toward initiating the construction of a memorial to Jefferson.

3. Architect John Russell Pope designed and oversaw the construction of the Jefferson Memorial. After his death in 1937, architects Otto Eggers and Daniel Higgins assumed the project.

4. Until the end of the 19th century, the site on which the memorial is located was under water.

5. In November 1938, work was started on the memorial.

6. On December 15, 1938, President Franklin Roosevelt (1933-1945) presided over the official groundbreaking for the memorial. (The same spade (shovel) that was used for the ground breaking for the Lincoln Memorial and Arlington Memorial Bridge was used for the Jefferson Memorial.)

7. On November 15, 1939, President Roosevelt was present at the laying of the memorial cornerstone. The cornerstone contains copies of the Declaration of Independence; the Constitution of the United States; *The Life and Morals of Jesus of Nazareth* (written by Jefferson); *The Writings of Thomas Jefferson* (10 volumes), edited by Paul Ford; the 1939 Annual Report of the Thomas Jefferson Memorial Commission; the signatures of Franklin D. Roosevelt and members of the Memorial Commission; and copies of the four leading Washington newspapers at the time (Washington Post, Washington Evening Star, Washington Times-Herald, and Washington Daily News).

8. On April 13, 1943, fifty-five years after the dedication of the Washington Monument, the Jefferson Memorial was dedicated in Potomac Park. (President Roosevelt was present at the ceremony.)

The Jefferson Memorial

9. The original cost of the memorial totaled $3,192,312.

10. The memorial stands on a 2.5-acre site.

11. The memorial is an adaptation of the Pantheon in Rome, Italy.

12. The memorial has a full diameter of 183 feet, 10 inches.

13. The height of the memorial from the roadway to the top of the dome is 129 feet, 4 inches.

14. The exterior of the memorial's dome is 103 feet from the ground.

15. The diameter of the Memorial Room within the memorial is 86 feet, 3 inches.

16. The height of the memorial from the floor to the ceiling of the dome is 91 feet, 8 inches.

17. The height of the memorial from the floor to the top of the dome (exterior) is 95 feet, 8 inches.

18. The dome is 4 feet thick.

19. The memorial weighs 32,000 tons.

20. The piers that support the memorial were driven 138 feet, 3 inches into the ground and bedrock.

21. The memorial stands on a granite circular base.

22. The exterior dome and columns of the memorial were constructed from Danby Imperial Vermont marble.

23. The interior wall panels of the memorial were constructed from Georgian white marble.

24. The ceiling of the dome to the memorial was constructed from Indiana limestone.

25. The floor of the Memorial Room was constructed from Tennessee pink marble.

26. The pedestal to the memorial was constructed from Missouri gray marble.

27. Fifty-four columns support the memorial. The exterior columns are 41 feet high, and the inner columns are 39 feet, 2 inches high. The columns are approximately 5 feet in diameter.

28. There are four entrances to the memorial. The main entrance (north) faces the White House.

29. The main entrance to the memorial is 8 columns wide and 4 columns deep.

30. In 1941, Rudolph Evans was awarded a $35,000 contract to provide preliminary models of Jefferson and the final plaster cast from which the statue of Jefferson would be cast from bronze.

31. The bronze statue of Jefferson is 19 feet tall, and stands on a 6-foot-high black (Minnesota) granite pedestal. A ring of Missouri marble surrounds its base. (Jefferson was actually 6 feet, 2 inches tall. The same height as George Washington.)

The Statue of Thomas Jefferson

32. The statue of Jefferson is 6 feet, 5 1/2 inches wide.

33. The statue of Jefferson was initially formed from plaster and painted to look like bronze. Use of these materials was due to the shortage of bronze during World War II (1941-1945).

34. On April 22, 1947, a full bronze statue replaced the plaster statue of Jefferson.

35. The bronze statue of Jefferson was cast in a dozen pieces. It was completed in nine months after 21 separate castings.

36. The statue of Jefferson is hollow.

37. The bronze forming the shape of Jefferson is 3/16 inch thick and weighs 10,000 pounds.

38. The four panels surrounding the statue contain a series of Jefferson's best quotations. A fifth quotation is found above the panels. The quotations are from the following works:

- The first panel is quoted from the Declaration of Independence of 1776.

- The second panel is quoted from the Act for Religious Freedom, passed by the Virginia Assembly in 1779.

- The third panel is a composite of thoughts from Jefferson's Summary of a View of Rights, Notes on Virginia, a January 4, 1787 letter to George Washington about the business of state, a August 13, 1780 letter to George Wythe about laws for educating the common people, and Jefferson's autobiography.

- The fourth panel provides insight into how Jefferson regarded the evolvement of the Constitution and other aspects of government. (It was quoted from a July 12, 1810 letter to Samuel Kercheval.)

- The quote "I have sworn upon the altar of God eternal hostility against any form of tyranny over the mind of man." is taken from a September 23, 1800, letter by Jefferson to Dr. Benjamin Rush, and circles the dome above the four panels.

39. Above the north entrance portico of the memorial, facing the Tidal Basin, is a 10-foot high, 65-foot wide pediment. The pediment (relief) is titled *The Drafting of the Declaration of Independence.*

40. Adolph A. Wineman completed the pediment (relief).

41. The figures in the pediment represent the men who worked with Jefferson in writing the Declaration of Independence. Seated on the right of Jefferson are Benjamin Franklin and John Adams. On the left of Jefferson are Roger Sherman and Robert Livingston.

UNIQUE FACTS ABOUT THE JEFFERSON MEMORIAL

1. On April 13, 1943, the original Declaration of Independence was displayed at the Jefferson Memorial during the dedication ceremony. It was the 200th anniversary of Jefferson's birth.

2. Because of their concern for the cherry trees growing in the tidal basin, several women protested the building of the memorial at this particular site by chaining themselves to the trees.

3. The problem with the women protesters was resolved when the government assured the protesters that not only were the selected trees to be transplanted without harm, but a thousand additional cherry trees were to be planted around the memorial and basin. (The existing trees were transplanted and the additional trees were planted as the government had assured.)

4. In 1909, the original cherry trees were presented as gifts from the city of Tokyo, Japan. However, because the Department of Agriculture determined that the trees were infested with insects and had fungus disease, they were destroyed. Serious diplomatic problems were avoided when the United States asked the government of Tokyo to send replacement trees. In 1912, the first of the new trees were planted during a simple ceremony. The ceremony was attended by Mrs. Helen Taft (wife of President William Taft (1909-1913)), and by the wife of the Japanese ambassador.

5. The 3,020 cherry trees of twelve varieties were given to the United States by Japan as a symbol of peace between the two nations.

6. Japanese cherry trees are unlike other cherry trees. They bloom for a very short time and do not bear fruit.

7. There are currently more than 3,700 cherry trees surrounding the Tidal Basin in West Potomac Park.

8. Only about 150 of the original 3,020 cherry trees remain.

9. Four of the cherry trees were vandalized a few days after the bombing of Pearl Harbor in December 1941.

10. During the spring of 1999, a family of beavers felled four cherry trees and damaged others. The beavers were captured and then safely released at a location far from the basin.

11. Near the Jefferson Memorial, close to the intersection of Ohio and West Basin Drive, is a Japanese Pagoda. In 1957, it was gifted to the city of Washington, D.C. by the mayor of Yokohama, Japan. The pagoda, which was sculptured around 1600, weighs 3,800 pounds.

12. Hidden among the cherry trees near the Tidal Basin rests a 20-ton stone lantern. The lantern, constructed in 1651, was presented to the city of Washington, D.C. in 1954 as a symbol of Japanese-American friendship.

The Japanese Lantern – Constructed in 1651

- The lantern is located on the opposite side of the Tidal Basin from the Jefferson Memorial (off to the left) near Independence Avenue.

- The lighting of the lantern, which once stood on the grounds of the To-ei-zan Temple in Tokyo, has for years signaled the start of the Cherry Blossom Festival.

- The lantern consists of a cube that forms the base, on top of which is a cylinder-shaped stone, then a sphere, a truncated pyramid, and finally a pointed ball. The lantern represents five elements: earth, water, fire, air, and ether (ether is an imaginary substance that fills all space beyond the sphere of the moon, and makes up the stars and planets). Chinese philosophy believes these five elements make up the universe.

FACTS ABOUT THE FRANKLIN DELANO ROOSEVELT MEMORIAL

Franklin Delano Roosevelt is believed by many historians and citizens to be one of the most capable presidents ever elected to the nation's highest public office. Born in 1882 into a wealthy New York family, Roosevelt enjoyed a privileged and sheltered life. But even with his background as a member of the socially elite, he is recorded in history as the key to the survival of many poverty stricken Americans during the *"Great Depression,"* and the world's defense and victory against the dictatorships of Germany, Japan, and Italy during World War II. The memorial to *"FDR"* is a tribute to a man who forbade physical limitations from keeping him from fulfilling his destiny, and to his wife Eleanor, who did much to influence the greatness of the 32nd President of the United States.

THE LIFE OF FRANKLIN DELANO ROOSEVELT

1. The name Roosevelt means *"Field of Roses"* in Dutch.

2. The Roosevelt family crest is *"Three Roses."*

3. On January 30, 1882, Franklin Delano Roosevelt was born in Hyde Park, New York. (He was an only child.)

4. Roosevelt's middle name *"Delano"* was his mother's maiden name.

5. Roosevelt's father, James, was age 54 when Franklin was born.

6. Roosevelt's mother, Sara, was age 28 when Franklin was born.

7. Roosevelt graduated from Harvard University and Columbia Law School.

8. In 1905, Roosevelt married Eleanor Roosevelt (a distant cousin). (President Theodore (Teddy) Roosevelt (1901-1909), the brother of Eleanor's father, attended the wedding ceremony.)

9. Franklin and Eleanor were the parents of six children: Anna Eleanor (1906-1975), James (1907-1991), Franklin Delano Jr. (1909), Elliott (1910-1990), Franklin Delano Jr. (1914-1988), and John (1916-1981). (Because the first son to be named Franklin died in infancy, another son was also named Franklin.)

10. From 1910 through part of 1913, Roosevelt served as a state senator for the state of New York. From 1913 through part of 1920, he served as Assistant Secretary of the Navy, and was the unsuccessful Democratic nominee for Vice President of the United States in 1920.

11. In 1921, at age 39, Roosevelt was disabled from the waist down by poliomyelitis (polio).

12. From 1928 until he took office as President of the United States in 1933, Roosevelt served as Governor of New York.

13. In November 1932, Roosevelt was elected the 32nd U.S. President. In March 1933, he took the oath of office for president.

14. Roosevelt was elected to an unprecedented four terms as President of the United States (1933-1945). He was the first and only president to serve more than two full elected terms.

15. Roosevelt served as president for 12 years and 39 days, from March 1933 to April 1945.

16. Roosevelt was the only president to be sworn into office during the months of January and March: March 1933, January 1937, January 1941, and January 1945. (Presidents elected since Roosevelt have all been sworn into office during the January following the November they are elected.)

17. Although known for his radio *"fireside chats,"* Roosevelt was the first president to give a speech through the new media of television. The speech was presented at the New York World Fair of 1939.

18. After his death on April 12, 1945, Roosevelt was buried at Hyde Park, New York, near the home where he was born and raised.

THE LIFE OF ANNA ELEANOR ROOSEVELT

1. On October 11, 1884, Anna Eleanor Roosevelt was born. (She was the oldest of four children. The other siblings were: Elliott (1889-1893), Gracie (1891-1941), and Margaret (1892-1941).

2. In 1892, when Eleanor was only eight years old, her mother, Anna, died of diphtheria.

3. In 1893, Eleanor's brother, Elliott, died of scarlet fever.

4. In 1894, Eleanor was only nine years old when her father, Elliott, died from depression and alcohol related illnesses.

5. As a child, Eleanor endured pain from a curvature of the spine, which required her to wear a steel brace for years.

6. Because many of Eleanor's relatives considered her homely, slow moving, and uncoordinated, they called her *"Granny"* for many of her early years.

7. After the death of her mother, Eleanor lived with her grandmother. She also spent much of her young life in boarding schools in the United States and abroad.

8. Similar to Franklin Roosevelt, Eleanor was raised in a privileged class. But unlike Franklin, Eleanor had, during her younger years, contact with needy and impoverished people through charity programs supported by her family.

9. Due to Franklin's disability, Eleanor became his legs. She traveled an average of 200 days each year during the presidency of her husband, talking to people from all walks of life, and reporting her findings to the president. These trips included the slums of the inner cities, the mines of Pennsylvania, and overseas military sites during World War II. (Eleanor was assigned the call sign "Rover" by the Secret Service.)

10. Eleanor's strong influence on the American civil rights movement benefited minorities, especially African-Americans and women. Prior to World War II there were only five African-American officers in the military, at war's end this number had grown to over 7,000. The number of women working in the factories had grown from less than one percent to sixty percent of the work force during the same period. Over 100,000 African-American workers were employed in factories as well. (Because Eleanor was such a thorn in the military's backside, General George Marshall, the Army's Chief of Staff, assigned a general officer to handle the demands of the first lady.)

11. After World War II, Eleanor was appointed a member of the United States' delegation to the United Nations, and played an important part in drafting and gaining approval of the United Nations' Declaration of Human Rights.

12. After her death on November 10, 1962, Eleanor was buried beside her husband at Hyde Park, New York.

THE FRANKLIN DELANO ROOSEVELT MEMORIAL

1. In 1946, the idea for a Franklin Delano Roosevelt (FDR) Memorial was conceived.

2. In 1955, a commission to plan the memorial was established.

3. In 1959, the site for the memorial was selected.

4. Consideration of the initial designs for the memorial were begun in the mid-1970s, and were approved by the Memorial Commission and the Commission of Fine Arts in 1978.

5. Tennessee Senator Claude Pepper was the driving force behind the approval of the FDR Memorial. Senator Pepper, an avid supporter of Roosevelt and his New Deal policy, died shortly after the project was approved.

6. Prior to the current design being accepted, two previous more grandiose designs for the memorial were accepted, but acceptance was later withdrawn. The 1960 design looked like great slabs of paper on edge containing engraved FDR memorandums. The 1966 design consisted of a series of high walls at various angles containing engraved FDR memorandums.

7. In September 1991, the ground was broken for the memorial.

8. In October 1994, on-site construction of the memorial was begun.

9. On May 2, 1997, President William Clinton (1993-2001) dedicated the memorial.

10. The memorial is located on a 7.5-acre site in West Potomac Park.

11. The final cost of the memorial totaled $48,500,000. Of this amount $42,900,000 was funded through federal appropriations, with the remaining $5,600,000 donated by private contributors.

12. Lawrence Halprin designed the memorial.

13. Leonard Baskin, Neil Estern, Robert Graham, Thomas Hardy, and George Segal sculptured the memorial.

14. President Roosevelt's words are engraved into Red Dakota granite.

15. John Benson engraved the large and small quotations into the stones.

16. John Benson's prior works included the inscriptions on the John F. Kennedy Memorial at Arlington Cemetery, and the East and West Buildings of the National Gallery of Art. He also participated in designing the inscriptions for the Vietnam Veterans Memorial.

17. Visitors wander through a zigzag path among the rough granite walls to pass by the sculptures, the engraved quotations, and the waterfalls.

18. Because water was a constant in Franklin Roosevelt's life, it was chosen as the theme for the memorial. Roosevelt was an avid boater and a former Assistant Secretary of the Navy, held wartime summits aboard Navy ships, and died in Warm Springs, Georgia, a health spa he helped create and frequently visited.

19. Approximately 100,000 gallons (378,500 liters) of water are recycled every minute through the entire monument.

20. The memorial consists of 9 artworks.

21. The memorial contains 6 waterfalls.

22. There are 21 FDR quotations engraved into the memorial.

23. Construction of the memorial required 31,439 pieces of cut stone (75,000 square feet of granite pavers) and ten miles of steel.

24. Four thousand pieces of granite blocks were used to form the walls.

25. The memorial walls are 12 feet high.

26. Four rows of granite blocks are in each wall.

27. The walls and paving stones are Pink Carnelian granite.

28. The benches and other gray stones are Minnesota granite.

29. Over 8,200 cubic yards of concrete were used to construct the memorial.

30. The memorial contains enough stones to erect an 80-story building.

31. The memorial stones weigh 6,000 tons.

32. Nine hundred steel pilings were used to support the memorial stones. The pilings were sunk 80 feet deep before they hit bedrock.

33. If a flood washed the ground away from under the memorial, the memorial would still remain standing.

34. The memorial is divided into four rooms, punctuated by three meditative spaces. Each period of Roosevelt's presidency is engraved in the granite walkway at the entrance to each room.

35. Each room not only represents one of Roosevelt's four terms, but the social climate of the country at the time (depression, social reforms, war, and peace).

36. The journey through the memorial begins in a paved forecourt, where a long granite wall announces the memorial's subject – *"Franklin Delano Roosevelt, 1882-1945."*

37. A statue of President Roosevelt welcomes visitors to the memorial near the gift shop. The bronze statue, dedicated by President Clinton (1993-2001) on January 10, 2001, shows Roosevelt in a wheelchair similar to the one Roosevelt designed. (See notes at the end of this section about the controversy surrounding the statue.)

Statue - President Roosevelt in Wheelchair

Room 1 - "The Early Years (1932-1936)"

1. This room houses the photo exhibit, a gift shop, and a bookstore.

2. The displayed Presidential Seal on the wall is an interpretation of the Presidential Seal at the time of FDR's first inauguration in March 1933. The seal is to remind visitors that FDR is being remembered above all else for his role as President of the United States.

3. A 30-foot-wall titled *"The First Inaugural"* represents optimism and new beginnings in the midst of the Great Depression. FDR waves from an open car during his first inaugural parade in 1933.

4. The Presidential Seal weighs 1,000 pounds, and represents a *"bird in flight."* The bird is an American Bald Eagle.

5. The Presidential Seal consists of sheet bronze that has been arc welded together.

6. Sculptor Tom Hardy was age 77 when he completed the Presidential Seal.

The Presidential Seal as of 1933

Room 2 – "Social Policy (1936-1940)"

1. This room represents the social programs of the New Deal, many of which were intended to combat the Great Depression.

2. The *"Breadline"* is a sculpture of five men in a bread line outside a closed door. It represents unemployment and the hard times of many citizens during the depression. (Unemployment at the peak of the depression (1933) was 24.9% of the workforce, or 13,000,000 workers.)

3. The *"Fireside Chat"* is a sculpture of a man listening to one of Roosevelt's many speeches that were broadcasted from the White House or Hyde Park, New York. (These so called chats were attempts by the president at keeping the average citizen informed, and providing encouragement at a time when almost everything was going wrong.)

4. The *"Rural Couple"* is a sculpture of a weary couple set against an old barn door. (Times were hard for people in both rural and urban areas. Many farmers lost farms that had been in their families for many generations. The movie *"The Grapes of Wrath"* depicts the hard times endured by many rural families.)

Room presents the social programs of the "New Deal"

5. Real people modeled for all of the figures depicted in the *"Breadline,"* the *"Rural Couple,"* and the *"Fireside Chat."*

6. In this room is a thirty-foot-long bronze mural that depicts 54 social programs implemented during Roosevelt's presidency. The five bas-relief panels titled *"Social Programs"* pay tribute to FDR's New Deal legislation. The five nearby columns carry the images of the mural in reverse, as if one had been cast from the other. (Some of these New Deal programs still exist today - Social Security, Unemployment Insurance, and Workman's Compensation.)

7. Robert Graham, who sculptured FDR's first inaugural and the five bas-relief panels and columns, is also credited with casting the *"Olympic Gateway"* at the entrance to the Los Angeles Memorial Coliseum for the 1984 Olympic Games.

8. Visitors can view the Potomac River from an opening in the landscape of the memorial.

9. The four-tiered waterfall pays homage to the Tennessee Valley Authority (TVA). (Established in 1933, the dams constructed by the TVA were instrumental in providing jobs, preventing floods, and providing electrical power.)

Room 3 - " The War Years (1940-1944)"

1. The piles of rough and broken granite blocks depicted in *"I Hate War"* represent the bombed-out ruins of World War II.

2. On September 1, 1939, war began in Europe. The United States entered the war as a result of Japan's bombing of Pearl Harbor on December 7, 1941.

3. The bronze statue of Roosevelt is 8 feet, 7 inches tall.

The Statue of Roosevelt and his dog "Fala"

4. The chair on which Roosevelt is seated has casters on the legs. This is the only suggestion that Roosevelt was handicapped. (The leg braces worn by Roosevelt weighed nearly 10 pounds.)

5. Prior to contracting polio, Roosevelt stood 6 feet, 2 inches tall.

6. The dog next to Roosevelt is his Scottish terrier, Fala. Fala was a 1940 Christmas gift from Roosevelt's cousin Margaret Suckley.

7. The statue of Fala stands 34-inches high from the front paws to the tips of its ears. Its length totals four feet from the tip of Fala's tail to the tip of his nose.

8. Fala was known to stand on his hind legs when the national anthem was played.

9. Fala died in 1952, and is buried at the foot of FDR's gravesite at Hyde Park, New York.

10. Room 3 contains the largest stone in the memorial. This stone is 21 feet, 6 inches long by 6 feet high.

Room 4 – " Seeds of Peace (1944-1945)"

1. The "*Funeral Cortege*" is a 30-foot long by 6-foot high bas-relief depicting the grief of mourners following on foot behind FDR's horse-drawn coffin. (Roosevelt died on April 12, 1945, at age 63, of a cerebral hemorrhage.)

2. The sculptor, Leonard Baskin, drew inspiration for this bronze relief from studying ancient Greek, Egyptian, and Chinese sculptures.

3. The statue of "*Eleanor Roosevelt*" stands in front of the seal of the United Nations. (Eleanor was a member of the U.S. delegation to the United Nations (U.N.), and she played an important part in drafting the U.N. Declaration of Human Rights.)

4. The bronze statue of Eleanor is the only statue of a first lady displayed at any of the presidential memorials or monuments within Washington, D.C.

5. The statue of Eleanor is 7 feet, 3 inches tall. (Eleanor has been the tallest first lady. She was 6 feet tall.)

6. After studying several pictures of Eleanor, the sculptor, Neil Estern, noticed that the lapels on Eleanor's overcoats were often folded over and unpressed. This observation caused Mr. Estern to insert this notable trend into his likeness of the first lady.

The Statue of Eleanor Roosevelt

7. The water of the final waterfall, "*The Grand Finale*" symbolizes the excitement at the end of World War II. It cascades over orderly granite blocks in a loud grand finale. Flat stones leading into the fountain invite the visitors to enter. (War ended in Europe in May 1945, and in the Pacific in September 1945.)

8. Upon leaving the Roosevelt Memorial, visitors can see the Jefferson Memorial across the basin. (Roosevelt influenced the decision for a memorial to Jefferson after he was sworn in as the 32nd president.)

9. A series of granite steps near the last waterfall were constructed in the shape of an amphitheater. On the steps are inscribed the major events of FDR's life.

10. Weighing 76,000 pounds, the heaviest stone in the memorial is located in Room 4 (foundation block).

NOTES

1. As a rebuttal to those who believed Franklin Roosevelt should be portrayed in a wheelchair or on crutches, Lawrence Halprin stated *"he didn't want people to focus on it"* (Roosevelt's handicap). *"This memorial is not meant to solve the problems of the handicapped. It is meant to be historically correct."*

2. Just weeks prior to the dedication of the memorial, President William Clinton (1993-2001) bowed to pressure. He directed that a figure of President Roosevelt (1933-1945) showing him in a wheelchair be included in the memorial. (Only a few pictures and a 15 second film clip are known to exist that show President Roosevelt on crutches or unable to walk on his own.)

3. Prior to his death, Franklin Roosevelt requested that no memorial be dedicated to him after his death. However, in 1965, friends and admirers of Roosevelt placed a small memorial near the National Archives. The memorial consists of a piece of granite the size of Roosevelt's desk with the inscription *"In Memory of Franklin Delano Roosevelt, 1882 – 1945"* engraved into it.

FACTS ABOUT THE KOREAN WAR VETERANS MEMORIAL

In a short period of five years after the end of World War II, the United States was again engaged in a conflict far from its shores. This time it was Korea, an Asian country divided at the 38th parallel between a communist north and a more democratic south. After the initial attacks and victories by North Korea, the combined forces of South Korea, the United States, and their allies forced the armies of North Korea beyond the 38th parallel to a point close to the border of Communist China. These victories prompted military intervention by China, and led to a long and destructive conflict that threatened to explode beyond the borders of Korea. The Korean War Veterans Memorial is a tribute to the men and women who served and sacrificed in what became known as the *"Forgotten War."*

THE KOREAN WAR

1. In 1945, near the end of World War II, the Allies agreed that in order to expedite the surrender of the Japanese military forces on the Asian peninsula, the Soviet Union would accept the surrender of the Japanese above the 38th parallel, and the United States would accept the surrender of the Japanese below the 38th parallel.

2. Instead of the areas above and below the 38th parallel reuniting after the surrender of the Japanese military, they remained divided, and became known as North Korea and South Korea.

3. On June 25, 1950, the military forces of North Korea invaded South Korea.

4. The United States and 21 other members of the United Nations immediately went to the aid of South Korea. (Fifteen countries actually provided combat troops, with the United States providing most of the armed forces and supplies.)

5. For political reasons, President Harry Truman (1945-1953) referred to the war as a conflict. (Only Congress can declare war.)

6. On October 14, 1950, Chinese forces crossed into North Korea.

7. On July 27, 1953, an uneasy armistice agreement was signed. (Many historians believe threats by President Dwight Eisenhower (1953-1961) to use atomic weapons forced China and North Korea to negotiate.)

8. Of the 1,500,000 U.S. servicemen and servicewomen who served in the Korean War, 33,651 died of battle wounds, and 3,262 died of accidents, disease, and other non-battle related incidents. Over 103,000 U.S. servicemen and servicewomen were wounded during the conflict.

9. To compare the casualties of the Korean War with those of World War II and the Vietnam War: Deaths resulting from World War II totaled 292,131 killed in battle and 115,185 non-battle related deaths. Vietnam had over 47,000 service personnel killed in battle and over 10,000 non-battle related deaths.

10. The following is a breakdown of the number of casualties, captured personnel, and missing in action for U.S. troops, and the total for all United Nations (U.N.) troops:

CASUALTIES OF THE KOREAN WAR		
STATUS	U.S. MILITARY FORCES	UNITED NATIONS FORCES
Killed	36,913	610,987
Wounded	103,284	1,064,453
Missing	8,177	470,267
Captured	7,140	92,970

See notes on next page.

*Official Department of Defense records support the number of service members who died of combat and non-combat incidents in the immediate Korean area as 33,651 combat deaths and 3,262 non-combat deaths, for a total of 36,913. Previously, the total was listed as 54,246 deaths attributed to the Korean War. However, on June 25, 2000, the Department of Defense corrected the 54,246 total fatalities previously attributed to the Korean War period as 33,651 combat deaths, 3,262 non-combat deaths within Korea, and an additional 17,333 non-combat deaths that occurred outside Korea (i.e., United States, Europe, etc.).

**Resulting from a correction of non-combat casualties suffered by the United States in Korea, the number of U.N. deaths associated with the Korean conflict was dropped from 628,833 to 610,987.

11. It has been estimated that North Korea and China lost over 2,000,000 servicemen and servicewomen in the conflict.

12. It is also estimated that over 3,000 advisors from the former Soviet Union provided in-country support to North Korea during the Korean War.

13. A total of 131 U.S. servicemen were awarded the Medal of Honor as a result of their military service in Korea. Of this number, 94 sacrificed their lives performing their heroic acts of valor.

14. There were two commanders of U.S. military forces over the course of the war. The first was General Douglas MacArthur, who was relieved of duty by President Harry Truman (1945-1953) in April 1951. The second was General Matthew Ridgeway, who replaced MacArthur. (MacArthur was age 71 when Truman relieved him of his duties.)

THE KOREAN WAR VETERANS MEMORIAL

1. In October 1986, Congress authorized the creation of a Korean War Veterans Memorial.

2. President Ronald Reagan (1981-1989) appointed a 12-member board of Korean War veterans to direct the construction of the memorial.

3. In 1989, a team from State College, Pennsylvania, submitted the plan initially approved for the memorial. However, the board later withdrew its acceptance of the plan.

4. The 1992 memorial plan submitted by Cooper-Lecky Architects was accepted and implemented.

5. On June 14, 1992, President George H. W. Bush (1989-1993) formally broke ground for the memorial.

6. On July 27, 1995, the memorial was dedicated. This date marked the 42nd anniversary of the armistice that ended hostilities in the Korean War. President William Clinton (1993-2001) and South Korean President Kim Young Sam attended the dedication.

7. The total cost of the memorial was $16,500,000.

8. The memorial stands on a 2.2-acre site.

9. A total of 223 piles were driven into bedrock 30-60 feet deep to support the statues and the wall.

10. The memorial's most prominent feature is the triangular *"Field of Service."*

11. There are nineteen U.S. servicemen depicted in the *"Field of Service."*

The Servicemen in "Field of Service"

12. The lines of trees behind the servicemen are being used as a background. They also symbolize the act of United Nations troops coming to the aid of South Korea from west to east.

13. World War II veteran Frank Gaylord sculptured the servicemen.

180

14. The formation of the servicemen depicts a squad on patrol, and evokes the experience of American ground troops in Korea.

15. The actual statues and their reflections on the wall total 38 servicemen. The number 38 is symbolic of the 38th parallel, which is the border between North Korea and South Korea. The number 38 can also represent the number of calendar months in which combat actions were conducted (June 1950 through July 1953) before a ceasefire was agreed to by the combatants.

16. The nineteen stainless steel figures stand between 7 feet, 3 inches and 7 feet, 6 inches tall.

17. Each figure weighs approximately 1,000 pounds.

18. Of the nineteen figures, one figure represents the Air Force (observer); one represents the Navy (medic); and the others represent the Army and Marines.

19. Of the nineteen figures, twelve represent Caucasian servicemen; three represent African-American servicemen; two represent Hispanic servicemen; one represents Asian servicemen; and one represents Native-American servicemen.

20. The figures of the servicemen are shown walking through a simulated rice paddy on a windy and cold day. Strips of granite and scrubby juniper bushes suggest the rugged Korean terrain. (The strips also help limit erosion.)

21. The servicemen are wearing cold weather clothing and ponchos. Mr. Gaylord chose this particular design for two reasons: (1) To provide motion to the figures as the ponchos flow in the wind, and (2) To represent the type of weather the soldiers often fought in during the war. (During the winter-months, troops fighting in the mountains had to deal with temperatures as low as 30 degrees below zero.)

22. Fully equipped, a combat soldier carried an average of between 75 and 80 pounds of food, clothing, and equipment.

23. The clothing and equipment used by the military during the Korean War was largely left over from World War II. Poorly equipped, the following list provides the average equipment issued to an American soldier (excluding weapons):

- M1 Steel Helmet with liner. (This 1940 helmet replaced the M1917A helmet used by U.S. troops during World War I.)
- M1928 Haversack (Backpack)
- M1923 Dismounted Cartridge Belt
- M1938 Dismounted Leggings
- M1940 Boots (Replaced by black boots during the 1950s.)
- M1910 Canteen, Cup & Cover
- M1910 Entrenching Tool & Cover (Shovel)

24. The "*M*" before a type of weapon, clothing, etc. represents the word "*Model*" and does not represent "*Military*" as many non-military visitors might believe. The numbers following the letter "*M*" usually represent the year the item was first manufactured or accepted by the government.

25. Many of the servicemen in the squad carry an M1 rifle, the standard weapon for U.S. ground troops in Korea. Designed by John Garand, these semi-automatic (fires a round each time the trigger is pulled) rifles fire .30 caliber bullets from an 8-round clip loaded through the top of the weapon. The clip is automatically ejected when the last round is fired. The rifle weighs 11.2 pounds, has a rate of fire of 16-32 rounds per minute, and an effective range of 500 yards. (Over 5.5 million M1 rifles were produced.)

26. One of the servicemen walking near the front of the squad is carrying a Browning Automatic Rifle (BAR). This weapon was used during World War I, World War II, and the Korean War. An extremely effective and reliable weapon, it provided squads with powerful cover-fire, while at the same time allowing mobility. The automatic/gas operated BAR fires a .30 caliber bullet from 20-round clips, weighs 20 pounds, has a firing rate of between 300-600 rounds per minute, an effective firing range of 500 yards, and a maximum firing range of 3,500 yards.

27. The one member of the squad wearing a winter cap versus a helmet is an Air Force observer.

28. The weapon carried by the Air Force member of the squad is an automatic/semi-automatic M1 carbine. These carbines were previously used during World War II, fires .30 caliber bullets from 30-round clips, weighs 6 pounds, 9 ounces, with a rate of fire of 700 rounds per minute, and a maximum range of 300 yards. Considered both an offensive and defensive weapon, the M1 carbine is smaller, lighter, and faster firing than the M1 rifle, but its effective firing range is 200 yards less than the M1 rifle. (Korean War veterans described the M1 carbine as very ineffective after 150 yards. Beyond this range, the bullet seldom passed through the winter clothing of the enemy.)

29. Two squad members are carrying a .30 caliber air-cooled Browning machine gun, tripod, and ammunition. This machine gun was used previously during World War II, fires .30 caliber bullets, weighs 31 pounds, with a length of 3 feet, 6 inches. The gun's rate of fire is 450-550 rounds per minute at a maximum range of 3,500 yards, and an effective range of 500 yards. Even though it is heavier and less mobile than the BAR, it was an effective offensive and defensive weapon. Because of the gun's importance to the squad, the gunner usually held the rank of sergeant and the feeder the rank of corporal. (The .30 caliber water-cooled version of the machine gun weighs 41 pounds. The .50 caliber air-cooled machine gun weighs 126 pounds.)

30. The officer/squad leader is probably carrying under his poncho a gas pressured .45 caliber automatic pistol. The weapon weighs 2 pounds, 5 ounces, has a 7-shot magazine, and an effective firing range of 50 yards. (The Model 1911 Colt 45 was first fielded in battle in the Philippines during 1911 and 1912. The Colt remained the standard pistol used by the U.S. military for nearly 80 years. The number *"1911"* represents the year the pistol was manufactured for the first time.)

31. One of the squad is carrying a large radio, evident by the large hump on his back and an antenna sticking out from beneath his poncho. This radio, referred to as an *"Angry 29,"* could transmit long and short distances.

32. Two members of the squad are carrying a small portable radio capable of receiving and transmitting over short distances. This radio, known as a *"PRCY,"* could be used to contact other squads in the area or low flying aircraft. The servicemen are probably lieutenants or a rank no higher than captain and no lower than corporal.

33. The high mural on the south side of the statues pays tribute to the military personnel who served in many roles during the Korean War.

34. The mural was designed by Louis Nelson.

35. The mural was constructed from "Academy Black" granite from California.

Reflections of Servicemen and Servicewomen on the Mural

36. The mural consists of 41 panels, is 164 feet long by 13 feet high at its highest point, and is 8 inches thick.

37. The mural weighs 100 tons.

38. Displayed on the surface of the mural are more than 2,500 photographic archival images. These images show various support and combat personnel in their military roles. The images were selected from over 15,000 images obtained from the National Archives.

39. The images on the mural were formed by first scanning period photographs into a computer, then using a computer-generated stencil to sandblast the images onto the surface of the mural.

40. The images of the servicemen and servicewomen on the mural represent the common foot-soldier, artillery, armor, medical services, air forces, supply organizations, general administration, and several other organizations associated with combat and support functions.

41. In addition to the sandblasted images of servicemen and servicewomen on the mural, there are images of several types of military equipment used during the conflict. Among these images are a B29 - capable of delivering six tons of bombs; a field hospital known as MASH (Mobile Army Surgical Hospital); a B36 jet bomber; a F4U close-air-support-aircraft; a F86 Sabre jet – a highly successful jet fighter against the Soviet built M16; a H5 light observation helicopter - the primary helicopter used to evacuate wounded from the battlefield; M4 Sherman, M26 Pershing, M26 Chaffe, and M46 Patton tanks - all used extensively during the war; and 155MM Long Tom Guns and 76MM Howitzer - two of the primary artillery pieces used by U.S. forces and their allies in Korea.

42. The *"United Nations Wall"* is the granite curb on the north side of the statues. It lists the twenty-two United Nations countries that provided combat troops or medical support in defense of South Korea.

43. Encircled by a grove of linden trees at the top of the *"Field of Service"* is the *"Pool of Remembrance."* It is dedicated to the servicemen and servicewomen who sacrificed their lives during the Korean War.

44. Engraved on a nearby wall are the total casualties of both the United States and the United Nations' forces along with the words *"FREEDOM IS NOT FREE"*.

45. The *"Pool of Remembrance"* is 30 feet in diameter, and was constructed from black granite from Canada.

46. To the south of the memorial are three beds of Rose of Sharon hibiscus plants. This plant is the national flower of South Korea.

FACTS ABOUT THE LINCOLN MEMORIAL

As the 16th President of the United States, Abraham Lincoln (1861-1865) led the United States through one of the most trying times in its short history - the American Civil War (1861-1865). This is a notable accomplishment considering Lincoln was born and raised in the wilderness, lost his mother at an early age, taught himself how to read and write, educated himself in the practice of law, and served as a state legislator and U.S. Congressman without the aid of formal schooling. Many historians rate Lincoln as a man of considerable personal strength, political savvy, and compassion, whose presidency is equal to those of Washington and Jefferson.

Immediately after Lincoln's death, efforts were begun to erect a memorial in Washington, D.C. to honor the man who "Saved the Union." However, it was not until the 20th century that any successful steps were taken by Congress to erect a memorial to Lincoln in the nation's capital.

THE LIFE OF ABRAHAM LINCOLN

1. The Lincoln family originated from England.

2. Lincoln's parents were Thomas Lincoln and Nancy Hawks.

3. On February 12, 1809, Abraham Lincoln was born at Nolin Creek, near Hodgenville, Kentucky.

4. Lincoln was born in Kentucky, raised in Indiana, and spent his adult life in Illinois.

5. In 1812, Lincoln's brother, Tom, died in infancy.

6. In 1818, Lincoln's mother, Nancy, died at age 34. She died from milk sickness, a disease obtained from drinking the milk of cows that had grazed on poisonous white snakeroot.

7. In 1819, Lincoln's father married Sarah Bush Johnson. Lincoln was very close to his stepmother. (Lincoln's stepmother outlived her stepson. She died in 1868 at age 80.)

8. In 1828, Lincoln's sister, Sarah, died at age 20 while giving birth to her child.

9. In 1832, Lincoln lost his bid for the Illinois General Assembly.

10. In 1834, Lincoln was elected to the Illinois General Assembly. It was also at this time he began his studies of law.

11. In 1836, Ann Rutledge, who is believed to be Lincoln's first love, died at age 22.

12. In 1838, Lincoln was re-elected to the Illinois General Assembly.

13. In 1839, Lincoln met Mary Todd.

14. On November 4, 1842, Lincoln married Todd. He was age 33, and she, 24.

15. In 1846, Lincoln was elected to the U.S. House of Representatives as a member of the Whig party.

16. In 1851, Lincoln's father, Thomas, died at age 73.

UNIQUE FACTS ABOUT ABRAHAM LINCOLN

1. Between the period when he left the U.S. House of Representatives in 1848, and his election as President of the United States in 1860, Lincoln practiced law; fathered two additional sons to increase his family size to four sons; buried his son, Edward, in 1850; was elected to the Illinois legislature; and was defeated in his bid for a seat in the U.S. Senate.

2. Lincoln served a full term as President of the United States from March 4, 1861 to March 4, 1865, and started a second term on March 4, 1865.

3. Lincoln was the first president to be born outside the thirteen original states of the United States.

4. At 6 feet, 4 inches tall, Lincoln has been the tallest president. On this tall frame rested an average weight of only 185 pounds, and was carried over size 14 shoes.

5. Lincoln was the first president to wear a beard while in office. His decision to grow a beard was influenced by an October 15, 1860, letter he received from Grace Bedell, an 11 year old girl from Westfield, New York, who wrote that "If you let your whiskers grow......you would look a great deal better for your face is so thin." (Lincoln and Grace later met at the train depot in Westfield on February 16, 1861, during Lincoln's trip to Washington, D.C. to be sworn in as president.)

6. After his death on April 15, 1865, Lincoln's body was returned to his hometown of Springfield, Illinois, for burial. He is buried in a magnificent tomb with his wife, Mary, and sons, Edward, William, and Thomas. His oldest son, Robert, is buried at Arlington Cemetery with his wife and son.

THE LINCOLN MEMORIAL

1. In 1901, the site for the Lincoln Memorial was selected. At the time the construction site was selected, the land was a malarial swamp with marshy pools and limited access by bridge or road. The place where the Lincoln Memorial is located is known as *"Foggy Bottom."*

2. On February 19, 1911, Congress created the Lincoln Memorial Commission. The chairperson for this commission was President William Taft (1909-1913).

3. In 1911, Congress authorized $2,000,000 for construction of the memorial.

4. On February 1, 1913, the memorial, designed by Henry Beacon, was approved by the Lincoln Memorial Commission.

5. On February 12, 1914, the groundbreaking ceremony took place.

6. On February 12, 1915, the cornerstone was dedicated.

7. Beacon was paid $150,000 for his work on the memorial.

8. Beacon used a Greek design for the structure, which is modeled after the Parthenon in Athens.

9. The memorial is on a 6.3-acre site.

10. The memorial weighs an estimated 38,000 tons.

11. To support the memorial, 122 solid concrete piers with steel reinforced rods were driven into the bedrock at depths ranging from 44 feet to 65 feet.

12. The memorial (colonnade) is 188 feet long by 118 feet wide.

13. The height of the memorial building is 99 feet above grade and 80 feet above the foundation.

14. There are 36 marble exterior columns in the memorial, one for each state in the Union at the time of Lincoln's death on April 15, 1865.

The Lincoln Memorial from the Reflecting Pool

15. The columns are 44 feet high.

16. The diameter of the columns at the base is 7 feet, 5 inches.

17. The exterior walls of the memorial and the columns were constructed from Colorado Yule marble.

18. The columns supporting the memorial are not fully vertical. They tilt slightly inward. This eliminates an optical illusion of having the structure appear to bulge outward. The Greeks were the first to use this technique to solve the problem of bulging.

19. The exterior tripods were constructed from Pink Tennessee marble.

20. The names of the 36 states in the Union at the time of Lincoln's death are engraved on the frieze above the memorial's colonnade. (The word colonnade means a series of columns set at regular intervals.)

21. The Doric colonnade around the memorial is 188 feet in length by 118 feet, 6 inches in width. (The Dorics were Greek citizens whose architecture style was basically simple.)

22. The attic parapet (railing) is capped with a frieze (horizontal band) of 48 bas-relief festoons (carved or molded decoration), each representing one of the 48 states in the Union at the time the memorial was dedicated. (There was an unsuccessful attempt at adding two festoons when Alaska and Hawaii became states in 1959. Instead of adding festoons to the memorial, a plaque with the names of the 49th and 50th states was attached to the memorial. The plaque is located at the bottom of the steps leading up to the memorial.)

23. The interior Ionic columns that divide the three chambers are 50 feet high.

24. The diameter of the interior columns is 5 feet, 6 inches.

25. The central chamber containing the Lincoln statue is 60 feet wide by 74 feet deep.

26. The two side chambers containing Lincoln's speeches are 63 feet wide by 38 feet deep. The speech on the north wall is the *Gettysburg Address* of November 19, 1863, and on the south wall is Lincoln's *Second Inaugural Address* of March 4, 1865.

Lincoln's Gettysburg Address

27. Some of the stones used to construct the memorial weigh as much as 23 tons.

28. The interior walls and columns of the memorial were constructed from Indiana limestone.

29. The interior floor was constructed from two-inch thick Tennessee marble.

30. The ceiling of the memorial was constructed by using bronze beams and one-inch thick Alabama marble.

31. To enhance lighting (translucency), the Alabama marble in the ceiling of the memorial was soaked in paraffin prior to assembly.

32. The murals at the top of the north and south walls are 60 feet long by 12 feet high, and each weighs 600 pounds.

33. Jules Guerin painted the murals, which depict principles evident in Lincoln's life.

34. The main theme of the mural on the south wall above the Gettysburg Address is *"The freedom of slaves."* (Includes an angel, representing truth, freeing a slave.)

35. The main theme of the mural on the north wall above the Second Inaugural Address is *"The reunification of the North and South after the Civil War."*

36. On December 8, 1914, at age 64, Daniel Chester French was selected to sculpture the Lincoln statue. (French is also famous for sculpturing the statue of the *"Minuteman"* in Concord, Massachusetts.)

37. Prior to French completing the final version of the Lincoln statue, he completed 3-foot by 7-foot clay models of the president, and a 10-foot plaster model. The plaster model was assembled in the memorial to help determine the final size of the Lincoln statue.

38. The statue of Lincoln was sculptured from 28 identical blocks of White Georgia marble.

39. The pedestal and platform for the statue were constructed from Tennessee marble.

40. It took French four years to complete the statue of Lincoln.

41. Under the watchful eye of French, the six Piccirilli brothers of New York carved the Lincoln statue. It took one year to complete the task. (The Piccirilli brothers also carved the urns at the front of the memorial.)

42. The statue of Lincoln is 19 feet high from his foot to the top of his head.

43. The statue of Lincoln is 19 feet wide at its widest point.

44. The chair is 12 feet, 6 inches high.

45. The pedestal is 10 feet high.

46. The estimated weight of the Lincoln statue is 120 tons.

47. The figure of Lincoln is sitting for two reasons: (1) A standing figure among the columns would create too much vertical thrust, and (2) A standing figure would place the head of Lincoln too far away from the eyes of visitors.

48. The chair on which Lincoln is sitting is a formal chair from Roman antiquity. The drapery on Lincoln's chair is intended to soften the hard lines of the chair.

The Statue of Abraham Lincoln

49. Directly behind the Lincoln statue are the words of Royal Cortissoz carved into the wall: "IN THIS TEMPLE AS IN THE HEARTS OF THE PEOPLE FOR WHOM HE SAVED THE UNION THE MEMORY OF ABRAHAM LINCOLN IS ENSHRINED FOREVER." (Cortissoz was an art critic and lecturer who wrote inscriptions for many memorials.)

50. On November 19, 1919, the Lincoln statue was completed.

51. During December 1919, the assembly of the Lincoln statue in Washington, D.C. was started.

52. In addition to the works of French and the Piccirilli brothers, Ernest Bairstow sculptured other features of the memorial with the assistance of Evelyn Beatrice Longman, French's 19-year-old apprentice.

53. On May 30, 1922, the memorial was dedicated.

54. Among the guests at the dedication was Lincoln's only surviving son, Robert Lincoln. Robert had been present at the deaths of three presidents: Abraham Lincoln (1861-1865), James Garfield (1881), and Rutherford Hayes (1877-1881). (Lincoln and Garfield were assassinated. Hayes died of natural causes in 1893.)

55. Robert Lincoln's tomb is located at Arlington Cemetery, where he is buried with his wife Mary, and young son Abraham Lincoln II, who died at age 17. (The Lincoln Memorial can be seen from the site of the tomb.)

56. Other guests at the dedication were President Warren Harding (1921-1923), former President William Taft (1909-1913), and Doctor Robert Moton, President of Tuskegee Institute, who was the principal speaker.

57. The final cost of constructing the memorial totaled $2,957,000.

58. The cost of the Lincoln statue was $88,400.

59. Henry Beacon died in 1924. Daniel French died in 1931.

60. Some historians and visitors believe the left side of Lincoln presents him as a president of war. The right side presents him as a president of peace.

61. It is said that French, who had a hearing-impaired daughter, carved Lincoln's hands to sign the letters "A" and "L" in American Sign Language. (Shortly before French sculptured the statue of Lincoln, he sculptured a memorial to Thomas Hopkins Gallaudet at Gallaudet College, a college for the hearing impaired.)

62. Below Lincoln's hands, the Roman fasces, symbols of the authority of the Republic, are sculpted in relief on the seat.

63. On the back of Lincoln's head is what some visitors believe is the faint outline of the face of Confederate General Robert E. Lee.

64. For several years, tours could be taken beneath the foundation of the memorial. The visitors could see the graffiti left there by the workers who assembled the memorial.

65. In July 2003, stone carver Andrew Del Gallo etched five lines into the steps of the Lincoln Memorial that mark the exact spot where Rev. Martin Luther King Jr. delivered his "*I Have a Dream*" speech on August 28, 1963. The inscription, which is located near the top-center of the steps, cost $8,300 to complete, is 24 inches wide by 10 inches high, and consists of the following words:

I HAVE A DREAM
MARTIN LUTHER KING, JR.
THE MARCH ON WASHINGTON
FOR JOBS AND FREEDOM
AUGUST 28, 1963

66. One of the earlier plans for a memorial to honor Lincoln called for 6 equestrian and 31 pedestrian statues, with a statue of Lincoln in the middle.

67. In 1909, the United States one cent piece with the image of Abraham Lincoln was release, and in 1914, the five dollar bill with his image was released. The Lincoln Memorial is also on both.

THE REFLECTING POOL

1. Henry Beacon and Charles McKein designed the Reflecting Pool.

2. The Reflecting Pool contains an estimated 6,750,00 gallons of water.

The Reflecting Pool as seen from the Lincoln Memorial

3. The Reflecting Pool is 2,029 feet long by 167 feet wide.

4. The Reflecting Pool is 18 inches deep on the sides and 30 inches deep in the center.

5. Construction on the Reflecting Pool was started in November 1919, and was completed in December 1922.

6. Construction of the Reflecting Pool cost $600,000.

7. It takes 24 hours to fill or empty the Reflecting Pool.

8. The Reflecting Pool is drained and cleaned annually. A front-loader tractor is used to load into dump trucks the thick and sticky mixture of dead leaves, sediment, and other debris from the bottom of the pool. (Any necessary repairs to the pool are also made at the same time.)

9. Because of the need for office space during World War II, temporary multi-story office buildings were constructed around the Reflecting Pool. Ramps were constructed over the Reflecting Pool to carry workers from one side of the pool to the other. (The bridges and buildings were removed after the end of World War II.)

FACTS ABOUT THE SIGNERS OF THE DECLARATION OF INDEPENDENCE MEMORIAL

No other document is considered more important to the birth of the United States than the Declaration of Independence. And if not for the bravery and sacrifices of the men who drafted and signed this national treasure, the future of the nation and its citizens would have been much different than it is today. The Signers of the Declaration of Independence Memorial honors these men, who through their support of the Declaration of Independence; pledged their lives, fortunes, and sacred honor.

THE MEN WHO SIGNED THE DECLARATION OF INDEPENDENCE

1. The following are the names of the 56 signers of the Declaration of Independence and the colonies they represented. The numbers in the brackets ( ) show the number of representatives from each colony.

Delaware (3) – George Read, Thomas McKean, and Caesar Rodney; Pennsylvania (9) – George Clymer, Benjamin Franklin, Robert Morris, John Morton, Benjamin Rush, George Ross, James Smith, George Taylor, and James Wilson; Massachusetts (5) – John Adams, Samuel Adams, John Hancock, Elbridge Gerry, and Robert Treat Pain; New Hampshire (3) – Josiah Bartlett, Matthew Thornton, and William Whipple; Rhode Island (2) – Stephen Hopkins and William Ellery; New York (4) – Lewis Morris, Francis Lewis, Philip Livingston, and William Floyd; Georgia (3) – Button Gwinnett, Lyman Hall, and George Walton; North Carolina (3) – William Hooper, Joseph Hewes, and John Penn; South Carolina (4) – Thomas Lynch, Thomas Heyward, Edward Ruthledge, and Arthur Middleton; New Jersey (5) – Abraham Clark, John Hart, Francis Hopkinson, Richard Stockton, and John Witherspoon; Connecticut (4) – Samuel Huntington, Roger Sherman, William Williams, and Oliver Wolcott; Maryland (4) – Charles Carroll, Samuel Chase, Thomas Stone, and William Paca; Virginia (7) - George Wythe, Richard Henry Lee, Thomas Jefferson, Benjamin Harrison, Thomas Nelson, Jr., Francis Lightfoot Lee, Carter Braxton

2. The number of professions represented by the signers are:

    Planters (Plantation Owners) – 9; Physicians – 4; Lawyers – 19; Merchants - 10; Landowners – 2; Statesmen -1; Surveyors - 1; Politicians -2; Judges – 3; Farmers – 2; Writers – 1; Clergymen – 1; and Iron Masters -1

    (The above professions are listed on the granite stones of the memorial.)

3. Five signers of the Declaration of Independence were later captured by the British and imprisoned. The signers were Thomas Heyward, Arthur Middleton, Edward Rutledge, Richard Stockton, and George Walton. (Only Stockton was arrested as a political prisoner. The remaining four men were prisoners of war. All five men were later released from custody.)

4. Some signers of the Declaration of Independence lost most, if not all, of their wealth.

5. At age 70, the oldest signer of the Declaration of Independence at the time it was signed was Benjamin Franklin from Pennsylvania.

6. At age 26, the youngest signer of the Declaration of Independence was Edward Rutledge from South Carolina.

7. John Morton was the first signer of the Declaration of Independence to die after the document was signed. He died in April 1777, at age 53, of natural causes. One month later Button Gwinnett died, at age 42, from a wound he received during a duel.

8. Thomas Jefferson, John Adams, and Charles Carroll lived the longest after signing the Declaration of Independence. The deaths of Jefferson, at age 83, and Adams, at age 90, on July 4, 1826, left Carroll as the last surviving signer. Carroll died in 1832, and was at age 96, the oldest and last surviving signer of the Declaration of Independence. He represented the colony of Maryland.

9. Three of the signers of the Declaration of Independence later became Vice Presidents of the United States. These signers were John Adams (1st), Thomas Jefferson (2nd), and Elbridge Gerry (5th). In 1814, at age 70, Gerry died in office while vice president.

10. Two of the signers of the Declaration of Independence later became Presidents of the United States - John Adams (2nd) and Thomas Jefferson (3rd). Both men died on July 4, 1826, the 50th anniversary of the approval of the Declaration of Independence. (Jefferson died just a few hours prior to Adams.)

11. At age 33, Thomas Jefferson was the leading draftsman of the Declaration of Independence. He was assisted by John Adams, Benjamin Franklin, Robert R. Livingston, and Roger Sherman.

12. John Hancock was President of the Continental Congress at the time the Declaration of Independence was signed. He was born on January 23, 1737, and died on October 8, 1793.

13. After Congress approved the Declaration of Independence on July 4, 1776, John Hancock was the first person to sign the document, thereby authenticating it. Secretary Charles Thomson attested to it with his signature. After Hancock and Thomson signed the document, it was delivered to the print shop of John Dunlap for reproduction.

14. It is believed Thomas McKean of Delaware was the last person to sign the Declaration of Independence. When Congress authorized the printing of an official copy with the names attached in January 1777, McKean's name was not included. It is believed that one of two events may have occurred: (1) McKean signed the document in 1781, or (2) The printer made a mistake by omitting his name.

THE SIGNERS OF THE DECLARATION OF INDEPENDENCE MEMORIAL

1. The Signers of the Declaration of Independence Memorial is located in Constitution Gardens along the Constitution Avenue side of the Mall between the World War II Memorial and the Lincoln Memorial.

2. The memorial honors the 56 signers of the Declaration of Independence.

3. The memorial is a gift from The American Revolution Bicentennial Administration.

4. Joseph Brown sculptured the memorial.

5. The memorial was constructed from granite.

6. In 1976, the memorial was dedicated and opened to the public.

The Signers of the Declaration of Independence Memorial

7. There is a large granite stone for each of the men who signed the Declaration of Independence. Engraved into each large stone is the name of the signer, his occupation, the location of his home, and a reproduction of his signature.

8. The stones are grouped together by colony.

9. Engraved at the base of each series of large stones is the name of the colony the signers represented.

10. At the entrance to the memorial is a quote from the Declaration of Independence – *"And for the support of this Declaration, with firm reliance on the protection of Divine Providence we mutually pledge to each other our lives, our fortunes, and our sacred honor."*

FACTS ABOUT THE VIETNAM VETERANS MEMORIAL

The Vietnam War, officially a conflict because only Congress can declare war, was not only the longest war ever fought by the United States, officially from 1955 to 1975, but it was also a war that divided the country more than any other conflict since the American Civil War. It pitted families and friends against each other in their support or condemnation of what many viewed as a civil war in a foreign country, while others viewed it as an invasion by one country against another. Young American men left the country rather than serve, and demonstrations at Kent State University, Ohio, resulted in the deaths of four students protesting the war. It was also the first war where current events could be viewed on television during the evening news.

Since the end of hostilities, most Americans have come to view the Vietnam War as a conflict that went very badly. Poor leadership by a U.S. President and his advisors, corruption in the government of South Vietnam, a lack of clear objectives, and the dwindling support on the home front all contributed to the withdrawal of U.S. troops from Vietnam without victory. Time does heal wounds, and with time it became apparent by both the supporters and opponents of the war that the men and women who served in Vietnam should not be criticized for the failure of their government, but should be recognized for their sacrifices. This recognition came in the form of "*The Wall*," and the surrounding statues honoring the men and women who served in a very difficult and unpopular war.

THE VIETNAM WAR

1. Prior to the war, Vietnam was a divided country in Southeast Asia. Divided at the 17th parallel, the communist controlled North Vietnam, and a government backed by the United States controlled South Vietnam.

2. As was often the case during the "*Cold War*," the efforts of the United States in Vietnam were intended to hold back the spread of communism.

3. Military advisors from the United States were first sent to South Vietnam in 1955. The first U.S. death in Vietnam occurred in 1956 (non-combat casualty). The first combat casualty occurred in 1959.

4. In March 1965, the first large troop contingency arrived in Vietnam.

5. On April 30, 1975, North Vietnam conquered South Vietnam.

6. The president largely responsible for the U.S. commitment to Vietnam was Lyndon Johnson (1963-1969). The president largely responsible for the withdrawal of the military was Richard Nixon (1969-1974).

7. A total of 2,600,000 servicemen and servicewomen served in-country in Vietnam. In addition to the ground forces and air forces actually stationed in Vietnam, an additional 500,000 supporting personnel, such as naval forces off the coast of Vietnam and air forces as far away as the Philippines and Okinawa also supported the war efforts.

8. In addition to fighting in Vietnam, U.S. forces served in Thailand, Cambodia, and Laos.

9. The number of servicemen and servicewomen in Vietnam at any one time peaked at 543,482 in April 1969. This number dropped constantly until all of the military forces were withdrawn.

10. The average age of the infantrymen who fought in Vietnam was age 22. The average age of the nurses who served was age 23.

11. The servicemen and servicewomen who served in Vietnam served on a rotating basis, usually one-year tours.

12. Over 58,000 American deaths resulted from service in the Vietnam War. An additional 303,000 were wounded, with 153,000 requiring hospitalization because of their wounds. Over 17,000 of the dead were married. An estimated 20,000 children lost their fathers.

13. The worst year for U.S. casualties in the Vietnam War was 1968. In this year, 16,592 servicemen and servicewomen died in the war.

14. To provide an example of how fierce the fighting in Vietnam was, 22% of the U.S. Marines who went into battle in Vietnam were either killed or wounded (13,091 dead and 51,392 wounded).

15. It is estimated that between 2.5 million and 3 million Vietnamese and other Asian lives were lost during the war.

16. In addition to the human costs, the United States spent over $111 billion supporting the war.

17. A total of 244 servicemen were awarded medals of honor for their heroic actions in the Vietnam War. Of this number, the names of 153 or 63% of the recipients are listed on the "Wall" of the Vietnam Veterans Memorial.

THE VIETNAM VETERANS MEMORIAL – "THE WALL"

THE PLANNING AND CONSTRUCTION EFFORTS – "THE WALL"

1. In 1979, Jan C. Scruggs started the first successful movement for the construction of the Vietnam Veterans Memorial. A native of Maryland, Mr. Scruggs served in Vietnam in 1969-1970 in the 199th Light Infantry Brigade of the U.S. Army.

2. Mr. Scruggs determined that the memorial must meet four criteria:

   - Harmonize with its surroundings;
   - Be reflective and contemplative in character;
   - The memorial would show the name of every American soldier, airman, sailor, marine and member of the Coast Guard who had died as a result of service in Vietnam or was missing in action; and
   - It must not make a political statement.

3. Maryland Senator Charles Mathias introduced a bill for the memorial site. On July 1, 1980, President Jimmy Carter (1977-1981) signed the bill approving the memorial site.

4. A $20,000 prize was offered for the best design for the memorial.

5. The winning design was selected on May 1, 1981, from the 1,421 designs offered for consideration. The designs were displayed in an airplane hangar at Andrews Air Force Base, Maryland, just outside Washington, D.C.

6. Maya Lin, a 21 year-old Chinese-American from a small Ohio town, submitted the winning entry. At the time of her submission she was an architect student at Yale University. (Lin's name, as well as the names of the other people involved in the project, is listed at the top of the apex of the Wall, which can't be seen from the front of the Wall, and access is restricted.)

7. On March 16, 1982, work was begun on the site of the memorial, with a groundbreaking ceremony on March 26, 1982.

8. On November 13, 1982, the memorial was dedicated.

9. The construction cost of the memorial totaled $4,284,000.

THE VIETNAM VETERANS MEMORIAL – "THE WALL"

1. The Wall is on a 2-acre site between the Lincoln Memorial and Washington Monument.

2. The Wall runs east to west. The east side of the memorial points to the Washington Monument, the west points to the Lincoln Memorial.

3. The design of the Wall is in the shape of a chevron, not a "*V*". The chevron is close to the wing shape of a jet aircraft.

4. Each of the two walls that form the chevron is 246 feet, 9 inches (246.75 feet) in length, at an angle of 125 degrees, 12 minutes.

5. The full length of the Wall is 493 feet, 6 inches. (Based on 246.75 feet per each wall.)

6. The size and weight of the Wall are 3,000 cubic feet at a weight of 175 pounds per cubic foot. Total weight of the granite without foundation is 525,000 pounds.

The Vietnam Memorial Wall

7. Black granite was transported from the mines near Bangalore, India to the state of Vermont, where it was given its finish. (Black granite was selected because of its reflecting qualities, and the color allows the names to be read more easily.)

8. The Wall consists of 148 panels. Each panel is 2.75 inches thick and 40 inches wide.

9. The panels of the Wall vary in height from 8 inches (ends), to 10 feet, 1.2 inches (10.1 ft at center of chevron).

10. At the time of the dedication, there were 70 separate inscribed panels for each wall, plus 4 panels at each end without names.

Some of the names on "The Wall"

11. There are from 1 to 137 lines per panel, and from 5 to 6 names per line. The letters on the memorial are .53 inch high and approximately .015 inch deep.

12. The granite panels are supported by 140 concrete pilings driven approximately 35 feet into bedrock.

13. Among the inscriptions on the Wall are the following.

At the beginning of the memorial (Panel 1 East) - "IN HONOR OF THE MEN AND WOMEN OF THE ARMED FORCES OF THE UNITED STATES WHO SERVED IN THE VIETNAM WAR. THE NAMES OF THOSE WHO GAVE THEIR LIVES AND OF THOSE WHO REMAIN MISSING ARE INSCRIBED IN THE ORDER THEY WERE TAKEN FROM US."

14. At the time the Wall was dedicated on November 13, 1982, a total of 57,939 names had been stenciled onto the Wall.

UNIQUE FACTS ABOUT THE VIETNAM WAR AND THE VIETNAM VETERANS MEMORIAL – "THE WALL"

1. Initially, a 1973 Department of Defense directive set the date for being considered a military casualty of the Vietnam War as anyone killed or declared missing on or after January 1, 1961. Then the date was changed to 1959, and in 1998, the eligibility date was again changed to November 1, 1955.

2. On July 8, 1959, Major Dale R. Buis and Master Sergeant Chester N. Ovnand, became the first combat related casualties of the Vietnam War. In 1998, the Department of Defense recognized Air Force Technical Sergeant Richard B. Fitzgibbon Jr. as a casualty of the Vietnam War. Sergeant Fitzgibbon became a non-combat casualty on June 8, 1956, and is considered the first United States casualty of the Vietnam War.

3. When Sergeant Fitzgibbon was recognized as a casualty of the Vietnam War, he and his son, Marine Lance Corporal Richard Fitzgibbon III, killed in 1965, became one of two pairs of fathers/sons who lost their lives in Vietnam. The other pair was Leo Hester Sr., killed in 1967, and his son, Leo Hester Jr., killed in 1969.

4. Twenty-three sets of brothers were killed in the Vietnam War. Sixteen chaplains also lost their lives.

5. As of May 2006, the number of names on the Wall totaled 58,253. An increase of 314 names over the number of names that had been stenciled onto the Wall on the date it was dedicated.

6. The names on the Wall were stenciled by using a then new computerized gritblasting system developed by Larry Century.

7. The names on the Wall are listed in the order the service member died as a result of his or her service in Vietnam or was declared missing in action. This is because there would be a great deal of confusion if the names were listed alphabetical. For example, there are fifteen Thomas Smiths on the Wall. And as prescribed by Maya Lin, The Wall's designer, "this arrangement allows those service members who died together to forever be linked." She also wanted the names to be arranged in an almost circular manner, having the first names reaching out and combing back to touch the last names of those killed or missing.

8. To find a name on the Wall, a visitor can search the available lists for the name under the year the service member died from his/her injuries or was declared missing in action. Listed under the year is the name of the service member and the state he or she represents. For example, *"PA"* for Pennsylvania or *"VA"* for Virginia. The panel number and the line on the panel where the name is located follow the state name. Reference to an individual would be as follows: *"Joseph Franks (Name), PA (State), 21E (Panel), 23 (Line)."*

9. A *"diamond"* at the end of a name of a casualty indicates the service member's death was confirmed or declared deceased. A plus (cross) "+" at the end of a name of a casualty indicates the service member is missing and unaccounted for. It can easily be changed to a diamond. A *"circle around a cross"* at the end of a name of a casualty indicates he was previously listed as killed or missing and has been determined alive. No circles appear on the Wall as of 2006, however, there have been servicemen declared alive after their names were placed on the wall.

10. If the names of the servicemen and servicewomen who died while serving their country in other parts of the world during the period of the Vietnam War were added to the Wall, an additional 20,000 names would have to be added.

THE ADDITIONS TO THE SITE OF THE VIETNAM VETERANS MEMORIAL

THE STATUE – "THREE SERVICEMEN"

1. Since the dedication of the Vietnam Veterans Memorial - Wall, two statues have been added to the memorial site.

2. Frederick Hart sculptured the first addition, *"Three Servicemen,"* also known as *"Three Soldiers."* The bronze statue shows three servicemen (Caucasian, African-American, and Hispanic – modeled after a Cuban-American), looking toward *"The Wall."*

Statue of "Three Servicemen"

3. The 7-foot tall statue was dedicated on November 9, 1984.

4. The 60-foot bronze flagpole next to the *"Three Servicemen"* was installed in 1983.

5. At the base of the flag staff are the seals of the five military services: Air Force, Army, Coast Guard, Marine Corps and Navy.

6. The following inscription is inscribed around the base of the flag:

   "THIS FLAG REPRESENTS THE SERVICE RENDERED TO OUR COUNTRY BY THE VETERANS OF THE VIETNAM WAR. THE FLAG AFFIRMS THE PRINCIPLES OF FREEDOM FOR WHICH THEY FOUGHT AND THEIR PRIDE IN HAVING SERVED UNDER DIFFICULT CIRCUMSTANCES."

7. In July 2004, a plaque was added to the site of the "Three Servicemen Statue" that reads: *"In memory of the men and women who served in the Vietnam War and later died as a result of their services. We honor and remember their sacrifice."* (The primary purpose of the plaque is to honor the memory of the servicemen and servicewomen whose names are not on the Wall, but their service in Vietnam may have caused physical or mental conditions that contributed to their deaths.)

THE VIETNAM WOMEN'S MEMORIAL

The Vietnam Women's Memorial

1. Glenna Goodacre sculptured the second addition, the *"Vietnam Women's Memorial."*

2. The memorial shows three servicewomen (one hidden in picture), one of whom is aiding a wounded soldier.

3. The bronze memorial weighs one-ton (2,000 pounds).

4. The memorial symbolizes the service, dedication, and compassion of the women who served in Vietnam.

5. The paving stones are Carnelian Red granite.

6. The approximate size of the memorial is 8 feet by 15 feet.

7. The eight yellowwood trees surrounding the statue represent the eight servicewomen (nurses) who died while serving in Vietnam.

8. The sculpture cost nearly $4,000,000 to construct.

9. On Veterans Day, November 11, 1993, the memorial was dedicated.

10. The Veterans Administration lists 7,484 servicewomen who served in the Vietnam War. Of this number 6,250 were nurses. (Because of inconsistencies in available records, the number who served in Vietnam could be as high as 11,000.)

11. The names of eight servicewomen are honored on the Vietnam Veterans Memorial - Wall. Only one of the eight women died from enemy actions. Lt. Sharon Ann Lane died from shrapnel wounds when rockets hit the 312th Evacuation Hospital at Chu Lai on June 8, 1969. Of the remaining seven servicewomen, five died as a result of aircraft accidents, and two died from natural causes.

FACTS ABOUT ARLINGTON NATIONAL CEMETERY
(BACKGROUND ABOUT THE CUSTIS AND LEE FAMILIES, THE FOUNDING OF ARLINGTON, AND ITS DESIGNATION AS A NATIONAL CEMETERY)

Very few of the over 4,000,000 international visitors who visit Arlington National Cemetery each year know much about these hallowed grounds. Seldom will visitors be familiar with how Arlington was settled, who were the first settlers to settle on the land, its pre-Civil War history, and how it became the most sacred and honored cemetery in the United States. As with any end, the history of Arlington had a beginning. This beginning has since been sculptured into what is now known as *Arlington National Cemetery*.

THE ARLINGTON HOUSE

1. George Custis, the foster grandson of George Washington, decided to establish a memorial to his grandfather on one of the several land parcels he owned. This was the basis for the start of the Custis-Lee Mansion, better known as the Arlington House. (The original size of the Arlington estate totaled 1,100 acres.)

2. Initially, the estate was to be named *"Mount Washington."* However, when Custis concluded several towns, cities and estates across the country had already been named in honor of the first president, he decided to name the estate *"Arlington"* after the Custis family's ancestral homestead on Virginia's Eastern Shore.

The Arlington House

3. The Greek Revival mansion, modeled after the Temple of Theseus in Athens, Greece, took sixteen years to complete. The delay was due largely to the wildly fluctuating cash situation of George Custis.

4. Construction on the mansion began in 1802, when Custis was just age 21, and was completed in 1818. In 1802, the north wing with its six rooms was the first to be completed. The south wing was completed in 1804. After the completion of the central section in 1818, the mansion totaled 140 feet wide from the north wing to the south wing. Custis displayed the artifacts of George and Martha Washington in the south wing of the mansion.

5. The eight columns supporting the portico are five feet in diameter at the base.

THE FAMILIES WHO LIVED IN THE ARLINGTON HOUSE

1. George Custis married his wife, Mary Lee Fitzhugh (Molly), in 1804, and they lived the remainder of their lives in the Arlington House.

2. Molly died in 1853, and George died in 1857. They are buried in the Custis Family plot (Section 13).

3. At the time of his death, George Custis owned 196 slaves. They were to be given their freedom within five years after the death of Custis. (Robert E. Lee intended to abide by the terms of George Custis' will, but war came in 1861.)

4. Under the terms of George Custis' will, Mary Anna Randolph Custis, the wife of Robert E. Lee, was given the right to inhabit and control Arlington House for the rest of her life. At the time of her death, full title of the property would be transferred to Mary's oldest son George Washington Custis Lee. (Mary was the only child of four children to survive to maturity.)

5. Mary Anna Randolph Custis, a distant cousin of Robert E. Lee, married Lee on June 30, 1831. (Robert was born in 1807, Mary in 1808.)

Close-up view of the Arlington House

210

6. Mary and Robert were married in the main hall of Arlington House, and six of the seven Lee children were born in Arlington House.

7. On April 17, 1861, Virginia seceded from the Union.

8. On April 18, 1861, President Abraham Lincoln (1861-1865) offered Robert E. Lee command of the Union Army.

9. On April 20, 1861, Lee turned down command of the Union Army, and left Arlington to take command of the Confederate Army. He never returned to Arlington.

10. Mary Lee left Arlington on May 15, 1861. She returned once after the war, which was in 1873, only to see the destruction to her estate.

11. Robert and Mary resided at Arlington for 30 years.

12. Robert E. Lee died in 1870, and Mary Custis Lee died in 1873. Both are entombed in the walls of the Lee Chapel on the grounds of the Washington and Lee University in Lexington, Virginia.

THE OCCUPATION & SALE OF ARLINGTON

1. A force of 14,000 Union soldiers occupied Arlington on May 23, 1861. Two Union forts were constructed on the estate. The larger of these forts was Fort Whipple, later renamed Fort Myer. The other was Fort McPherson.

2. After taking over the mansion, the Union Army made it an unofficial officers club, providing both housing for lower-ranking Union officers and a venue for frequent balls and galas for the commissioned staff.

3. During the Civil War, President Abraham Lincoln (1861-1865) occasionally visited the mansion.

4. In 1862, the federal government enacted legislation to collect property taxes from the *"insurrectionary districts,"* meaning land claimed by the Confederacy.

5. The property tax on Arlington totaled $92.10 on an assessed value of $26,810. The landowner was the only person who could pay the taxes, and the taxes had to be paid in person. Mary Custis Lee was considered the owner of the property.

6. Since Mary Lee had become an invalid, confined to a wheelchair because of arthritis, she sent a cousin to pay the taxes on her property. Her representative was turned away, and the government confiscated the estate for tax default.

7. Due to the non-payment of the property taxes, the property was offered for public sale on January 11, 1864, and was purchased by a tax commissioner for "government use, for war, military, charitable, and educational purposes."

8. General Montgomery Meigs, the Quartermaster of the Union Army, had served with Robert E. Lee. However, because of Meigs' hatred of Lee after Lee accepted command of the Confederate Army, Meigs convinced Secretary of War Edwin Stanton to turn 200 acres of the estate into a federal cemetery. The 200 acres closest to the Custis Mansion (Arlington House) were designated a national cemetery on June 15, 1864. (Meigs served under Lee while both were stationed at St. Louis, Missouri. Meigs was also a southerner from the state of Georgia, but chose his country over his state, whereas Lee chose his state over his country.)

9. On the day the estate was declared a national cemetery, 65 soldiers were buried on the land, including several in Mrs. Lee's famous rose garden. By the end of the Civil War, 16,000 graves filled the spaces close to the Custis Mansion (Arlington House).

10. However, two months prior to June 15th, Private William Christman, a 21-year-old farmer from Pennsylvania, became the first soldier to be buried on the plantation. He is buried in what is now Section 27.

11. After President Lincoln issued his *Emancipation Proclamation*, thousands of refugee slaves from the South streamed North into Washington, D.C. To house the refugees in a safe location, the Union Army dedicated a Freedman's Village near Arlington Cemetery on December 4, 1863. Freedman's Village, consisted of over 100 buildings, including a hospital, a school, churches, and shops. The community existed until the 1890s.

12. At its peak, Freedman's Village stretched from near what is now the Tomb of the Unknowns to near the Pentagon.

13. James Parks was the only former slave to have been born and died at Arlington. At the time of his death in 1929, the government permitted his burial in Section 15.

14. More than 3,800 inhabitants of Freedman's Village are buried in the Jim Crow section of the cemetery, Section 27. Their headstones are marked *"Civilian"* or *"Citizen."*

Headstone marked "Citizen"

15. Other headstones in Section 27 have headstones marked *"USCT."* These headstones cover the graves of <u>U</u>nited <u>S</u>tates <u>C</u>olored <u>T</u>roops.

16. In April 1866, General Meigs took another step toward ensuring the mansion would not be returned to the Lee family. He ordered that the remains of all unidentified soldiers recovered from battlefields within a twenty-five mile radius of Washington, D.C. be gathered and placed in a common vault in the rose garden near Arlington House. Most of the 2,111 remains were recovered from the battlefield at Bull Run. The vault is located near the Arlington House and stands today as Arlington's Memorial to the Unknown Civil War Dead.

17. General Meigs, his wife, father, and a son who was killed during the Civil War, are all buried near the rose garden of Arlington House.

18. In 1877, George Washington Custis Lee, Robert and Mary's oldest son and heir to the estate, sued the federal government for trespassing on his property. The case went to the U.S. Supreme Court, which ruled 5-4 in Lee's favor.

19. In March 1883, Lee agreed to sell the property to the government of the United States for $150,000. The sale became final in May 1883, when the deed was approved by then Secretary of War Robert Todd Lincoln (son of President Lincoln).

20. Arlington House served as quarters for the cemetery staff until 1925.

21. A 1955 act of Congress dedicated Arlington House as a monument to Robert E. Lee.

FACTS ABOUT ARLINGTON NATIONAL CEMETERY
(SIZE, REQUIREMENTS FOR BURIAL, CEREMONIES, NOTABLE SITES, AND EVENTS WITHIN THE CEMETERY)

The burial of President John F. Kennedy (1961-1963) at Arlington National Cemetery turned the cemetery into one of the most sought after places to spend eternity. Requests for burials at Arlington rose as much as 400 percent after the death of the president. This surge in requests prompted changes to the rules that governed who qualified for burial in this hallowed ground, how and where in the cemetery the remains would be honored, and what alternatives were needed to accommodate the wishes of the families who's loved ones served their country honorably.

But even without the tragedy of 1963, Arlington National Cemetery had become the final resting place for several notable Americans. These statesmen, generals, admirals, inventors, explorers, recipients of the Medal of Honor, and many common soldiers, sailors, airmen and marines who made the ultimate sacrifice for their country, had for 100 years prior to the death of *"JFK"* been honored with ceremonies and burial at Arlington.

WHO IS AUTHORIZED BURIAL AT ARLINGTON NATIONAL CEMETERY

1. To qualify for in-ground burial at Arlington National Cemetery, a deceased must meet at least one of the following requirements:

   - Died on active duty.

   - Served at least 20 years of active duty and qualified to receive retired pay.

   - Retired reservists, who have reached age 60 prior to death, were drawing retired pay, and served a period of active duty other than for training.

- Veterans honorably discharged with at least 30 percent disability before October 1, 1949.

- Holders of the nation's highest military decorations. These medals consist of one or more of the following: Medal of Honor, Distinguished Service Cross, Distinguished Service Medal, Silver Star, or Purple Heart.

- Any person who held the office of President of the United States.

- Any former member of the U.S. armed forces who served on active duty (other than for training) and who held any of the following positions: (1) An elective office of the U.S. Government; (2) Office of the Chief Justice of the United States Supreme Court or of an Associated Justice; (3) Select U.S. government offices; and (4) Certain chiefs missions.

- Former prisoners of war who died on or after November 30, 1993.

- The widow or widower of: (1) A member of the armed forces who was lost or buried at sea or officially determined to be missing in action; (2) A member of the armed forces who is interred in a U.S. military cemetery overseas that is maintained by the American Battle Monuments Commission; and (3) A member of the armed forces who is interred at Arlington Cemetery as part of a group burial.

- The spouse or unmarried minor child (under age 21) of any of the above, or of any person already buried at Arlington Cemetery. An unmarried dependent student qualifies up to age 23.

2. A veteran who does not qualify under the above rules may be buried in the same grave as a previously buried brother, sister, parent, or child. The veteran's spouse must waive his or her eligibility for Arlington, and the veteran can have no dependent children at the time of death.

3. In addition to in-ground burials, and as of 1980, the remains of qualified personnel may also be interred in the Arlington Cemetery's Columbarium. The columbarium consists of nine courts containing 60,000 niches. The niches are capable of holding a maximum of 100,000 cremated remains. Persons eligible for burial in the Columbarium are:

-   Any former member of the armed forces who served on active duty (other than for training), and whose last service ended honorably.

-   Certain reservists and ROTC members who die while on active duty, while performing training, or while traveling to or from training.

-   Certain former military personnel who were being hospitalized for injuries or diseases incurred while on active duty.

-   Members of 37 civilian groups who served their country during wartime. Included in these groups are World War II veterans who were members of the Women Air Service Pilots (WASPs), U.S. Merchant Marines, civilians involved in the defense of Bataan in the Philippines, and members of the Women's Auxiliary Ferrying Squadron (WAFS).

-   Certain commissioned officers of the U.S. Coast and Geodetic Survey (National Oceanic and Atmospheric Administration), or of the U.S. Public Health Service.

-   The spouse or unmarried minor or permanently dependent child of any of the above, or of any person already in the Columbarium. A student qualifies up to age 23.

4. Normally, an authorized family will be allowed one niche in the Columbarium.

5. The President of the United States or Secretary of the Army may waive the qualifications for burial at Arlington Cemetery under special circumstances. For example, President Reagan authorized the interment of Joe Louis in April 1981. (Because veteran groups saw this waiver as being abused, it has become very difficult for a person who does not qualify under the normal criteria to be laid to rest at Arlington.)

BURIAL AT ARLINGTON NATIONAL CEMETERY

1. Except for federal holidays, funeral services are conducted Monday through Friday, from 9 a.m. through 3 p.m.

2. The burial services of veterans buried at Arlington Cemetery range from services where only a single representative of the cemetery is present at the burial, to a burial with full honors requiring the services of nearly 60 military personnel.

3. Burial services for enlisted personnel consist of graveside honors by military members of the appropriate branch of the service (Army, Navy, Air Force, etc.). The honors include body bearers, firing party, and a bugler. Upon request, the cemetery staff will provide a military chaplain.

4. In addition to the graveside honors provided to enlisted personnel, burial services for officer personnel may also include a caisson, band, and escort troops. For Army and Marine officers in the rank of full colonel and higher, the riderless horse is used. For Navy, Coast Guard, and Marine Flag Officers (admirals and generals), the Minute Guns (Gun Salute) is executed.

5. The flag of the United States that is presented to the next of kin of an active duty member at a funeral is provided by the deceased's branch of service. The Department of Veterans Affairs provides the flags for non-active duty veterans.

6. The services with full honors consist of an escort officer, a flag bearer, an 18-person band, a 4-person color guard, a 18 members marching platoon, a horse-drawn caisson pulled by 6 horses, 4 army riders, 8 body bearers, and a 7-person firing party. (The firing party fires 3 volleys at the gravesite.)

Uniform Layout of Military Graves – Standard Headstones

7. Flags flown at Arlington Cemetery are lowered to half-staff 30 minutes before the first burial of the day, and remain lowered until after the last funeral is completed.

8. The draping of the U.S. flag over the casket is symbolic of the services provided soldiers during the Civil War. Because caskets were seldom available for the thousands of soldiers killed in battle, the flag was often used in lieu of a casket while transporting the body to a grave. (The flag was not buried with the body.)

9. The firing of three volleys of rifle fire at a gravesite is also symbolic of the Civil War. At pre-arranged times, soldiers from the opposing sides would agree to a cease fire to allow the recovery of the wounded and dead from the battlefield. The cease fire was started when soldiers from both sides showed themselves, one side fired a volley in the air to show that their rifles were empty, the other side responded in kind. After the wounded and dead had been cleared from the field, a third fired volley would signal the renewal of hostilities.

10. The playing of *taps* at a gravesite had its origin in the Civil War, when it was originally used as a signal for "lights out" at military camps. Later, because of concerns that firing a volley of shots at a gravesite might prompt an attack from the enemy, *taps* replaced the volley. The U.S. Army officially adopted *taps* in 1874, and since 1900, *taps* has been played at the funerals of military personnel. (The term *taps* originated from the fact that the call was often tapped out on a drum in the absence of a bugler.)

11. The two black artillery caissons that are used to transport the veterans to their last resting place have been in service since 1918. These caissons are also used for transporting the bodies of former Presidents of the United States and other honored dead to the Capitol Building to lie in state or to other ceremonies within the Washington area. (Arlington is the only national cemetery authorized to use horses and caissons on a regular basis for funeral ceremonies.)

12. The tradition of using a caisson to carry the body of the honored dead dates back to the reign of Henry VIII of England (reigned 1509-1547), when the bodies were transported on cannon wagons. As part of the history of the United States during time of war, both the Union and Confederate armies transported their dead on caissons during the Civil War.

13. Six horses pull the caissons, with riders only on the left side of the team. This is symbolic of how the caissons were used during the Civil War: Riders on the left side, with supplies being carried on the horses on the right side.

14. The average weight of these strong horses is 1,800 pounds.

15. On average, 28 funerals are conducted each day at Arlington Cemetery, totaling 6,400 each year. (Due to the projected increase in the number of World War II, Korean War, and Vietnam War deceased veterans, this number is expected to peak at 30 per day. At this rate the cemetery will be full between the years 2050 and 2060.)

16. In 1948, the wives of active duty and retired Air Force members began to attend and participate in the funerals at Arlington. Since 1972, the *"Arlington Ladies"* as they are known, and who consist of the wives and widows of military members from all of the military branches attend the burials. Their attendance symbolizes the honoring of a lost family member.

17. At the end of the burial services, the *"Arlington Ladies"* present a letter of appreciation and thanks to the family of the deceased.

18. Above ground interments (crypts) are no longer permitted at Arlington Cemetery.

19. The government provides a headstone for each gravesite at Arlington. The headstone is formed from white marble, measures 13 inches wide by 42 inches high, and is 4 inches thick. Twenty-four inches of the white marble headstone are above ground. (The Veterans Administration provides the headstones.)

20. Servicemen and servicewomen who are entitled to a headstone at a national cemetery are those: (1) Whose remains have not been recovered; (2) Buried at a cemetery not managed by the Veterans Administration; or (3) Buried overseas in a military cemetery. The words "*In Memory Of*" are inscribed above the name on the headstone.

21. Over 300,000 service members and their family members are buried in over 200,000 graves at Arlington Cemetery.

SOME OF THE NOTABLE PEOPLE BURIED AT ARLINGTON NATIONAL CEMETERY

1. Born on August 2, 1754, Pierre Charles L'Enfant, was a Frenchman who served as an engineer during the American Revolution, and is credited with designing what is now Washington, D.C. On June 14, 1825, L'Enfant died penniless and was buried on farmland in what is now Prince George's County, Maryland. In 1909, L'Enfant's remains were reburied at a site just in front of the Arlington House.

2. On May 22, 1911, the marble monument over the gravesite of L'Enfant was dedicated.

3. L'Enfant has been credited with designing the Purple Heart, which is awarded to wounded American servicemen and servicewomen. (The Purple Heart was originally presented for acts of valor.)

Burial site of Pierre Charles L'Enfant

4. In 1828, Mary Randolph was the first person buried on the grounds of what became Arlington Cemetery. (Mary was the cousin of General Robert E. Lee's wife Mary.)

5. There are six five-star admirals and generals buried at Arlington. (There have been no five-star generals or admirals in the U.S. military since Omar Bradley died in 1981.) These officers are:

    *   General Blackjack Pershing led U.S. forces in Europe during World War I.

    *   General George C. Marshall was sworn in as the Army Chief of Staff on the same day Germany invaded Poland (September 1, 1939). He held this office for the duration of the war. After World War II, Marshall was appointed special ambassador to China, and later as Secretary of State under President Harry Truman (1945-1953). Marshall is credited with the success of the Marshall Plan, an economic plan that was instrumental in rebuilding the countries of Western Europe after World War II. Prior to his retirement, Marshall served as President of the Red Cross, and was awarded the Nobel Peace Prize for the Marshall Plan.

    *   Admiral William "*Bull*" Halsey was instrumental in several victories against Japanese forces in the Pacific theater of World War II.

    *   General Henry "*Hap*" Arnold commanded the United States Army Air Forces during World War II.

    *   Admiral William D. Leahy performed duties as Chief of Staff for Presidents Franklin Roosevelt (1933-1945) and Harry Truman (1945-1953).

    *   General Omar Bradley was Commander of the Allied forces during the invasion of Normandy, and the Army Chief of Staff during the Korean War.

6. The actor Lee Marvin served in the U.S. Marines during World War II, and is buried next to Joe Louis.

7. Joe Louis Barrow ("The Brown Bomber") was twice the heavyweight boxing champion of the world. He was awarded the Legion of Merit for his services in the U.S. Army during World War II. (Louis donated over $100,000 to the Army and Navy relief efforts during World War II.)

8. Audie Murphy was the most decorated combat soldier for the United States during World War II. He is buried near the Memorial Amphitheater.

9. Robert E. Peary was credited with being the first person to reach the North Pole.

10. Matthew Henson was credited with being the first African-American to reach the North Pole.

11. General Jimmy Doolittle led U.S. bombers on the first mission over Japan during World War II. (He was awarded the Medal of Honor for his actions.)

12. President William Taft was the 27th President of the United States (1909-1913), and later a Chief Justice of the United States Supreme Court.

13. Oliver Wendell Holmes was a notable Supreme Court Justice of the United States.

14. General Arthur MacArthur was the father of General Douglas MacArthur. (Arthur was awarded a Medal of Honor for his actions during the Civil War. His son, Douglas, was awarded his Medal of Honor for his actions during World War II.)

15. General Abner Doubleday was a Union general during the Civil War, and is credited with developing the rules for the game of baseball. (Doubleday was a member of the Union forces garrisoned at Fort Sumter, South Carolina, when the Confederate forces fired on the fort. This action was the beginning of hostilities between Northern and Southern states during the Civil War.)

16. Doctor Walter Reed was credited with discovering the causes of and treatment for yellow fever. (Doctor Reed served in Cuba during the Spanish-American War of 1898.)

17. General Montgomery Meigs, a Union Civil War general, was responsible for Arlington being dedicated a national cemetery, was instrumental in the construction of the dome to the U.S. Capitol Building, oversaw the construction of a modern sewage and water system for Washington, D.C., and oversaw the construction of the U.S. Pension Building in Washington, D.C.

18. The Apollo 1 Astronauts - Virgil Grissom, Roger Chaffee, and Edward White. They were killed in a fire on January 27, 1967, while training for the first Apollo mission, a 14-day trip into space.

19. William Jennings Bryan - Notable politician, presidential candidate, and U.S. Secretary of State.

20. Robert Todd Lincoln - The son of President Abraham Lincoln (1861-1865). In his own behalf, he was a successful lawyer and businessman, and was appointed the Secretary of War in 1881, and the U. S. Minister to Great Britain.

21. General Philip H. Sheridan was a successful Union general during the Civil War.

22. General Jonathan M. Wainwright commanded American and Filipino forces in the Philippines after General MacArthur was directed to leave the Philippines during World War II. He surrendered these forces to the Japanese in 1942. (He was awarded the Medal of Honor.)

FACTS ABOUT SOME OF THE UNIQUE HEADSTONES AND MONUMENTS

1. Most of the opulent (crypts, large headstones) graves are clustered in the Officer's Section - Section 1.

2. Between 1885 and 1895, twenty-six men who had served as generals during the Civil War were buried in Section 1 at Arlington. Many Civil War veterans had unique markers placed at the head of or over their final resting places.

3. Colonel Joseph Cates requested that a huge cannonball formed from polished black marble be placed over his gravesite.

4. The remains of Wallace Fitz Randolph, and those of his wife and daughters, are buried under an actual Civil War-era cannon. (He told his wife that he'd slept under a cannon all of his life, and he wanted to be buried under one.)

5. Lt. John Meigs, the son of General Montgomery Meigs, was killed in action near Harrisonburg, Virginia, in 1864. After his death and burial in Section 1, Lt. Meigs' gravesite was marked with a metal sculpture that shows the young man lying dead in his uniform, his pistol near his boot, and hoof-prints from the Rebels' horses around his body. (Impressive – worth locating.)

6. General Meigs had the remains of unknown soldiers removed from the battlefields surrounding Washington, D.C. and brought to Arlington for burial in a common grave. This tomb was later designated as the Tomb of the Unknown Dead of the Civil War. The remains were broken down by the type of bones, i.e. skulls in one section, legs in another, arms in a third, etc. The remains were sealed in a vault in September 1866. The vault is capped with a granite sarcophagus that reads *"Beneath this stone repose the bones of 2,111 unknown soldiers."* (The vault is located near the Arlington House.)

The Tomb of the Unknown Dead of the Civil War

7. General Meigs had a *"Temple of Fame"* erected near the Arlington House. The monument, which consists of eight marble columns supporting a marble roof, is a dedication to President George Washington and eleven Union Civil War generals.

8. The site of the Temple of Fame was used for memorial services and other events until the Memorial Amphitheater near the Tomb of the Unknowns was dedicated in 1920.

9. The mast of the USS Maine is a memorial to the men who were killed on the battleship in 1898. The remains of 266 of the men are buried at the site. (This tragedy ignited hostilities between Spain and the United States - The Spanish-American War.)

10. One of the most notable memorials at Arlington Cemetery is the Confederate Memorial. This memorial, which is located near the entrance to Fort Myer, is dedicated to the Confederate soldiers who served in the Civil War. Some facts about the memorial are:

The Confederate Memorial

- In 1900, Congress authorized that a section of Arlington Cemetery be set aside for the burial of Confederate dead.

- On March 4, 1906, a request for a Confederate Memorial was granted by then Secretary of War William Howard Taft.

- The Daughters of the Confederacy funded the construction of the Confederate Memorial.

- Former Confederate soldier Moses Ezekiel, a VMI cadet who fought in the Battle of New Market, Virginia, created the Confederate Memorial. (He is buried at the base of the memorial.)

- On November 12, 1912, the cornerstone was laid.

- Was dedicated on June 4, 1914, the 106th anniversary of Jefferson Davis' birth. The dedication was before 3,000 Union and Confederate veterans.

- President Woodrow Wilson (1913-1921) presided over the dedication.

- The memorial is 32 feet high.

- The figure of a woman at the top of the memorial is symbolic of *"Peace."* She faces south and is crowned with olive leaves. In her left hand extends a laurel wreath toward the South, acknowledging the sacrifice of her fallen sons. Her right hand holds a pruning hook resting on a plow stock, which symbolizes the biblical passage "And they shall beat their swords into plows shares and their spears into pruning hooks."

- The plinth on which she stands is embossed with four cinerary urns, symbolizing the four years of the Civil War. Supporting the plinth are 14 inclined shields on the frieze, which depict the coat-of-arms for each one of the 13 Confederate states and Maryland, which supported the South during the war.

- Another frieze is of life-sized figures depicting mythical gods and Southern soldiers. It also includes 6 vignettes illustrating the effect of the war on Southerners of all races.

- There are 482 persons buried around the Confederate Memorial, including 397 Confederate soldiers. Note that unlike the rounded Union headstones, the Confederate headstones are pointed. (It was a common joke by the southerners that the headstones were pointed, so *"No damn Yankees could sit on the stone during their visits to Arlington."*)

OTHER FACTS ABOUT ARLINGTON NATIONAL CEMETERY

1. The initial acreage of Arlington National Cemetery totaled 200 acres. For several years the cemetery totaled 624 acres. Recent acquisitions will enlarge the cemetery to approximately 674 acres.

2. John Metzler Jr. is the current cemetery superintendent. He was appointed in 1991. His father, John Metzler Sr., was a sergeant in the U.S. Army during World War II, and the cemetery's superintendent for 21 years beginning in 1951.

3. Initially, the men and women buried at Arlington were separated by rank (officer/enlisted). This practice has been discontinued.

4. Initially, there were three entrance gates (arches) to Arlington Cemetery. One of the gates honored Union Generals Edward Ord and Godfrey Weitzel, and a second honored Union General Philip Sheridan. The third, and only remaining gate, honors the memory of Union General George B. McClellan, Commander of the Army of the Potomac. It was constructed in 1879, and stands at the original site of the cemetery's main entrance.

The McClellan Arch

5. Until the turn of the 20th century, many different types and sizes of headstones were authorized at Arlington Cemetery. This policy gradually changed to the current one, where there are very few exceptions to a small white headstone.

6. Initially, the government used wooden headboards to mark the gravesites. Cast iron markers later replaced the wooden headboards, which cost $1.23 each. In 1873, Congress approved the shape and size of the current marble headstones.

7. Only government regulation tombstones are allowed in sections opened after 1947.

8. In 1961, Arlington became the first national cemetery to abolish the traditional practice of side-by-side burials. The coffins of family members eligible to be buried at Arlington are buried over each other in a single grave.

9. In 1868, Arlington Cemetery was the site where the first Memorial Day was officially declared and first commemorated.

FACTS ABOUT THE TOMB OF THE UNKNOWNS AT ARLINGTON NATIONAL CEMETERY

The participation of the United States in World War I was short when compared to the fighting endured by the European countries of Great Britain, France, Germany, Austria, and Italy. Hostilities in Europe began in 1914, but it wasn't until 1917 that the United States declared war against the Axis powers (particularly Germany and Austria-Hungry). But even with its delayed entry into the conflict, the United States suffered over 116,000 dead and missing during the period of the war.

After this *"Great War,"* the Allied powers of Great Britain, France, Italy, and the United States took steps to honor their dead and missing warriors. Great Britain and France were first. In 1920, the Unknown Soldier for Great Britain was entombed in the floor of Westminster Abby in London. France honored its Unknown Soldier on the same day with ceremonies at the Arc de Triomphe in Paris. Italy was the next to honor its unknown patriot with ceremonies in Rome on November 4, 1921. And finally, on Armistice Day (now known as Veterans Day), November 11, 1921, the United States honored its Unknown Soldier of World War I through ceremonies at Arlington National Cemetery.

THE TOMB OF THE UNKNOWNS

THE TOMB OF THE UNKNOWN OF WORLD WAR I

1. Of the 4,355,000 servicemen and servicewomen who served in the military during World War I, a total of 116,516 lost their lives while serving their country. Of the total deaths, 53,513 were combat deaths.

2. At the end of World War I, there were 1,237 graves of Americans at cemeteries in the United States and overseas that were marked *"Unknown."* The remains of several other soldiers have never been recovered.

3. In 1921, Congress approved a resolution providing for the burial of an unidentified American soldier at Arlington Cemetery to represent the unknown soldiers of World War I.

4. On March 4, 1921, the last day of his presidency, President Woodrow Wilson (1913-1921) signed a bill authorizing the selection and burial of an unknown American soldier at Arlington Cemetery.

5. In 1921, the remains of four unknown soldiers were exhumed from cemeteries in France, placed in identical caskets, and taken to Charlons-sur-Marne, France.

6. In a formal ceremony, Sergeant Edward F. Younger, a highly decorated combat infantryman of World War I, selected the soldier who would be returned to the United States and entombed in a crypt at Arlington Cemetery. (After his death, Sergeant Younger was buried in Section 18 at Arlington.)

7. Sergeant Younger selected the soldier by placing a spray of white and pink roses on one of the four coffins.

8. The remaining unselected soldiers were reburied at the Romagne Cemetery, France.

9. The remains of the soldier selected as the American Unknown for World War I were returned to the United States onboard the USS Olympia, a cruiser and the former flagship of Admiral Dewey. (The Olympia was decommissioned after carrying the remains of the Unknown Soldier to the United States, and is currently a floating museum on the Delaware River in Philadelphia, Pennsylvania.)

10. On November 9, 1921, after arriving at the U.S. Navy Yard in Washington, D.C., the Unknown Soldier was transported to the Capitol Rotunda to lie in state for two days.

11. The Unknown Soldier was placed on the same catafalque that was used to support the casket of President Abraham Lincoln in 1865.

12. On November 11, 1921, President Warren G. Harding (1921-1923), former President William Taft (1909-1913), and General John "Blackjack" Pershing (Commander of the United States Forces in Europe during World War I) were among those who accompanied the casket to Arlington Cemetery.

13. Former President Woodrow Wilson (1913-1921) attempted to attend the ceremony, but due to ill health, was unable to travel any farther than the White House.

14. The traffic around Arlington Cemetery on the day of the ceremony was so congested that President Harding had to get off the road and travel through Potomac Park on the grass. He was late for the ceremony.

15. To accommodate the over 100,000 people who attended the funeral ceremony, large loud speakers were installed at the ceremony site at Arlington Cemetery.

16. The American Unknown Soldier for World War I was awarded the Medal of Honor and the Distinguished Service Cross.

The Tomb of the Unknowns

17. After the ceremonies, the casket was lowered into a crypt that had been layered with two inches of French soil.

18. Many attending the ceremony believed the highlight of the ceremony occurred when Chief Plenty Coup, a Crow Indian, placed his war bonnet on the sarcophagus in tribute to the Unknown Soldier.

19. Lorimer Rich designed the Tomb of the Unknown. (Rich is buried in Section 48 at Arlington.)

20. Thomas Hudson Jones shaped the Tomb of the Unknown.

21. The Tomb of the Unknown was constructed from Yule marble quarried in Colorado.

22. The Tomb of the Unknown, without the crypt, weighs 79 tons.

23. The Tomb of the Unknown consists of seven individual pieces assembled into four primary sections. These primary sections consist of:

   - A one piece, 16-ton Base

   - A four piece, 15-ton Sub-base

   - A one piece, 36-ton Dye

   - A one piece, 12-ton Cap

24. The dimensions of the Tomb of the Unknown are:

   - At its highest point, the Tomb is 10 feet, 3/4 inches high.

   - The width at the bottom of the Tomb is 8 feet.

   - The length at the bottom of the Tomb is 13 feet, 11 inches.

25. The three figures on the shrine represent *"Peace," "Victory,"* and *"Valor."* Peace is holding a dove, Victory is holding a palm branch, and Valor is holding a sword – *"Peace through Victory by Valor."*

26. On each of the north and south faces of the Tomb are three wreaths. Each wreath represents one of the six major campaigns of World War I that American servicemen fought in. These campaigns consist of Chateau-Thierry, Ardennes, Oise-Aisne, Meuse-Argonne, Belleau Wood, and the Somme.

27. The wreaths are inverted to represent mourning.

28. No one knows who authored the phrase *"Here Rests in Honored Glory An American Soldier Known but to God"* that is engraved into the Tomb of the Unknown of World War I.

29. On December 28, 1931, the cap to the Tomb of the Unknown was installed.

30. On April 9, 1932, the Tomb of the Unknown was opened to the public.

31. The construction cost of the Tomb of the Unknown totaled $48,000.

THE TOMBS OF THE UNKNOWNS OF WORLD WAR II AND THE KOREAN WAR

1. After World War II, it was decided to bury the remains of a World War II unknown soldier in a duplicate tomb just below the tomb of the unknown soldier of World War I. However, because of the United States' combat action in the Korean War at the time, construction of the tomb was delayed.

2. During World War II (1941-1945), there were 87,976 American servicemen (excluding merchant marines) whose remains could not be identified or recovered.

3. During the Korean War (1950-1953), there were 9,037 servicemen whose remains could not be identified or recovered.

4. After the end of the Korean War, it was decided to honor the unknown soldiers of both World War II and the Korean War on the same date - Memorial Day, May 30, 1958.

5. The procedures for selecting the Unknown Soldiers of World War II and the Korean War were:

   • On May 12, 1958, at the Epinal American Military Cemetery in France, thirteen unidentified American remains from Europe and North Africa were brought together for selection.

233

- On May 12, 1958, Major General Edward O'Neil placed a wreath before one of the coffins. This act designated the remains as a candidate for the Tomb of the Unknown Soldier of World War II.

- On May 15, 1958, Master Sergeant Ned Lyle selected the Korean War Unknown on the island of Oahu, Hawaii. The wreath of blue and white carnations represented the Korean Service Medal.

- On May 16, 1958, six remains from the Pacific theater of World War II were brought to Hickam Air Force Base, Hawaii.

- On May 16, 1958. Colonel Glenn Eagleston placed a lei on the selected candidate from the Pacific theater of World War II.

- On May 26, 1958, the remains of the World War II and Korean War casualties were placed in new bronze caskets and arranged on the deck of the USS Canberra off the coast of Cape Henry, Virginia. (The Canberra was a heavy cruiser that was named in honor of the Australian cruiser HMAS Canberra, which was severely damaged by gunfire and torpedoes from Japanese warships, and subsequently sunk by USN warships at the Battle of Savo Island in 1942.)

- The casket of the Korean War Unknown was placed between the two Unknowns of World War II.

- Seaman First Class William R. Charette, the Navy's only active duty Medal of Honor recipient, placed a floral wreath in front of the casket containing the remains of the soldier selected as the World War II Unknown.

6. The remains of the unselected serviceman from World War II were buried at sea 8 miles off the coast of Cape Henry, Virginia. (This distance from the shore is required for deep sea burials.)

7. The remains of the Honored Unknowns of World War II and the Korean War were returned to the United States onboard the USS Blandy. (The USS Blandy was a destroyer that was named for Admiral William H. P. Blandy.)

8. On May 27, 1958, the Honored Unknowns arrived at the U.S. Navy Yard in Washington, D.C.

9. On May 28, 1958, the Honored Unknowns were transported to the Capitol Rotunda to lie in state.

10. On May 30, 1958, the Unknowns were buried at Arlington Cemetery in a ceremony that was attended by 216 surviving Medal of Honor recipients. (A total of 464 Medals of Honor were awarded for services during World War II, and 131 for services during the Korean War.)

11. Both unknown servicemen were presented the Medal of Honor by President Dwight D. Eisenhower (1953-1961).

THE TOMB OF THE UNKNOWN OF THE VIETNAM WAR

1. The latest unknown serviceman represented the dead and missing of the Vietnam War (1958 - 1975).

2. Over 58,000 servicemen and servicewomen sacrificed their lives or were declared missing in action while participating in this very unpopular war.

3. As of 2006, over 1,800 servicemen remain missing.

4. Of all the remains recovered from the battlefields of North Vietnam, South Vietnam, Laos, and Thailand, only one set of recovered remains was unidentifiable at the time the Unknown of the Vietnam War was laid to rest at Arlington Cemetery.

5. Even though there was only one set of remains, tradition called for a dockside ceremony in Pearl Harbor, Hawaii, where Sergeant Major Kellog selected the remains of the Vietnam War Unknown. Sergeant Kellog was the recipient of the Medal of Honor from the Vietnam War. (He threw himself on a live hand grenade in order to save his comrades.)

6. This one set of remains was transported from Hawaii to Washington, D.C. On May 25, 1984, upon arriving at Washington, D.C., the remains were transported to the Capitol Building, where they lay in honor for three days.

7. On May 28, 1984, the remains were transported on a caisson to Arlington Cemetery.

8. President Ronald Reagan (1981-1989) presented the unknown serviceman with the Medal of Honor during the ceremonies.

9. On May 14, 1998, the remains of the Unknown of the Vietnam War were disinterred for DNA testing to determine if the remains could be identified.

10. On June 30, 1998, it was announced that the remains had been identified as those of Air Force Lieutenant Michael J. Blassie. The 24-year-old flyer, who was shot down near An Loc, South Vietnam, on May 11, 1972, was later reburied at the Jefferson Barracks National Cemetery near St. Louis, Missouri.

11. A request from Lieutenant Blassie's family for the Medal of Honor that was awarded to him when he represented the Unknowns of the Vietnam War was denied. The medal will remain displayed next to the other medals awarded to the Unknowns of World War I, World War II, and Korean War in the amphitheater, and will represent the other unknowns of the Vietnam War.

12. The Department of Defense decided in 2000 that no remains from the Vietnam War would be placed in the crypt at the Tomb of the Unknowns unless it is proven that they will never be identified.

13. An inscription has been placed on the crypt cover of the Vietnam War Unknown that reads *"Honoring and Keeping Faith with America's Missing Servicemen, 1958-1975."*

UNIQUE FACTS ABOUT THE TOMB OF THE UNKNOWNS

1. Unlike the Tomb of the Unknown of World War I, a large exterior marble cap does not cover the Unknowns from World War II, the Korean War, and the Vietnam War. However, the remains of these honored dead are very well protected. On top of each tomb is a four-ton piece of marble inscribed with the name of the war in which the Unknown made the ultimate sacrifice for his country. Below the marble, eight tons of concrete add even more protection. And finally, a one-inch steel plate covers the steel vault containing the casket of the Unknown. The marble covering each crypt is 42 inches wide by 98 1/4 inches long, and is 10 inches thick.

2. When the remains of the Unknowns were buried, U.S. Presidents or Vice President represented the next of kin. President Warren Harding (1921-1923) represented the Unknown of World War I, President Dwight Eisenhower (1953-1961) represented the Unknown of World War II, Vice-President Richard Nixon (1953-1961) represented the Unknown of the Korean War, and President Ronald Reagan (1981-1989) represented the Unknown of the Vietnam War.

3. On June 2, 1958, each crypt of the Unknowns of World War II and Korean War were filled with a concrete slab and topped with white marble. The marble tops bore only dates: 1941-1945 for the World War II Unknown, and 1950-1953 for the Korean War Unknown. At the same time, the dates 1917-1918 were carved into the pavement in front of the Tomb of the Unknown for World War I.

4. The Medals of Honor awarded to the honored unknowns <u>are not</u> buried with their remains. After the ceremonies the medals are secured in the Trophy Room of the Amphitheater.

THE HISTORY OF THE 3rd INFANTRY - "OLD GUARD"

1. The origin of the American version of the *"Old Guard"* was the First American Regiment, who fought under the command of George Washington during the American Revolutionary War.

2. General George Washington chose the color blue for the uniform of the First American Regiment.

3. During 1846-1848, the 3rd Infantry fought in Mexico.

4. The 3rd Infantry was first referred to as the *"Old Guard of the Army"* by General Winfield Scott as a testimony to the 3rd Infantry's service during the war with Mexico.

5. The 3rd Infantry fought in many major battles during the American Civil War. Over 90% of the soldiers in the 3rd Infantry became casualties during the conflict.

6. Because of its outstanding service during the Civil War, the 3rd Infantry was selected to lead the Union armies during the Grand Review (parade) down the streets of Washington, D.C. at the end of the Civil War.

7. In November 1946, because of budget cuts and the restructuring of the U.S. military, the 3rd Infantry was deactivated.

8. In April 1948, because of its notable history, the 3rd Infantry was reactivated to provide security for Washington, D.C., and to participate in ceremonies.

9. The 3rd Infantry is headquartered at Fort Myer, Virginia, an Army installation adjacent to Arlington Cemetery.

10. The strength of the *"Old Guard"* number between 1,200 and 2,000 personnel.

11. The 3rd Infantry is the official ceremonial unit for the U.S. Army.

12. The 3rd Infantry is the oldest active infantry unit of the U.S. Army.

13. In addition to duties at Arlington Cemetery, the *"Old Guard"* participates in between 3,000 and 4,000 ceremonies annually at the White House, Pentagon, and national memorials and cemeteries.

14. The 3rd Infantry is the only U.S. military unit that has a Fife and Drum Corps. (This is the corps that performs in colonial dress.)

15. It is the 3rd Infantry that places the flags before each of the headstones just before Memorial Day. Since 1948, this tribute, which is known as "Flags-in," calls for a small United States flag to be placed one foot from and centered in front of each headstone. Flags are also placed before each columbarium niche and before each of the four crypts at the Tomb of the Unknowns.

16. Until 1994, because the *"Old Guard"* is a combat unit, women were not assigned to the unit.

THE HONOR GUARD AT THE TOMB OF THE UNKNOWNS

1. From November 1921 to 1925, there was no watchman or Honor Guard assigned to protect the Tomb of the Unknown. This lack of security allowed people to walk over the crypt of the honored dead, many actually enjoyed picnics on the plaza.

2. From 1925 to 1926, a civilian watchman was responsible for protecting the Tomb of the Unknown. (At this time only the remains of a soldier killed in World War I were buried at the site.)

The Changing of the Guard at the Tomb of the Unknowns

3. From 1926 to 1937, a military guard was posted at the Tomb of the Unknown during daylight hours only.

4. In 1937, the twenty-four-hour military Honor Guard at the Tomb of the Unknown was established.

5. On April 6, 1948, the 3rd United States Infantry assumed the sole responsibility for guarding the Tomb of the Unknown.

6. Members of the Honor Guard are assigned to Company "E" of the 3rd United States Infantry.

7. Members of the Honor Guard perform their duties at the Tomb of the Unknowns for an average period of between 12 and 18 months. (There is no set period for assignment.)

8. Both men and women may be selected to perform duties as an Honor Guard.

9. Only 20 percent (one out of every five) of the soldiers who apply for duties as an Honor Guard are selected.

10. All soldiers, including female soldiers, who are selected for Honor Guard duties at the Tomb of the Unknowns must be between 5 feet, 10 inches and 6 feet, 4 inches tall. Depending on their height, each soldier is assigned to what is referred to as a "Relief." The height of the members assigned to each Relief consists of the following:

   - 1st Relief – 6 feet, 2 inches to 6 feet, 4 inches
   - 2nd Relief – 6 feet to 6 feet, 2 inches
   - 3rd Relief – 5 feet, 10 inches to 6 feet

11. Each Relief (shift) consists of a Relief Commander and about 6 Sentinels. (The number of Sentinels is dependent on the number of proficient Sentinels available.)

12. A Relief (shift) of Honor Guards is commanded by Non-commissioned Officers (NCOs). There are five levels of responsibilities at the Tomb of the Unknowns. These levels consist of the following:

   - Sentinel (soldier who stands watch at the Tomb). They usually serve in the ranks of Private First Class through Specialist. Average age is 22.

240

- Assistant Relief Commander (ARC). They serve in the rank of Corporal or Sergeant, and are the Relief Commander's chief assistants. Average age is 24.

- Relief Commander (RC). They serve in the rank of Staff Sergeant, and are responsible for conducing the Changing of the Guard, and the welfare and morale of the Relief as a whole. Average age is 27.

- Assistant Sergeant of the Guard (ASOG). They typically serve in the rank of senior Staff Sergeant in the platoon, and are primarily responsible for conducting the daily administrative duties associated with the Relief, including the initial training of the new Sentinels. Average age is 28-29.

- Sergeant of the Guard (SOG). They serve in the rank of Sergeant First Class, whose primary duties and responsibilities include Presidential Wreath Ceremonics, as well as the overall responsibility for the conduct and actions of the platoon. Average age is 30.

13. For several weeks after being selected as an Honor Guard, the *"New Man"* is trained by experienced members of the Honor Guard, and performs duties as an Honor Guard during night walks only. His shift is usually two hours in length.

14. After approximately nine months of duty, the *"New Man's"* knowledge of the cemetery and the history of the military are evaluated. A score of at least 95% must be obtained. The *"New Man's"* dress, walk, and how he presents himself are also rated.

15. The Tomb Guard Badge was first authorized on September 9, 1957. It was created in February 1958.

16. The Tomb Guard Badge is a silver color metal badge 2 inches in width by 1 15/32 inches in height, consisting of an inverted open laurel wreath surmounted by a representation of the front elevation of the Tomb of the Unknown Soldier, the upper section containing the three figures of Peace, Victory, and Valor, the base bearing in two lines the words "HONOR GUARD", all in low relief.

17. The members of the Honor Guard must serve honorably for nine months before they are authorized to wear the badge permanently.

18. If the *"New Man"* is deemed proficient, he is entitled to wear the Tomb Guard Badge on a temporary basis.

19. If soldiers are awarded the Tomb Guard Badge, and they fail to conduct themselves at the level required of an Honor Guard, even if they leave the Army, then the authorization to wear and even possess the badge is revoked. (Each badge awarded is assigned a number, and the number is hung on the office wall of the Honor Guards. If the wearing of the badge is revoked, then the round metal tag that has the number of the badge is removed, and is replaced by one that has the word "Revoked" imprinted on it.)

20. Because wool is the only fabric that will adequately hold a crease in hot weather, it is the only fabric used for the blouse worn by the Honor Guard.

21. During the hours Arlington Cemetery is open to the public; all uniforms are dress Army blues, reminiscent of the uniforms worn by the Continental Army during the American Revolution and the Union soldiers during the Civil War. The style currently worn by the Honor Guards is similar to the style worn by Army personnel in the late part of the 1800s.

22. The uniforms are not tailored, so excess material is tucked into the belt issued to the Honor Guard.

23. The shoes worn by the Honor Guard are standard Army issue, with additional layers of soles to protect the soldier's feet from heat and cold.

24. During the hours Arlington Cemetery is closed to the public, the Honor Guards wear what is referred to as BDUs (Basic Drab Uniform). This uniform consists of camouflaged fatigues and combat boots. Subdued Honor Guard badges are authorized in cloth on the BDUs. The cloth badge consists of an olive green base cloth with the badge in black and olive green embroidery.

25. The Honor Guard may wear an overcoat when the temperature falls below 45 degrees, and a raincoat during inclement weather.

26. The Honor Guards (Sentinel) currently carry an M14 rifle, which weighs 9.5 pounds. (The M14 rifle has been used by the Honor Guards since 1960. It replaced the Garand M1 rifle, which weighs 11.2 pounds and was used by the Honor Guards from 1948 to 1960.)

27. The M14 rifle is basically a product improved M1 Garand. The M14 has an effective range of 500 yards, uses a 7.62 cartridge in a 20-round magazine.

28. The bayonet/knife on the M14 is an M6 bayonet with a total length of 11.5 inches (6.75 inch blade). It has been used by the Honor Guards since 1960.

29. To provide a better grip on the custom-made, wood-handled M14 rifle, the Honor Guards (Sentinels) may dampen their cotton gloves with water prior to assuming their duties at the Tomb of the Unknowns.

30. As the Honor Guard paces, which is referred to as the "Walk", the rifle is always on the shoulder away from the Tomb. The rifle is on the left shoulder when the guard paces north, and is on the right shoulder when the guard paces south. This right and left shoulder arms symbolizes the act of protecting the Tombs.

31. The Honor Guard paces in front of the Tomb at a pace of 90 steps per minute.

32. The handgun carried by the Sergeant of the Guard is a M9 Baretta 9mm.

33. The duties of the Tomb Guard are staffed using a rotating system. Each relief has the following schedule: First day on, one day off, second day on, one day off, third day on, four days off. Then their schedule is repeated. (Much of the off time is used for preparing for the next shift, training, etc.)

34. During the daylight hours of winter (October 1 through March 31), the Changing of the Guard ceremony occurs on the hour.

35. During the daylight hours of summer (April 1 through September 30), the Changing of the Guard ceremony occurs every 30 minutes.

36. At night, whatever the season, the Honor Guard is on duty for a 2-hour shift.

37. The black mat on the plaza in front of the crypt is 63 feet long, and is replaced each Memorial Day.

38. The Honor Guard takes 21 steps across the mat, faces the Tomb for 21 seconds, and then turns for the return 21 steps. The number 21 (i.e., 21 gun salute etc.) is considered the highest level of honor bestowed on the subject receiving the honor. The *"New Man"* is tested for the correct and consistent number of steps and seconds.

39. The Honor Guard paces north to south, then retraces his steps.

40. A shelter, which is referred to as the "Box", is located to the left of the Tomb as visitors look from the Memorial Amphitheater steps. The "Box" is used by the Sentinel to retreat to while flowers and Taps are being presented. There is also a phone with a direct line to the Tomb Guard Quarters for emergencies.

41. The Honor Guards participate in more than 1,500 ceremonies at the Tomb of the Unknowns each year.

42. The first female to serve as an Honor Guard at the Tomb of the Unknowns was Sergeant Heather Lynn Johnsen. The 5 feet, 11 inches tall former military policewoman was awarded the Tomb Guard Identification Badge on March 25, 1996. (The license plate on her car during the time she served read "TOMB GRL.")

43. Twenty-one year old Sergeant Danyell Wilson was the second woman, and first African-American woman, to earn the privilege of serving as an Honor Guard at the Tomb of the Unknowns. This occurred in 1997.

FACTS ABOUT THE MEMORIAL AMPHITHEATER AT ARLINGTON NATIONAL CEMETERY

Initially, the Memorial Amphitheater was constructed to pay homage to the servicemen and servicewomen who died in conflicts fought by the United States prior to World War I. The conflicts include the Revolutionary War, War of 1812, Mexican War, Civil War, and Spanish-American War. Since the Tomb of the Unknown Soldier was dedicated in 1921, the Amphitheater has played a significant part in the ceremonies rendered to the servicemen who rest in the Tomb of the Unknowns, and to all American servicemen and servicewomen who have made the ultimate sacrifice for their country.

THE MEMORIAL AMPHITHEATER

1. On October 13, 1915, construction on the Memorial Amphitheater was started.

2. The Amphitheater was designed to hold crowds of up to 5,000 people.

3. President Woodrow Wilson (1913-1921) dedicated the cornerstone to the Amphitheater.

The Exterior of the Amphitheater on the side of the Tomb of the Unknowns

4. The cornerstone to the Amphitheater contains the designs for the structure, an autographed photo of President Woodrow Wilson (1913-1921), a copy of the day's program, and other memorabilia from the period.

5. On May 15, 1920, the dedication ceremonies for America's "*Temple of Patriotism*" were conducted.

6. A United States flag, with a field of 36 stars, was flown on a special flagpole until the cornerstone was installed. The flag signified the 36 states in the Union at the end of the Civil War. (The 36 states consisted of the 34 states in the Union at the beginning of the Civil War, plus the 2 states that entered the Union after the start of the Civil War. The additional states were West Virginia in 1863, and Nevada in 1864.)

7. Once the cornerstone was installed, the Civil War era flag was replaced with one consisting of a field of 48 stars, one star for each state in the Union at the time of the ceremony.

8. The Amphitheater was originally constructed with 48 crypts under the colonnade.

9. Even though the crypts were intended to accommodate the remains of citizens from the individual states, they were never used for this purpose.

The Interior of the Amphitheater

10. President Woodrow Wilson (1913-1921) established the precedent for presidential visits to the Amphitheater.

11. In 1976, the Amphitheater was renovated to create office space and install new restroom facilities. This renovation eliminated many of the crypts. The Honor Guards use some of the remaining crypts for office space, storage, and drill practice.

12. The United States flags that covered the coffins of the Unknown Servicemen, and the medals awarded them, are displayed in a room of the Amphitheater. In 1997, the room that safeguards these treasures was renovated.

FACTS ABOUT THE KENNEDY GRAVESITES AT ARLINGTON NATIONAL CEMETERY

Almost from the day John F. Kennedy was elected to the Presidency of the United States in November 1960, he and his immediate family were considered the primary figures in an American version of "*Camelot.*" Young, full of energy, handsome, and beautiful, they were perceived as what was right with the world, and it would be through their efforts the world would be made safer and better for generations to come. However, this dream for the future was shattered on November 22, 1963, when a madman with a gun extinguished a glowing star in the form of John F. Kennedy. A second horrible tragedy occurred on June 5, 1968, when Robert F. Kennedy (the president's brother, former U.S. Attorney General, and U.S. Senator) was killed by a terrorist who chose to be remembered through one act of cowardliness versus a lifetime of good.

Gone, but not forgotten, John Kennedy, Jacqueline Kennedy, and Robert Kennedy rest with other distinguished Americans and fallen heroes at Arlington National Cemetery. They are visited by millions of visitors each year, many of whom bring with them memories of what it was, and what it could have been, if "*Camelot*" would have been allowed to flourish.

THE LIFE AND BURIAL OF JOHN F. KENNEDY

1. On May 29, 1916, John F. Kennedy was born in Brookline, Massachusetts.

2. Prior to being elected to the presidency, Kennedy graduated from Harvard, served in the U.S. Navy during World War II, and was credited with saving the lives of several of his men when their patrol boat (PT-109) was rammed by a Japanese destroyer. Kennedy also wrote the book "*Profiles of Courage*" and served as a member of the House of Representatives and a U.S. Senator from Massachusetts.

3. In November 1960, at age 43, Kennedy became the youngest man and first Catholic to be elected to the presidency.

4. On January 20, 1961, Kennedy was sworn in as the 35th President of the United States.

5. During his presidency, Kennedy was known for his fight against organized crime, support of civil rights, the failed *"Bay of Pigs"* invasion of Cuba, pushing for space explorations, and the 1962 crisis between the United States and the Soviet Union over the removal of Soviet made missiles from Cuba.

6. On November 22, 1963 (Friday) at 12:30 p.m. (Eastern Standard Time), in Dallas, Texas, President Kennedy was shot by an assassin using a high-powered rifle. The first shot struck him in the throat, the second in the head.

7. On November 22nd, at 1 p.m. (Eastern Standard Time), President Kennedy was pronounced dead. He was just age 46.

8. On November 22nd, President Kennedy's body was returned to Washington, D.C. on the presidential plane *Air Force One*. (The flight took 2 hours and 18 minutes.)

9. From late afternoon on November 23rd through early afternoon on November 24th, President Kennedy's body lay at rest in the East Room of the White House.

10. From the afternoon of November 24th through late morning on November 25th, President Kennedy's body lay in state in the Rotunda of the United States Capitol Building. An estimated 200,000 people viewed the closed casket containing his body.

11. On November 25th, services for President Kennedy were conducted at St. Matthew's Cathedral in Washington, D.C.

12. After the funeral services on November 25th, the body of President Kennedy was carried on a caisson to Arlington National Cemetery.

13. After President Kennedy's body arrived at the cemetery, fifty fighter jets, each one representing a state in the Union, flew directly over the gravesite, followed by *Air Force One*. (The pilot of *Air Force One* (Colonel James Swindal) dipped the wings of the aircraft in a final salute, once to the left and once to the right.)

14. On November 25, 1963, at 3:13 p.m. (Monday), Mrs. Jacqueline Kennedy, with the aid of Robert Kennedy (President Kennedy's younger brother), lit the eternal flame at Kennedy's gravesite.

15. Initially, there were three possible gravesites considered for the burial of President Kennedy at Arlington Cemetery. The first was near the mast of the USS Maine; the second was on Dewey Circle, and the third was below the Arlington House. Robert Kennedy chose the site below the Arlington House, which was later approved by Mrs. Kennedy.

16. Mrs. Kennedy requested that President Kennedy's burial be modeled after the ceremonies rendered to President Abraham Lincoln in 1865. She also requested that a contingency of the Irish Guards be present at the president's burial.

17. The mahogany coffin in which President Kennedy was buried weighs 1,200 pounds.

18. To prepare themselves for the weight of the coffin on the day of the burial, the honor guard practiced carrying a coffin similar in weight to that of the president's. To add to the weight, two men sat on the coffin while it was being carried during the practice sessions.

19. The bronze casket that contained President Kennedy's body from Dallas, Texas, to Washington, D.C. had a handle broken while it was being transported. To eliminate the possibility of the casket becoming a morbid piece of displayed history, it was flown to a spot off the Maryland-Delaware coast, and dropped in 9,000 feet of water.

20. On the day President Kennedy was buried, 23 other burials were performed at Arlington Cemetery.

21. The items buried with President Kennedy consist of three letters, a pair of cufflinks, a piece of scrimshaw (decorative work) engraved with the Presidential Seal, a silver rosary, and a PT-109 tie clasp. (PT-109 was the number of the patrol torpedo boat Kennedy commanded when it was sunk by the Japanese during World War II.)

22. Two of the Kennedy children were buried near their father on December 4, 1963. (Patrick, who predeceased his father by just 15 weeks, was moved from Brookline, Massachusetts, and an unnamed stillborn daughter from Newport, Rhode Island.)

23. Construction of President Kennedy's permanent gravesite began in 1965, and was completed on July 20, 1967.

24. The 3.2-acre site is just below where President Kennedy was first laid to rest.

25. During the night of March 14, 1967, the bodies of President Kennedy and his two children were moved to their permanent graves.

The Kennedy Gravesite

26. The Kennedy gravesite consists of Massachusetts granite selected by the Kennedy family and quarried from a site near the president's home in Massachusetts. The sedum and fescue plants between the stones are intended to give the appearance of stones lying naturally in a Massachusetts field.

27. It is believed Mrs. Kennedy got the idea for the *"eternal flame"* when she recalled the eternal flame at the Tomb of the Unknown Soldier of World War I at the Arc de Triomphe in Paris, France, during an earlier visit to the city.

28. The flame burns from the center of a five-foot circular flat-granite stone at the head of the grave.

29. To ensure the flame is not snuffed out by rain or snow, there is a constant electric spark at the tip of the nozzle.

30. The fuel used for the flame is natural gas mixed with a controlled quantity of air to achieve the color and shape of the flame.

31. While living at Arlington, Robert E. Lee and his family often enjoyed picnics on the site that is now the Kennedy gravesite.

32. President Kennedy was shot and killed in Dallas, Texas, while campaigning for re-election. A federal investigation committee determined Lee Harvey Oswald was the sole killer of the president. Jack Ruby, a Dallas strip-tease-club owner, killed Oswald on November 24, 1963, while Oswald was in the custody of the Dallas Police. In 1967, Ruby died of cancer while in prison.

33. There are several thoughts about whether Oswald was the sole perpetrator of the murder of President Kennedy. Some people believe the Soviets or Cubans were responsible for the killing, others believe the Central Intelligence Agency was involved, a third group believe organized crime (Mafia) wanted President Kennedy dead, and a fourth group felt Oswald was just a *"nut"* who wanted to be remembered in history for his infamous crime.

34. In 1972, a 23-year-old Army veteran from Michigan knelt down on Kennedy's grave and plunged a kitchen knife into his chest. He died seven hours later.

35. In 1982, an extremely intoxicated man went to the Kennedy gravesite during the night. While kneeling near the *"eternal flame"* he suffered a heart attack and died. His grotesquely burned body was found on the flame the next morning.

36. In 1997, someone made an unsuccessful attempt at removing some of the granite paving stones covering the Kennedy gravesite. An impossible task considering the stones extend several feet underground, weigh 500 pounds each, and are anchored to one another.

THE LIFE AND BURIAL OF ROBERT F. KENNEDY

1. On November 20, 1925, Robert F. Kennedy was born in Brookline, Massachusetts.

2. Robert graduated from Harvard University and the University of Virginia (law degree).

3. Robert was instrumental in the successful election campaigns of his brother John F. Kennedy; was the U.S. Attorney General from 1961-1964, and served as a U.S. Senator from New York from 1965 to his death in 1968.

4. On June 5, 1968, at age 42, Robert was shot while campaigning for the presidency of the United States in Los Angeles, California. He died the next day.

5. Robert left a widow and 11 children.

6. Robert's service in the Navy during World War II and his position as a U.S. Senator, qualified him for burial at Arlington Cemetery.

Gravesite of Robert Kennedy

7. Burial ceremonies were conducted at Arlington Cemetery after the funeral motorcade arrived at the cemetery at 10:30 p.m., June 8, 1968. Over 1,500 candles were distributed to the mourners.

8. The folded flag of the United States was presented to Robert's wife, Ethel, by former astronaut and U.S. Senator John Glenn.

9. In 1971, Robert's formal gravesite was completed.

10. Two of Robert's most notable addresses are inscribed at his gravesite. One of which is his 1968 self-evaluation *"Some men see things as they are and ask 'Why?', I dream of things that never were and ask, 'Why not'"*

11. Robert's burial has been the only nighttime burial conducted at Arlington Cemetery.

THE LIFE AND BURIAL OF JACQUELINE L. KENNEDY

1. On July 28, 1929, Jacqueline (Jackie) Kennedy was born Jacqueline L. Bouvier in South Hampton, New York.

2. Jacqueline Bouvier graduated from George Washington University.

3. On September 12, 1953, Jacqueline Bouvier married John F. Kennedy.

4. Jacqueline became first lady at age 31.

5. On November 22, 1963, Jacqueline was widowed as a result of the assassination of President Kennedy.

6. In 1968, Jacqueline married Aristotle Onassis.

7. On May 19, 1994, Jacqueline Bouvier Kennedy Onassis died of cancer at age 64. On May 23, 1994, she was buried next to her first husband, John Kennedy.

8. On October 6, 1994, Jacqueline's grave marker was installed.

9. On July 16, 1999, at age 38, her son, John F. Kennedy Jr., was killed in a plane crash with his wife, Carolyn Bessette Kennedy, age 33, and sister-in-law Lauren Bessette, age 34. Their remains were buried at sea off the coast of Massachusetts near the site of the accident on July 22, 1999. (John's grandmother, Rose Kennedy, was born on July 22, 1890.)

10. Her daughter, Caroline, survives Jacqueline.

COINCIDENCES BETWEEN PRESIDENTS LINCOLN AND KENNEDY

John and Jacqueline Kennedy admired the life and accomplishments of President Abraham Lincoln (1861-1865). After Kennedy's death it was determined that there were several coincidences between the lives and deaths of Lincoln and Kennedy. The coincidences include:

- Lincoln was elected president in 1860, Kennedy in 1960.
- Both were shot from behind and in the head.
- Their successors, both named Johnson, were southern Democrats (Andrew from Kentucky, Lyndon from Texas), and both were former senators.
- Andrew Johnson was born in 1808, and Lyndon Johnson was born in 1908.
- John Wilkes Booth was born in 1839, and Lee Harvey Oswald was born in 1939.
- Both presidents lost children through death while in the White House.
- Lincoln's secretary, whose name was Kennedy, advised him not to go to the theater.
- Kennedy's secretary, whose name was Lincoln, advised him not to go to Dallas.
- John Wilkes Booth shot Lincoln in a theater and ran to a warehouse.
- Lee Harvey Oswald shot Kennedy from a warehouse and ran to a theater.
- The names Lincoln and Kennedy each contain seven letters.
- The names Andrew Johnson and Lyndon Johnson each contain thirteen letters.
- The names John Wilkes Booth and Lee Harvey Oswald each contain fifteen letters.
- Both assassins were killed before being brought to trial.
- Both Johnsons were opposed for re-election by men whose names start with "G," Grant and Goldwater. (Grant won the election, Goldwater lost.)
- Both were married while in their 30s to women in their 20s.
- Lincoln won a seat in the House of Representatives in 1846. Kennedy won a seat to the House in 1946.

254

- Lincoln tried and failed to get his party's nomination for vice president in 1856, and Kennedy failed in 1956.
- Stephen A. Douglas, who was born in 1813, was defeated by Lincoln for the presidency in 1860. Richard Nixon, who was born in 1913, was defeated by Kennedy in 1960.
- Lincoln and Kennedy were both shot on a Friday as they sat next to their wives.

UNIQUE FACTS ABOUT THE PRESIDENTIAL PLANE – "AIR FORCE ONE"

1. Any plane that transports the President of the United States is designated "Air Force One" while the president is onboard. It is designated "Air Force Two" when it transports the Vice President of the United States.

2. The Boeing 707 that carried the body of John F. Kennedy from Dallas, Texas, to Washington, D.C. after his assassination on November 22, 1963, later carried Lyndon B. Johnson's body to Texas after his state funeral on January 24, 1973, in Washington, D.C. (Lyndon B. Johnson was sworn in as President of the United States on the plane after Kennedy's assassination.)

3. In March 1998, after 36 years of service, the plane designated SAM 26000, was retired from service, and is on display at Wright-Patterson AFB, Ohio.

FACTS ABOUT THE WOMEN IN MILITARY SERVICE FOR AMERICA MEMORIAL AT THE GATEWAY TO ARLINGTON NATIONAL CEMETERY

History has recorded countless acts of valor by women who have served their country during times of war and national crisis. From the days of the Revolutionary War, when Molly Pitcher replaced her husband as a cannoneer during the Battle of Monmouth, to the women in the cockpits of jets during the conflicts in the Middle East, American women have been quick to answer the call to duty. The Women In Military Service For America Memorial is a long overdue tribute to the service, bravery, and professionalism of the officers and enlisted women who have made unlimited contributions to the protection of the United States. To quote Vice President Gore at the memorial's dedication ceremonies, "*At long last, here in our nation's capital, we can unveil a memorial that says to every servicewoman, past and present, thank you for what you have done.*"

THE ARLINGTON CEMETERY HEMICYCLE

1. One of the highlights of the Women In Military Service For America Memorial is the Arlington Cemetery Hemicycle. The hemicycle is a 30-foot-high, neoclassical retaining wall that was designed by McKim, Mead, and White in 1927, and was dedicated in 1932 by President Herbert Hoover (1929-1933).

2. The Arlington Cemetery Hemicycle was initially intended to be a gateway to Arlington Cemetery. It was part of the construction plan that included the Memorial Bridge.

Women In Military Service For America Memorial

3. Due to the Great Depression of the late 1920s and 1930s, construction was halted on the Hemicycle. The Hemicycle was not completed until the construction of the Women In Military Service For America Memorial.

4. The basic building material of the Hemicycle is reinforced concrete, faced with Mount Airy Granite from a quarry in Virginia.

5. The Hemicycle is 226 feet long by 30 feet high.

6. The thickness of the front wall of the Hemicycle ranges from 2 feet, 6 inches to 3 feet, 6 inches.

7. Decorative elements of the Hemicycle wall include the symbolic laurel and oak leaf wreaths used to honor valor and sacrifice, Greek key patterns, rosettes, tridents, faces, and Roman sacrificial urns.

8. The wall of the Hemicycle includes 10 niches with pilasters on each side. The outer, center and middle niches on each side are semicircular 3 feet 6 inches deep. The two other niches on each side are rectangular 2 feet deep. All niches are 19 feet high by 9 feet across. There is an oak leaf wreath within the rectangular niches. At the center of the circular wall is a large semicircular niche, the Great Niche, which is 20 feet across by 30 feet high, containing accent panels and coffers of red Texas granite. At its base is a fountain. Forming the keystone of the Great Niche is the Great Seal of the United States of America. On each side of the Great Niche and slightly lower than the Great Seal of the United States are large Seals of the Department of War (now the Army) and the Department of the Navy.

9. On the sides of the Hemicycle are two large ornate wrought iron gates. The one on the north side is the Schley Gate, named after Admiral Winfield Scott Schley (Hero of the Battle of Santiago, Cuba, during the Spanish-American War of 1898). The one on the south is named in honor of President Theodore Roosevelt (1901-1909).

10. The iron gates were refurbished by the Women In Military Service For America Memorial Foundation as part of the restoration of the Hemicycle and construction of the Women's Memorial, and presented as a gift by the Foundation to the American public.

11. The seals for the U.S. Marine Corps and the U.S. Army are on the Roosevelt Gate. The seals of the U.S. Navy and U.S. Coast Guard are on the Schley Gate. (The U.S. Air Force was not established as a separate branch of the military until 1947, several years after the gates were installed in 1932.)

THE WOMEN IN THE MILITARY SERVICE FOR AMERICA MEMORIAL

1. The Women In Military Service For America Memorial is the only major national memorial dedicated to the over 2.5 million American women who have served in the nation's defense, beginning with the American Revolution.

2. On November 6, 1986, President Ronald Reagan (1981-1989) signed into law, legislation authorizing the Women's Memorial in Washington, DC, or its environs.

3. In 1989, the Weiss-Manfredi design for the memorial was chosen.

4. Michael Manfredi and Marion Gail Weiss, now a husband and wife architectural team from New York, submitted the winning 33,000-square-foot plan for the memorial. (Manfredi's mother served as an Army nurse for 11 years, part of which was during World War II and the Korean War.)

5. In 1995, President William Clinton (1993-2001) attended the groundbreaking for the memorial.

6. On October 18, 1997, the memorial was dedicated.

7. It took thirteen years from concept to dedication for the memorial to be constructed.

8. Vice President Gore represented President Clinton at the dedication ceremonies, which had over 40,000 attendees.

9. Retired Air Force Brigadier General Wilma L. Vaught was instrumental in guiding the construction of the memorial.

10. The oldest military member present at the ceremonies was Frieda Hardin, who at age 101 recalled her experiences in the Navy during 1918.

11. The memorial is on a 4.2-acre site.

12. The cost of the memorial totaled about $22,500,000.

13. The federal government contributed $9,500,000 toward the restoration and preservation of the original structures on the site.

14. The hemicycle forms one side of a semicircular sky-lit exhibition gallery.

15. A marble-paneled wall lines the opposite side of the below-grade exhibition gallery.

16. More than 3,500 truckloads of dirt were hauled away from behind the hemicycle to provide space for the 33,000-square-foot exhibit hall and education center.

17. The memorial's roof is a terrace that is 250 feet long with an arc consisting of 138 glass panels.

18. The glass panels are tilted upward at an angle of about 20 degrees, and are arranged around the balustraded-top of the hemicycle. Each of the rectangular panels is 1-inch thick and capable of sustaining an 800-pound load.

19. Scattered among the glass panels are 108 panels suitable for inscription, of which eleven have been etched with quotes by and about women who have served in America's defense.

20. Some of the 400-pound tablets also contain tributes to the service and sacrifices of the women, one of which is a 1961 tribute by President John F. Kennedy (1961-1963).

21. The memorial's 33,000 square feet education center houses the exhibit gallery and provides access to the gift shop, theater, Register, Hall of Honor, offices and other public spaces, some of which are underground, excavated into the hillside.

22. The memorial has a 196-seat theater, which frequently shows films about military women, their history and roles. The theater is also used for conferences, lectures, speeches and musical and theatrical productions.

23. The memorial contains a computerized, interactive database registry of names and stories of women who have served.

24. The memorial's Hall of Honor is dedicated to the women who died in service, were prisoners of war, or received the nation's highest awards.

25. Displayed in the Hall of Honor is a block of Colorado Yule marble, the companion piece to the one used for the Tomb of the Unknowns.

26. The memorial gallery includes 16 alcoves, 14 of which house special and permanent exhibits chronicling the history of women's service. The exhibits include unique artifacts and memorabilia, photographs and audio-visual displays relating to women's service, from the American Revolution to the present.

27. The memorial's reflecting pool is 80 feet in diameter and is covered with black granite from a quarry in Culpeper, Virginia. The reflecting pool holds 60,000 gallons of water.

28. The reflecting pool sits at the center of the Court of Valor, the grand plaza fronting the memorial.

29. The sound of the 200 jets of water coming from the fountain on the Court of Valor represents the individual voices of women blending in a collective harmony of purpose, coming to rest in the reflecting pool.

30. Another symbolic example of the challenges that have confronted women in the military is the four stairways penetrating through archways in the wall created by opening up four of the wall's original ten blank, statuary niches. The glass-enclosed stairways through the interior concourse *"create a passage from the old wall to the terrace above, symbolizing women breaking through the barriers."*

UNIQUE FACTS AND MILESTONES ABOUT WOMEN IN THE MILITARY (1775-PRESENT)

1. The following are statistics about women who served their country in the military as of 2006 (sources DOD and U.S. Coast Guard):

Women in Military Conflicts		Women Prisoners of War	
Spanish-American War	1,500	Civil War	1
World War I	35,000	World War II	88
World War II (Era)	400,000	Desert Storm	2
Korea (In Theater)	1,000	Operation Iraqi Freedom	3
Vietnam (In Theater)	7,500		
Grenada (Deployed)	170		
Panama (Deployed)	770		
Desert Storm (In Theater)	41,000		

2. During the American Revolution of 1775-1783, women served on the battlefields as nurses, water bearers, cooks, laundresses, and saboteurs.

3. In 1776, Margaret Corbin manned her husband's cannon when he was killed during the battle of Fort Washington, New York.

4. In 1778, Deborah Samson of Plympton, Massachusetts, disguised herself as a young man and served for the whole term of the war as Robert Shirtliffe.

261

5. During the War of 1812, women served as nurses aboard the ship *United States*.

6. During the Mexican War (1846-1848), women disguised themselves as men and served in the infantry.

7. During the Civil War (1861-1865), women provided casualty care and nursing to Union and Confederate troops at field hospitals and aboard the Union Hospital Ship *Red Rover*. They also disguised themselves as men in order to serve.

8. In 1866, Doctor Mary Walker was awarded the Medal of Honor. She is the only woman to date to be awarded the nation's highest award.

9. During the Spanish-American War (1898), the Army assigned 1,500 civilian contract nurses to Army hospitals in the United States, Hawaii, Cuba, Puerto Rico, Guam and the Philippines, as well as to the Hospital Ship *Relief*. Twenty nurses died during the term of their service.

10. In 1901, the Army Nurse Corps was established, in part due to the extraordinary performance of the contract nurses during the Spanish-American War, and the Navy Nurse Corps was established in 1908. The nurses served without rank or benefits.

11. During World War I (1917-1918), the Navy enlisted 11,880 women as Yeoman (F), the first women to serve in the United States military in an official capacity, other than nurses. In addition, the Marine Corps enlisted 305 women and the U.S. Coast Guard 2 women. All were discharged following the war.

12. In 1920, military nurses were granted "relative rank" from 2nd lieutenant to major, but not full rights and privileges.

13. During World War II (1941-1945), each of the services established women's components, and some 400,000 women served within the United States and overseas in nearly all non-combat jobs.

14. First Lieutenant Annie G. Fox was the first woman to be awarded the Purple Heart medal for wounds. The medal was awarded for wounds she sustained while serving at Hickam Field during the Japanese attack on Pearl Harbor on December 7, 1941.

15. In 1947, Army and Navy nurses were awarded permanent commissioned officer status. Lieutenant Colonel Florence Blanchfield, Chief of the Army Nurse Corps was the first woman to hold a permanent commission in the U.S. Army or any other military branch.

16. In 1948, the Women's Armed Services Integration Act granted women permanent status in the Regular and Reserve forces of the Army, Navy, Marine Corps, and Air Force up to the grades of lieutenant colonel/lieutenant commander (O-5).

17. During the Korean War (1950-1953), some 1,000 nurses were deployed to the combat theater and served on the ground, aboard hospital ships, and on evacuation aircraft.

18. In 1976, women were admitted to the service academies.

19. In 1978, the Coast Guard opened all assignments to women, including ships and aircraft. In the same year, the Navy opens non-combat ships to the assignment of women.

20. The first women to attain the rank of general or admiral in their respective branches of the military are:

- Army Nurse Corps - Brigadier General Anna M. Hayes in 1970
- Army - Brigadier General Elizabeth P. Hoisington in 1970
- Air Force - Brigadier General Jeanne M. Holm in 1971
- Navy Nurse Corps - Rear Admiral Alene B. Duerk in 1972
- Air Force Nurse Corps - Brigadier General E. Ann Hoefly in 1972
- Navy - Rear Admiral Fran McKee in 1976
- Marines - Brigadier General Margaret A. Brewer in 1978
- Coast Guard – Rear Admiral Vivien S. Crea in 2000

21. The first women to attain the highest enlisted rank – E-9 in their respective branches of the military are:

- Navy (WAVES) – Master Chief Anna Der-Vartanian in 1959
- Army (WAC) – Sergeant Major Carolyn H. James in 1960
- Marines (USMC) – Master Gunnery Sergeant Geraldine M. Moran in 1960
- Air Force (WAF) – Chief Master Sergeant Grace A. Peterson in 1960
- Coast Guard (SPARS) - Master Chief Yeoman Pearl E. Faurie in 1964

22. In 1986, Rear Admiral Grace Murray Hopper retired from the Navy at age 80. She was a mathematician, and a pioneer in data processing and computer science. Admiral Hopper invented COBOL and coined the term "bug" in computers when she actually discovered a moth in a malfunctioning mainframe computer.

23. In 1991, the 1948 legislation prohibiting women from serving aboard combat aircraft was repealed.

24. In 1993, the legislation banning women from serving aboard combat ships was repealed.

25. In 1995, Air Force Colonel Eileen Collins became the first woman pilot astronaut when she piloted STS-63 Discovery.

26. In 2005, Sergeant Leigh Anne Hester became the first woman to be awarded the Silver Star for combat actions. Sergeant Hester was deployed to Iraq as part of Operation Iraqi Freedom.

27. Enormous strides in the utilization of women have been made since the advent of the All Volunteer Force in 1973. Today, women serve in nearly every position in the U.S. military, except those in direct combat; and they have achieved every rank except four-star general/admiral. In addition, women are restricted from Special Forces and are not permitted to serve in submarines.

FACTS ABOUT THE UNITED STATES MARINE CORPS MEMORIAL
(IWO JIMA STATUE)

Since the United States Marine Corps was established on November 10, 1775, the Marines have been called to duty throughout the world to protect the interests of the United States, and to ensure the lives and property of its citizens are protected from outside forces. Always on alert, Marines are often the first to be placed in harms way on short notice. It was the Marines who carried *"the flag"* to the Barbary pirates on the coast of Africa, the Pacific islands of Tarawa and Okinawa during World War II, the jungles of Vietnam, and the deserts of the Middle East. The United States Marine Corps Memorial was established to honor the thousands of Marines who have sacrificed their lives in the defense of the United States.

THE ISLAND OF IWO JIMA & THE BATTLE

1. At 5 1/2 miles long by 2 1/2 miles at its widest point, the Pacific island of Iwo Jima is 660 miles from the mainland of Japan. Its importance to the Allies during World War II was to provide airfields in support of bombing raids on mainland Japan, and to eliminate the threat of enemy fighters shooting down American bombers.

2. The name *"Iwo Jima"* means *"sulfur island."* (The Marines described the terrain as a *"Jungle of Stone."*)

3. The Japanese had constructed on Iwo Jima an elaborate defensive system that included sixteen miles of tunnels connecting 1,500 man-made caverns. Above ground, Japanese defenses included 750 blockhouses and pillboxes. (One underground hospital could treat 400 injured men.)

4. The highest peak on Iwo Jima is Mount Suribachi, a 550-foot volcanic peak on the southern tip of the island. (Seizing Mount Suribachi cost the U.S. 28th Marine Regiment 500 casualties out of the approximate 1,000 Marines who attacked the fortifications.)

5. As part of Iwo Jima's defense system, the Japanese dug 7 layers of tunnels and rooms into the bowels of Mount Suribachi.

6. On February 19, 1945, after 74 days of almost constant bombing by allied pilots, Iwo Jima was invaded by 70,647 Marines and 570 Army assault troops. (The 15th Fighter Group, U.S. Army Air Force, arrived on Iwo Jima on March 6, 1945, and the Army's 147th Infantry Regiment arrived on March 20, 1945.)

7. On March 25, 1945, the battle for Iwo Jima ended. The victory over the Japanese resulted in 26,000 American casualties, including 6,825 deaths. These casualties included 17,372 Marines, including 5,931 deaths. Of the nearly 22,000 Japanese defenders, only 1,083 survived the 36-day battle. (The Marines suffered 20% of their World War II combat casualties on Iwo Jima.)

8. On April 18, 1945, the Marine invasion force left Iwo Jima.

9. The sacrifices of the American military on Iwo Jima is credited with saving the lives of an estimated 28,000 airmen who would have crashed due to damage or malfunctions to their aircrafts on their missions over Japan.

10. Twenty-two Marines and 5 Navy personnel who fought in the battle for Iwo Jima were awarded the Medal of Honor for bravery.

THE MEN WHO RAISED THE FLAG ON IWO JIMA

1. Six men were immortalized in the photograph taken by Joe Rosenthal as they raised the second flag of the United States atop Mount Suribachi.

2. The five Marines credited with raising the historical U.S. flag on Mount Suribachi are Michael Strank, Harlon H. Block, Franklin R. Sousley, Rene Gagnon, and Ira Hayes. All of the Marines were assigned to Easy Company, 2nd Battalion, 28th Regiment, 5th Division. The sixth man, John H. Bradley, was assigned to the company as a Navy Pharmacist Mate (medic).

3. Strank, Sousley, and Block were later killed on Iwo Jima.

4. Strank, Hayes, and Gagnon are buried at Arlington Cemetery.

5. On November 10, 1919, <u>Mychal</u> <u>Strenk</u> was born in Jarabenia, Czechoslovakia. In 1922, he migrated to Franklin Borough (near Johnstown), Pennsylvania, where he changed his name to <u>Michael</u> <u>Strank</u>. In 1939, at age 19, Strank enlisted in the Marines, and was assigned duties as a rifleman. In February 1942, he was promoted to sergeant, and served as a Marine Raider on Bougainville (Pacific island) in 1943. Sergeant Strank was the first of the six men to die. On March 1, 1945, at age of 25, Strank was killed when a shell exploded near him on Iwo Jima. In 1947, Sergeant Strank was buried at Arlington Cemetery after his body was returned from Iwo Jima.

The Men – Marine Corps Memorial

6. On November 6, 1924, Harlon Block was born on a small farm in Rio Grande Valley, Texas. In early 1943, at age 18, he enlisted in the Marines, and graduated from paratrooper school in May 1943. Block participated in the battle for Bougainville in 1943. On March 1, 1945, at age 20, Brock was killed by an exploding shell just a few hours after the death of Sergeant Strank. Until 1947, Corporal Block remained buried on Iwo Jima, when his body was returned to Weslaco, Texas, for burial.

7. On September 19, 1925, Franklin Sousley was born outside the small town of Hilltop, Kentucky. In 1944, at age 18, he enlisted in the Marines, and was assigned duties as a rifleman. Iwo Jima was the first and last battle for Private Sousley. On March 21, 1945, at age 19, Sousely was killed by a bullet to the back. In May 1947, Private Sousley's body was returned to Elizaville, Kentucky, for burial.

8. On January 12, 1923, Ira Hayes was born on the Gila River Indian Reservation in Arizona. He was a member of the Pima Indian tribe ("*Pima*" means "*River People*"). In 1942, at age 19, he enlisted in the Marines, and graduated from paratrooper school in November 1942. Hayes participated in the battles for Bougainville in 1943, and Iwo Jima in 1945. After his discharge from the Marines, Hayes was unable to adjust to life after the war. As an alcoholic, he died on January 24, 1955, of exposure to freezing cold on the Gila River Indian Reservation. At age 32, Private Hayes was buried at Arlington Cemetery.

9. On March 7, 1925, Rene Gagnon was born in Manchester, New Hampshire. In 1943, at age 17, he enlisted in the Marines, and was assigned duties as a rifleman. Iwo Jima was the first and only time Private Gagnon saw combat. After the war, Gagnon was assigned to China and was discharged in 1946. After returning home, he worked in the mills in Manchester. On October 12, 1979, at age 53, Gagnon died of a heart attack. In 1981, his body was reburied at Arlington Cemetery.

10. On July 10, 1923, John Bradley was born in Antigo, Wisconsin. In 1943, at age 19, he enlisted in the Navy, and was assigned duties as a Navy Pharmacist's Mate Second Class (medic). He was awarded the Navy Cross for his efforts in saving Marine lives on Iwo Jima, and a purple heart for the serious wounds to his legs during the battle. After the war, Bradley married, fathered 8 children, and owned a funeral home in Antigo. Of the 6 men, PM2/C Bradley was the last to pass away. He died on January 11, 1994, at age 70, and is buried in Antigo, Wisconsin.

THE UNITED STATES MARINE CORPS MEMORIAL

1. The United States Marine Corps Memorial shows the flag of the United States being raised over Mount Suribachi during the World War II battle of Iwo Jima. It honors all Marines who have died in the service of their country.

2.	On February 23, 1945, a 40-man combat patrol reached the top of Mount Suribachi and raised a small U.S. flag (54 inches by 28 inches) secured to a length of pipe weighing over 100 pounds. A larger flag measuring 96 inches by 56 inches later replaced this smaller flag. The replacement flag is the one shown in the photograph. It was obtained from the tank landing ship *LST-779,* and flew for three weeks before it was chewed up by strong winds and was removed.

3.	On February 23, 1945, photographer Joe Rosenthal, a 5 feet, 3-inch tall Associated Press photographer with very poor eyesight, took the photograph of the second flag being raised on Mount Suribachi. It took just $1/400^{th}$ of a second to take this historic picture. (Rosenthal died in 2006, at age 94.)

4.	The memorial was designed by Horace W. Peaslee.

5.	Felix de Weldon, an Austrian immigrant who served as a Navy Petty Officer during World War II sculptured the Marine Memorial. He later designed and created the Seabees Memorial and the Memorial to Admiral Richard Byrd. (These other memorials can be seen on Memorial Drive near the main entrance to Arlington Cemetery.) (De Weldon died in 2003, at age 97.)

The Marine Corps Memorial

6.	The men depicted in the memorial, starting at the bottom of the flagpole and working upward are: Corporal Harlon H. Block, Private First Class Rene Gagnon (whose down turned head is near Block's left elbow on the opposite side of the pole), PM2/C John H. Bradley (facing forward behind Block), Sergeant Michael Strank (leaning over Gagnon's back), Private First Class Franklin Sousley (immediately behind Bradley) and Private First Class Ira Hayes (the rear figure whose outstretched hands are not quite touching the flagpole).

7. In 1945, the planning of the memorial began.

8. The three survivors of the battle, Gagnon, Hayes, and Bradley volunteered to act as models for the memorial.

9. Photographs and physical data were used to build the models of the three deceased Marines.

10. A steel frame resembling the bone structure of a human body was assembled to support the huge figures under construction.

11. The figures were initially molded unclothed so the men's muscular strain would be evident after the clothing was added.

12. The figures were initially finished in plaster.

13. It took three years for the figures in the memorial to be cast in bronze after they were formed in plaster.

14. The figures were cast in bronze in Brooklyn, New York.

15. The memorial was assembled from twelve major pieces of casting, with the largest piece weighing more than 20 tons. (The twelve major pieces were formed from 108 smaller plaster molds.)

16. The figures of the men stand 32 feet high.

17. The figures are six times larger than life-size.

18. The figures, placed on a rock slope, rise about 6 feet from a 10-foot base, making the memorial 78 feet high overall.

19. The flagpole is 60 feet long.

20. The memorial weighs approximately 100 tons.

21. The concrete base is covered with blocks of polished Swedish black granite.

22. The inscription on the memorial reads "In honor and in memory of the men of the United States Marine Corps who have given their lives to their country since November 10, 1775."

23. Inscribed on the memorial is the tribute rendered the Marines on Iwo Jima by Fleet Admiral Chester W. Nimitz *"Uncommon Valor Was a Common Virtue."*

24. The principal Marine Corps engagements since the founding of the Marine Corps are inscribed on the base of the memorial.

25. In September 1954, the erection of the memorial was begun.

26. On November 10, 1954, President Dwight D. Eisenhower (1953-1961) dedicated the memorial. (The date marked the 179th anniversary of the Marine Corps.)

27. The construction cost of the memorial, donated by active and retired Marine and Navy personnel, totaled $850,000.

28. The memorial is on a 7.5-acre site.

29. The M1 rifle is 16 feet in length.

30. The M1 carbines are 12 feet in length.

31. The canteen, if filled, would hold up to 32 quarts (8 gallons) of water.

32. In accordance with President Kennedy's (1961-1963) Presidential proclamation of June 12, 1961, the flag over the memorial flies 24 hours a day.

33. The original first and second flags that were raised over Mount Suribachi on February 23, 1945, are displayed on a rotating basis at the Marine Corps Museum near the Quantico Marine Corps Base, in Triangle, Virginia.

FACTS ABOUT THE PENTAGON

On September 1, 1939, the day Germany invaded Poland, General George C. Marshall was appointed the Chief of Staff of the United States Army. It was also at this time the government took the first steps toward constructing the Pentagon. These steps were taken because the leadership of the United States foresaw the eventual entrance of the United States into World War II, and they hoped that by consolidating the leadership of the military at one location, they would be better prepared for war. However, not even the planners who witnessed the construction of a tall, five-sided building in Virginia could have imagined the significance of how the Pentagon would influence the military history of the United States.

THE CONSTRUCTION OF THE PENTAGON

1. The person largely responsible for supervising the construction of the Pentagon was Brigadier General (1-Star) Brehon B. Somervell, Chief of Construction for the War Department.

2. The chief architect was George E. Bergstrom, and the prime contractor was the John T. McShain Company of Philadelphia.

3. A pentagon is a plane figure with five angles and five sides. Thus the name of the structure – *"The Pentagon."*

4. The Pentagon appears to be in the shape of a fort, symbolic of an era in which forts were used widely to protect the citizens and interests of a nation.

The Pentagon

5. The initial plans for the Pentagon were designed in just 4 days.

6. On September 11, 1941, construction on the Pentagon was started.

7. At its peak, between 13,000 and 15,000 workers labored on the Pentagon on round-the-clock shifts.

8. Eight construction workers were killed during the construction of the Pentagon.

9. Skilled workers who worked on the Pentagon, such as carpenters and plumbers, were paid approximately $1.65 an hour.

10. On April 29, 1942, the first occupants moved into the Pentagon. Less than nine months after construction was started.

11. On January 15, 1943, construction on the Pentagon was completed, just one year and four months after construction was started. (This consolidated 17 buildings of the War Department.)

12. The Pentagon is located in the state of Virginia. Across the Potomac River from Washington, D.C.

13. The site of the Pentagon was originally little more than wasteland, swamp and dumps. (Five and one-half million cubic yards of earth were used to fill the wasteland.)

14. The swamp area on which the Pentagon was constructed was known as "*Hell's Bottom.*" It was also known as "*Arlington Farms.*"

15. The Pentagon was constructed from reinforced concrete. (By using reinforced concrete, the builders saved over 38,000 tons of steel, enough to build a battleship, and it made the building much more fire resistant.)

16. Construction of the Pentagon required the addition of 5.5 million cubic yards of earth, the installation of 41,492 concrete piles placed every 28 feet, and the use of 680,000 tons of sand and gravel processed into 435,000 cubic yards of concrete.

17. Each of the five outer walls of the Pentagon is 921 feet long, or longer than the length of three football fields.

18. The walls of the Pentagon consist of 6 inches of Indiana limestone (outer layer), 8 inches of brick (middle layer) and 10 inches of concrete (inner layer). A total thickness of 24 inches.

19. The height of the Pentagon is 77 feet, 3 inches.

20. There are five rings to the Pentagon. The most inner ring is "*A*" ring, the most outer ring is "*E*" ring.

21. The Pentagon consists of five floors, plus the mezzanine and basement.

22. The gross floor space of the Pentagon is 6,636,360 square feet.

23. The floors of the Pentagon are typically 5.5 inches thick and are designed to support a load of 150 pounds per square foot.

24. The initial cost of the Pentagon building was $49,600,000.

25. The Pentagon building covers 29 acres (3.7 million square feet).

26. The center court of the Pentagon covers 5 acres.

27. The cost of the land totaled $2,245,000.

28. The cost of the land, building, parking, etc. totaled $82,000,000, versus the initial estimate of $35,000,000.

29. There are 17.5 miles of corridors in the Pentagon. On the levels of the Pentagon, there are 10 corridors leading from the exterior wall to the offices near the interior wall facing the central courtyard.

30. There are also three corridors circling the Pentagon.

31. These corridors are set up in a way that it takes only 7 minutes to walk between any two points in the building.

32. The Pentagon was initially intended to provide working space for 40,000 civilian and military personnel. (Space was dramatically reduced with the installation of elevators, escalators, etc.)

THE PRESENT DAY PENTAGON

1. An extensive renovation of the Pentagon, which was begun in 1998, included the following reinforcements to the walls:

   • Blast-Resistant Windows – Each window cost $10,000, including installation. Each window and steel frame weighs about 2,500 pounds. The glass is nearly two inches thick.

   • Steel Beams – Structural steel beams were added through all five floors to strengthen the walls.

   • Inner Wall Coverings – Interior wall coverings are made from a blast-resistant cloth similar to Kevlar, which is used to make bulletproof vests. The fabric was stretched between the steel beams to prevent debris from becoming shrapnel in the event of an external explosion.

   On September 11, 2001, a hijacked Boeing 757, Flight #77, traveling at an estimated speed of 345 miles per hour struck the Pentagon. The impact caused the death of 64 innocent people on the plane and 125 people in the Pentagon when it struck rings "*E*" through "*C*". It was estimated that several more people working in the Pentagon would have been killed if it had not been for the recently installed renovated wedge described above.

2. A lattice of copper strands have been installed under each floor to filter out noise from external sources and also to cause signal interference if there are attempts to use listening devices from the floors above or below.

3. Working space in the Pentagon totals 3,705,793 square feet. (The Pentagon is the largest working office in the world.)

4. Over 30 miles of access roads have been constructed around the Pentagon. Near the Pentagon are 67 acres of parking space for 8,700 vehicles in 16 parking lots.

5. The Army Library in the Pentagon is the result of a 1944 consolidation of 28 government libraries in the Washington, D.C. area. The library is a direct descendant of the old War Department Library, established in 1800, and is the second oldest U.S. government library in existence. The oldest is the Library of Congress. The Library currently stores 300,000 publications and 1,700 periodicals in various languages.

6. The primary sources of heat for the Pentagon are oil and natural gas.

7. There are over 200,000 telephone calls made daily through 100,000 miles of telephone cable, and approximately 1,200,000 pieces of Pentagon mail handled monthly.

8. The Pentagon also consists of:

- 131 Stairways
- 19 Escalators
- 13 Elevators
- 284 Restrooms
- 691 Water Fountains
- 4,200 Clocks
- 16,250 Light Fixtures (An estimated average of 250 light bulbs are replaced daily.)
- 7,754 Windows

9. There are currently between 23,000 and 26,000 civilian (defense and non-defense) and military personnel working in the Pentagon.

10. Over two tons of classified documents are destroyed in the Pentagon every workday.

11. In 1992, the Pentagon was designated a national landmark by the Department of Interior.

FACTS ABOUT MOUNT VERNON
(HOME OF GEORGE AND MARTHA WASHINGTON)

No other man contributed more to the birth and infancy of the United States than George Washington. As a soldier he led a small and poorly equipped army to victory against the British Empire, as a statesman he was deeply involved in developing the guidelines that led to the formation of a federal government and the approval of the Constitution of the United States, and as a president, he did much to ensure a democratic government was formed that would serve its citizens. His skills also contributed immeasurably to the location of the nation's capital, and the building of the White House, Capitol Building, and other government buildings in Washington, D.C.

In taking note of his many accomplishments, it should be remembered that Washington was also a prosperous farmer and plantation owner. Skilled in crop rotation and the day-to-day management of his lands, Washington enlarged his holdings nearly four-fold during his lifetime. By touring Mount Vernon, visitors will not only view the beauty of a plantation on the banks of the Potomac River, but will walk in the footsteps of the first president, his family, and the workers who made the plantation a success.

THE MEMBERS OF THE WASHINGTON FAMILY

1. George Washington's grandfather, John Washington, was the first to settle on the land that became Mount Vernon.

2. The land acquired by John Washington in 1674 was previously known as *Little Hunting Creek Plantation.*

3. In 1726, Washington's father, Augustine Washington, acquired Little Hunting Creek.

4. Mary (Ball) Washington gave birth to George Washington on February 11, 1732, on the Pope's Creek Plantation in Virginia. His birth date was changed to February 22, when England adopted the Gregorian calendar in 1752. (The site of Washington's birth is near the site of General Robert E. Lee's birth.)

5. George Washington had no middle name.

6. As an adult, Washington was 6 feet, 2 inches tall, and weighed approximately 175 pounds during his younger years, and approximately 200 pounds during his older years. He had reddish brown hair and blue eyes.

7. Washington had a younger sister and three younger brothers. He also had two older half-brothers.

8. In 1735, Augustine Washington moved his family to Little Hunting Creek, when George was three-years-old.

9. In 1738, Augustine moved his family to the Ferry Farm near Fredericksburg, Virginia.

10. In 1743, Washington's brother, Lawrence, inherited the plantation upon the death of their father - Augustine Washington.

11. Washington was only 11 years old when his father died.

12. Lawrence changed the name of "Little Hunting Creek" to "Mount Vernon" in honor of British Admiral Edward Vernon. Lawrence served under Admiral Vernon in the Caribbean while serving in the Royal Navy.

13. In 1745, Washington moved in with Lawrence at Mount Vernon.

14. In 1752, Lawrence died.

15. In 1754, Washington acquired Mount Vernon by leasing it from Lawrence's widow Anne Washington.

16. In 1761, Washington inherited Mount Vernon after the death of Anne Washington.

17. From 1754 to 1799, Washington increased the size of his holdings from 2,126 acres to nearly 8,000 acres on five farms.

18. At their peak period, over 250 people lived and worked on these five farms.

19. From 1754 to 1759, Washington was away from Mount Vernon for long periods of time as he served as commander of the Virginia militia. (Washington served in the French and Indian War, and was with Braddock when the general was killed near Pittsburgh, Pennsylvania in 1755.)

20. While Washington was away, his brother, John Augustine, and cousin, Lund Washington, managed Mount Vernon.

21. In January 1759, Washington married Martha Dandridge Custis. Martha was a wealthy widow with two children, John Parke Custis and Martha Parke Custis.

22. At the time Washington married Martha, there were eleven rooms in the mansion at Mount Vernon.

23. From 1775 to 1783, Washington was again absent from Mount Vernon while he performed duties as Commander-in-Chief of the Continental Army.

24. From 1789 to 1797, Washington again served his country as the first President of the United States. During these years Washington visited Mount Vernon just sixteen times.

25. On December 14, 1799, George Washington died at age 67. (Some historians believe Washington would have lived longer if he had not been bled. Bleeding is when a patient is intentionally cut to allow the sickness to flow from the body.)

26. Constructed in 1758, the third floor of the mansion contains Washington's Study and Little Parlor. After Washington's death, Martha spent much of her time in a small bedchamber on this floor. (Because of the narrow stairwell leading to the room and the small size of the room, access is limited to special occasions. For example, during the annual Christmas tours.)

27. On May 22, 1802, Martha died at age 70.

THE DISPOSITION OF MOUNT VERNON AFTER GEORGE AND MARTHA WASHINGTON'S DEATHS

1. The Washington estate was divided after Martha Washington's death. The majority of the estate, including the mansion and 4,000 acres, was willed to Washington's nephew, Rushrod Washington, the son of John Augustine (Washington's brother).

2. In 1829, Rushrod Washington, an Associate Justice of the U.S. Supreme Court, left the mansion to his nephew John Augustine Washington.

3. In 1850, John Augustine Washington's widow deeded the property to her son, John Augustine Washington, Jr.

4. In 1850, John Augustine Washington, Jr. made an unsuccessful attempt at selling Mount Vernon to the federal government.

5. Between the years of 1829 to 1853, Mount Vernon had fallen from a productive and self-sustaining plantation, to a poorly run and dilapidated farm. (The mansion's roof had to be propped up with the masts of old ships.)

6. In 1853, the Mount Vernon Ladies' Association launched a campaign to save and restore the estate of Mount Vernon.

7. The person instrumental in purchasing Mount Vernon for the Mount Vernon Ladies' Association was Ann Pamela Cunningham. Ms. Cunningham was from South Carolina.

8. In 1858, with the support of a $69,000 contribution from Edward Everett of Massachusetts, the association purchased Mount Vernon from George Washington's great-grandnephew John Augustine Washington, Jr., for $200,000. (The mansion has been restored to its appearance in 1799, the final year of Washington's life.)

9. In 1860, Mount Vernon, located sixteen miles from Washington, D.C., was opened to the public.

THE BUILDINGS AND SITES ON THE MOUNT VERNON ESTATE

1. In 1735, Augustine Washington constructed the central part of the mansion, a one-and-a-half-story structure.

2. In 1757, George Washington enlarged the central part of the mansion to two-and-a-half-stories.

The entrance to Mount Vernon

3. The basic footprint of the mansion shows its dimensions to be 93 feet by 32 feet. This does not include the piazza or front porch of the mansion, which runs the length of the mansion and is 14 feet, 3 inches wide. The mansion is approximately 9,000 square feet, excluding the basement, piazza (large covered porch) and cupola (small dome on the roof). The mansion is 59 feet high from the ground to the top of the Dove of Peace weathervane.

4. The mansion was constructed from pine.

5. At the very top of the mansion Washington added a cupola, which served as both a decorative rooftop element and a practical device. With windows open, the cupola helped to cool the mansion on sultry summer days. In 1787, a Dove of Peace weathervane was placed atop the cupola.

6. The pine exterior of the mansion has been "rusticated." (This is a process involving the use of varnish, paint, and sand to create the appearance of stone.)

7. When Washington inherited the Mount Vernon estate in 1761, the mansion consisted of four rooms and a central passage on the first floor and three bedrooms on the second floor.

8. In 1774, the south wing was added to the mansion.

9. In 1776, the north wing was added to the mansion.

10. Between 1778 and 1780, the covered walks leading from both sides of the mansion were constructed.

11. Because good ventilation was enabled by having the two end doors to the hall opened, the center hall of the mansion was often used as a parlor in warm weather.

12. A key to the Bastille, in Paris, France, is displayed on the wall between the downstairs bedroom and dining room. The key was presented to George Washington by General Marquis de Lafayette in 1790.

13. The dining room is the largest room and last room added to the mansion. Completed in 1788, it was in the dining room that Washington received notice of his election to the presidency of the United States on April 14, 1789.

14. The decorative molding and plasterwork around the dining room reflect Washington's nationalism and his role as a leading agriculturist. The motifs include farming tools, oak leaves symbolizing national strength, olive branches for peace, grapevines for the harvest, and compotes signifying the abundance of the earth.

15. The mantel in the dining room was a gift from Samuel Vaughan, a friend of the Washington family. The bas-relief pastoral scenes on the mantel reflect Washington's love of farming.

16. The music room, or *"Little Parlor,"* contains a harpsichord - a musical instrument assembled in London in 1793. Washington purchased it for his granddaughter, Nelly Custis. (It was the first piece of original furniture to be returned to Mount Vernon after the Mount Vernon Ladies' Association assumed ownership.)

17. The front parlor is a formal room with paneled walls. The Washington Coat-of-Arms is carved into the pediment over the mantel. The Coat-of-Arms consists of a mythical griffin emerging from a ducal coronet. Stars and bands complete the shield.

18. Washington's study is also on the first floor. In this room, Washington shaved and dressed each morning between 4:00 and 5:00 a.m. The contents of his study include:

- A ceiling high bookcase filled with 884 books.

- Terrestrial (world) globe that was acquired from a source in England in 1790.

- A Hepplewhite secretary-bookcase that was designed and assembled by John Aitken in Philadelphia around 1797.

- A leather-covered revolving desk chair constructed in New York around 1790. Washington used this chair during his eight-year-presidency.

19. On the second floor of the mansion are six additional bedrooms, including the bedroom in which George Washington died in 1799. Martha Washington also used the room for her office.

20. Washington designed and installed the piazza (large covered porch; veranda) onto the mansion. The piazza, which faces the Potomac River, was constructed from English flagstone in 1777.

The piazza on the mansion at Mount Vernon

21. The view from the piazza is much the same today as it was when Washington lived at Mount Vernon. The National Colonial Farm directly across the Potomac River is a working farm. The 18th - century farm was created by private citizens to ensure the land was not developed in a way that would detract from the scenery visitors see from Mount Vernon.

22. The small dwellings surrounding the mansion consist of a kitchen, the butler's house, gardener's house, storehouse, smokehouse, washhouse, coach house, stables, spinning house, icehouse, greenhouse, and slaves' quarters.

23. Washington planned the upper garden as a pleasure garden.

24. The lower garden was used as a source of fresh vegetables.

25. It is estimated that between 50 and 100 slaves are buried in the Slave's Burial Ground. In 1929, a memorial marker was placed at the site. In 1983, a larger marker was placed at the site.

26. Washington's will directed that his slaves be freed at the time of his death.

THE BURIAL SITE OF GEORGE AND MARTHA WASHINGTON

1. The tomb of George and Martha Washington is located in what is known as the "*Vineyard Enclosure.*"

2. George Washington selected the site of the new tomb prior to his death.

3. In 1831, the bodies of George and Martha Washington were removed from the old family vault to another vault inside a brick enclosure.

The vault containing the remains of George and Martha Washington

4. In 1837, the bodies of George and Martha Washington were moved from the vault to two marble sarcophagi inside the brick enclosure.

5. On a stone tablet over the entrance to the vault is inscribed the brief legend, *"Within this Enclosure Rest the Remains of Gen. George Washington."*

6. On the sarcophagus that contains George Washington's body, under the Coat-of-Arms of the United States, is inscribed, *"WASHINGTON."*

7. On the sarcophagus that contains Martha Washington's body is inscribed, *"Martha, Consort of Washington."* On the foot is inscribed, *"Died May 22, 1802, aged 70 years."*

8. On the back wall of the open vault above the iron door of the inner vault, an insert stone bears the following passage, *"I am the resurrection and the life, saith the Lord, he that believeth in me, though he were dead, yet shall he live; and whosoever liveth and believeth in me shall never die."* Book of John, chapter 11, verses 25 & 26.

To order *Just The Facts About Washington, D.C.* directly from the author, please visit our website at www.home.earthlink.net/~abekennedy or write to A & N Books, LLC, P.O. Box 1094, La Plata, MD 20646-1094.